Building the Green Economy

Building the Green Economy

Success Stories from the Grassroots

Kevin Danaher, Shannon Biggs, Jason Mark

PoliPointPress

Building the Green Economy:

Success Stories from the Grassroots

This edition published in the United States of America by PoliPointPress, P.O. Box 3008, Sausalito, CA 94966-3008

www.p3books.com

Book design: Global Exchange and Ranch 7 Creative

Cover design: Ranch 7 Creative

Library of Congress Cataloging-in-Publication Data

Danaher, Kevin, 1950-

  Building the green economy : success stories from the grassroots / Kevin Danaher, Shannon Biggs, Jason Mark.

     p. cm.

  Includes bibliographical references and index.

  ISBN-13: 978-0-9778253-6-3 (alk. paper)

  ISBN-10: 0-9778253-6-1

  1. Sustainable development--Citizen participation. 2. Environmentalism--Economic aspects. 3. Green products. I. Biggs, Shannon. II. Mark, Jason. III. Title.

  HC79.E5.D3252 2007

  338.9'27--dc22

                              2007027163

Printed in the United States of America (2007)

Published by:

PoliPointPress, LLC

P.O. Box 3008

Sausalito, CA 94966-3008

(415) 339-4100

www.p3books.com

Distributed by Ingram Publisher Services

PRINTED ON 100% POST-CONSUMER RECYCLED PAPER

WITH SOY-BASED INK.

Our Gratitude

For my Mom, Eleanore, and the memory of my Dad, Albert. For Shane who put up with me.
                    Shannon B ggs

For Nell.
                    Jason Mark

With deepest love and thanks to Medea, Arlen, and Maya. They know why.
                    Kevin Danaher

CONTENTS

Section Three
From Mean Streets to Green Streets

Section Four
Power to the People

Section Five

The Freedom of Everyone to Be Enterprising

INTRODUCTION

LaDonna Redmond didn't think of herself as an activist, and she didn't set out to become a heroine. In 1999, when her son Wade was diagnosed with acute food allergies, Redmond was first and foremost a new mother, trying to figure out how best to care for her vulnerable child. Those basic maternal instincts would soon spur a campaign for community food security and spark a renaissance in her neglected Chicago neighborhood.

The doctors weren't much help in figuring out how to cope with Wade's food-based allergies, so Redmond had to give herself a crash course in nutrition. In the process of deciphering the ingredients in our food, Redmond got an eye-opening education in food politics. The more she read about the food system, the more she learned about how hazardous our industrial agriculture is for us and for the environment. That knowledge cultivated in Redmond an appreciation for locally grown, sustainable foods. But the price of supermarket organics proved to be a budget-buster. So Redmond came up with a better solution: She would grow the family's food herself.

First LaDonna and her husband, Tracey, converted their backyard into a "micro-farm." Then Tracey quit his job and, with some help from the city of Chicago, the couple took over a few nearby vacant lots and converted them into vegetable gardens. Neighbors became curious, then offered to pitch in. Soon the Redmonds were selling organic produce in the community and helping others take over abandoned lots and turn them into organic gardens.

Today, the Redmonds' organization, the Institute for Community Resource Development, manages an African-American farmers' market, helps neighborhood residents develop the skills to grow their own food, and is working to create a co-operative grocery story. Its network of gardens has become a model for how low-income communities can improve their quality of life.

"I really believe in the idea that people can change their community's circumstances," Redmond told us. "The community has the capacity to change; in fact, it has the right to change."

LaDonna Redmond's story is a powerful example of how a personal concern can grow into a political cause. Initially, Redmond was focused on the most basic of needs—keeping her child healthy. Because the stakes were so high, Redmond didn't have the luxury of complaining; she was forced to change to protect her family. When she saw that her personal issue was connected to a web of problems, she realized that the remedy her son needed was exactly what the neighborhood needed: healthy food. Redmond's individual difficulty took on a political dimension the minute she realized she was not alone.

At first glance, LaDonna Redmond's story may seem inspiring because it's exceptional. But if you look closely, you'll find that there are thousands of LaDonna Redmonds, people who are working diligently to safeguard their communities. In the process, they are laying the foundation for a new kind of economy: one that is ecologically sustainable, socially just, and locally controlled.

The days of a globalized, industrial economy based on ceaseless resource extraction are numbered. More people every day are realizing that the ecosystems on which we depend are collapsing. If we want to avoid ecological disaster—and the social catastrophes that will come with it—we must create a way of living that is more deeply connected to nature.

The pioneers of this local, green economy movement aren't pie-in-the-sky prophets. They are hard at work, on the ground, figuring out ways to reduce toxic emissions, grow organic food, build a clean energy system, enliven blighted city streets, and create companies whose business models are based on the cyclical logic of nature rather than the linear thinking of the market.

Each of those efforts is, in its own unique way, about knitting together community. Whether the story is about something as huge as climate change or as prosaic as selling worm poop in re-used plastic bottles, the protagonists in our success stories recognize the importance of bringing people together. They know that the answers to our global challenges rest on collective solutions. They know that there is no such thing as an individual solution—just individual coping mechanisms.

This ethos of collective responsibility is a sharp rebuke to the cultural mindset that says life is all about you, the individual. Fortunately, millions of people like LaDonna Redmond are waking up from their American Dreams.

The State of the American Dream

Somewhere between the sunny images on the television and the suffocating grind of the daily commute, the American ideal of success appears to have gone off track. To be sure, we enjoy luxuries that only a few societies in history have possessed. Yet our material wealth has failed to translate into equally abundant personal satisfaction. In the last 50 years, average income, adjusted for inflation, has doubled. But during the same period, the percentage of Americans describing themselves as "very happy" declined. A recent survey by the Gallup organization and the Pew Center found that the percentage of Americans believing they will live a "higher quality of life" in the future has dropped to 49 percent, from a high of 61 percent, the sharpest decrease in 40 years. It appears we are failing in that most American of pastimes—the pursuit of happiness.

How to explain the undercurrent of unease in the midst of such affluence? Could it be that millions of people sense that below the veneer of our prosperity lurk dirty secrets that distress us even as we pretend to be satisfied?

Perhaps it's the poisons we fear. Our luxurious lifestyles float on a sea of artificial chemicals that—while they give us conveniences like plastics and disposable packaging—also pose a clear risk to our health. Since World War II, the production of synthetic materials has increased 350 times, and billions of pounds of chemicals have been poured into the environment. Studies show that 287 toxins and chemicals are regularly found in the umbilical cords of newborns. During the post-World War II industrial age, the incidence of cancer has increased nearly 50 percent. Today, about half of all men and 38 percent of all women in the United States will be diagnosed with some form of cancer. That could be reason enough to be distressed.

The air we breathe is also cause for concern. By some estimates, 64,000 people die prematurely every year due to the soot from power plants. Rates of asthma are skyrocketing. An estimated 6.3 million children suffer from asthma, double the rate 20 years ago.

Our food, the very thing that should bolster our health, is doing exactly the opposite. In their relentless drive to maintain growth, food corporations encourage us to eat more and more. The result has been a national obesity epidemic. Sixty-five percent of adults are overweight or obese, as are one in six children. The excess weight contributes to heart disease, stroke, and respiratory problems. Most troubling is the increase in Type-2 diabetes. About one in three of children today are at risk of developing the disease, making them the first generation in U.S. history to have a shorter life expectancy than their parents. Such daily assaults on our personal health no doubt serve as a drag on national morale.

The problems are compounded by our political system's unresponsiveness to these crises. Our democracy—which of course has never been free from cronyism or corruption—seems to grow more distant from average citizens with every election cycle. While official Washington quarrels, the standard of living for millions deteriorates. Roughly 40 million Americans live without health insurance. Fifteen percent of all children in this country, and 30 percent of African-American children, live in poverty. Personal bankruptcies and household debt are at all-time highs.

The political class's neglect of these issues can be traced, in part, to the massive wealth disparities afflicting the nation. Our political leaders know they can stay in power as long as they enjoy the largesse of the wealthiest individuals. This includes the CEOs who today earn, on average, more than 400 times what the average worker makes.

The incompatibility of democratic principles and huge wealth gaps should be obvious. As Supreme Court Justice Louis Brandeis once warned: "We can have a democratic society or we can have the concentration of great wealth in the hands of a few. We cannot have both." Wealth without equity is not prosperity.

To add insult to injury, most Americans are working more and earning less. Since the 1970s, wages for blue-collar workers have been virtually stagnant. Salary stagnation is now hitting college-educated workers too; from 2000 to 2004, salaries for skilled workers dropped 5 percent. Yet we are working longer. Since 1980, Americans have tacked on more than 80 hours to their work year.

For the ecosystems on which we depend, our frenzied lifestyles result in a tangible loss of vitality. The evidence is all around us. The planet's ocean ecosystem is collapsing, with scientists predicting that by 2048 most fish populations will be depleted beyond the point of regeneration. Eighty percent of the globe's old growth forests have been stripped. About one-third of the earth's plants and mammals are at risk of extinction, a die-off of historic proportions. The earth's topsoil—the resource on which every terrestrial species, including us, depends—is eroding 10 times faster than the natural rate, in a kind of chemical peel of the earth's skin.

To put this in market terms, our demands are beginning to outstrip the planet's supply. The American Dream, it appears, is turning into a nightmare.

Expanding the Definition of Green

Heard enough doom and gloom? We have.

The good news is that the local green economy is changing the culture of the progressive movement from one of protesting what we don't like to one of creating what we do like. As our friend Van Jones is fond of saying, "Dr. King did not say, 'I have a complaint.' He said, 'I have a dream.'"

Our dream is the local green economy. Some of our stories will not fit what you think of as today's "green economy": solar panels, organic food, recycling. We are using the term to mean what it will inevitably mean in the not-too-distant future: a popularly controlled economy that can guarantee human survival without destroying other species. Given the accelerating collapse of all biological systems, there will soon be little choice. We will either make a transition to a sustainable economy or we will perish by the millions. Earth's biosphere cannot continue supporting the wasteful, nature-destroying economy that has dominated the planet for the past several centuries.

When—and it is a matter of when, not if—catastrophic environmental developments start cascading down on us, the grassroots heroes portrayed herein will look very prescient. Fifty years from now, when the historians look back at how we managed to save humanity from itself, they will mark the early years of this century as the period when many people realized that we must make a shift toward biomimicry. Biomimetics is the science of studying how nature operates and then engineering our economy and our society toward that model. It's a model in which there is no waste, where everything is recycled, and nothing gets thrown away—because there is no "away."

The green economy is no longer some quaint sideline. It is the most rapidly growing sector of the economy. Sales of organic food are skyrocketing; renewable energy is the hot frontier of venture capital; hybrid vehicles are all the rage; and green building technology is transforming the construction industry.

After centuries of an economic system built on extraction and exploitation, the two greens are finally merging. The green of money is synergizing with the green of nature as ecological enterprises prove themselves to be more profitable. As natural resources are depleted, business models that save or restore nature will increase in value.

No one knows exactly what the green economy will look like, but that's part of the beauty of the process. It's an organic, evolving being. There are, however, several fundamental features of the local, green economy. They include:

• *Eco-sustainability*: Safeguarding the biological systems on which we all depend so we can meet the needs of everyone today without compromising the ability of future generations to do the same. As green architect William McDonough says: "How do we love all the children of all species for all time?"

• *Social responsibility*: Ensuring no one is left out or abused, acknowledging the basic human rights principle that no group is inherently superior or inferior to any other, and institutionalizing that principle in law and policy.

• *Fiscal responsibility*: Making sure that costs and rewards are distributed evenly, and that those who can afford to carry more of the load compensate for those less able. For example, healthy adults should be expected to work harder than the young, the old, and the sick.

This green economy must also be a democratic economy. It must create the kinds of economic structures that give everyone a voice in the production and distribution of key resources. After all, no one wants to live near a dangerous chemical plant, or chooses to pay themselves a poverty wage. The ethos of creativity—allowing people to let their imaginations run loose while gaining control of their living conditions—is the backbone of the emerging green economy. If the top-down corporate economy is monotone and homogeneous, the green economy is the exact opposite: polyphonic and heterogeneous. It is based on nature's core principle—unity-of-diversity—whereby all living things are connected in webs of interdependence.

We must now incorporate that principle into every aspect of our lives. We are, in fact, part of nature and cannot escape Mother Nature's embrace. We can no longer afford to deceive ourselves about our ultimate dependence on sun, soil, air, and water. In everything we do, in every policy we enact, we must put our connectedness with nature and the environmental consequences of our actions at the center of our planning. We must internalize a green worldview.

But the local green economy movement is not yet a unified movement. You will notice that some of our stories are obviously green and others are more about local people asserting control of our society, with no obvious environmental angle. Yet we believe that these latter struggles are crucial to building a green economy. A necessary—but not sufficient—condition for creating a green economy is citizens learning to assert control over the institutions that govern their lives. The attitudes and organizing skills that people develop during the course of a struggle to shut down a bad prison or oppose the Patriot Act will be crucial ingredients in creating the green economy. Building the green economy will involve more than technology and economics; it will also require people empowering themselves to assert their authority over all aspects of our society.

Ecology teaches that all living things are interconnected. That insight can prompt an expansion of the definition of green, so that green also comes to mean empathy and solidarity, compassion and kindness. Ecological thinking says that we cannot afford to sacrifice the sweatshop worker or the sea turtle because those living beings are part of us, and we are dependent on them, whether we realize it or not.

If we fail to transform human consciousness so that people feel themselves to be part of nature, we will never achieve true sustainability, and we will pass on to our children and grandchildren a failure that will give new meaning to the word shame.

Movement Storytelling

Humans define themselves with stories. Narratives provide the scaffolding that gives shape to our lives. Stories put events in perspective, establish priorities, provide meaning to the flow of experience. Collectively, our shared stories form the backbone of tradition and culture.

Our goal in this book is modest. We want to share some stories with you. We strive to be movement storytellers.

The stories you read in newspapers or see on TV typically feature subjects who are "leaders"—senators, generals, pundits, and corporate chieftains. The news is often gloomy: dispatches of war, layoffs, natural disasters. Our stories are different. We focus on the little guy and the ordinary gal. These stories are about your neighbors, friends and co-workers. Our protagonists are neither politicians nor prophets. They are ordinary people, scrambling to find their way forward to something better.

Personally, we've had enough of the bogeyman fright tales, the reports about how bad everything is. With all due respect to those fine muckrakers whose work remains so important: We know already. Let's stop telling *their* story—the stories of abuse and corruption and injustice—and start writing our own, the stories that carry the pulse of struggle and the quick heartbeat of triumph over adversity. Enough with the hand-wringing. It's time for fists in the air.

In telling the stories in this book, we hope to contribute to the local, green economy movement by promoting a movement culture. Because stories allow us to ask "what if?," they reveal our aspirations, the kind of world we hope for and how we plan to get there. Stories also instruct behavior—illustrating right from wrong—establishing a moral code. By revealing our hopes and our beliefs, these stories give shape to the living culture that is the green economy movement. It is a culture of resistance to injustice. Beyond that, it's a culture of reconstruction and restoration, an effort to heal a wounded world.

By highlighting that culture, these stories demonstrate how the local, green economy movement fits within a long folklore of struggle. Our stories may be new, but they are only the latest chapters in a much older saga. Our grassroots heroes and heroines are part of an esteemed counter-narrative, a tradition that includes people—Ella Baker, Joe Hill, Sojourner Truth, William Lloyd Garrison, Tom Paine—who played vital roles in creating a more humane history.

The stories in this book are all true. At the same time, they are tales of imagination. They relate the histories of people who acted in the faith of a better future. In daring to imagine a higher order of human behavior, our protagonists prove the interlinked nature of courage and vision.

We hope that, in telling these stories, we are able to uncover some of the mystery of what we like to call "the alchemy of empowerment." That is, how does passing concern convert into lasting commitment? How do passive consumers and spectators transform themselves into active citizens? What is the magic spell that allows people to see themselves as the heroes of the story?

After a close examination, we are led to believe that the alchemy of empowerment is not all that magical. The philosopher's stone, we guess, is you. What we need, essentially, are more storytellers—and more story-makers. We need for everyone to find and undertake some act worthy of being retold, so that the story goes on.

That's what we're asking of you, the reader: to force us to have to write a sequel.

From Isolation to Community

We live, seemingly, in the United States of A"me"rica, the land of good and plenty where singular achievement is considered the pinnacle of success. The American Dream is based on pulling yourself up by your own bootstraps; it's not a group effort. On the rickety ladder to big-business success there is only room to reach the top by stepping over those you pass. We place a premium on those things that separate us from the pack.

If so, then mission accomplished. A recent study by the *American Sociological Review* showed that the social isolation of Americans has increased dramatically in the last 20 years. Today, one in four Americans say they have no one to confide in—not one person. Another 20 percent say they have only one confidante. The kinds of relationships that have been most affected are those outside the family, among neighbors and group associations. The collapse of our social networks should have been big news, but we hardly had the time to reflect on its meaning, because we were so busy trying to keep up with the Joneses.

The first steps we need to take are simple: Get to know your neighbors. Maybe invite them to a barbeque, or bring them a basket of fresh baked goodies. If that feels corny, then go for something simpler. Join a club. If you love to swim, then look for the local swimmers group. If knitting is your thing, then find the nearest knitting club. Take off your iPod at the gym and risk a conversation with the guy on the stationary bicycle next to you. Shop at the farmers market and talk to the vendors, who might ask you something besides "Paper or plastic?"

Author and activist Frances Moore Lappé reminds us that community shouldn't be a chore. "People are looking for community in all the wrong places," she says. "It's not goodwill and like-mindedness. It's daily experience in workplaces and neighborhoods and churches and civic groups."

Just as isolation breeds helplessness, real community is the cure to what ails our hometowns. Through the plain act of creating relationships with strangers, chances are you will come to recognize shared problems ("You hate that refinery too?") and you'll come up with common solutions ("Let's close it").

Novelist Barbara Kingsolver encourages people to consider that the collective effort is more impressive than the lone crusade. "There's no shame in depending on each other," she has said. "There's heroism in ordinariness and connectedness and using relationship skills to get through difficult times, as opposed to the isolated heroism of the cowboy." Only through community can the Lilliputians overwhelm the Gulliver of the corporate empire.

A term that is currently undergoing a makeover is the label "environmentalist." While one poll suggests that only 40 percent of Americans are "pro-environmentalist," another public opinion survey reveals that three-quarters of us identify as environmentalists or support environmental laws and goals. The disparity reveals confusion about what it means to be an environmentalist. Sure, most people are not going to chain themselves to a tree to save a redwood grove. At the same time, most people don't want to live next to a cancer-causing oil refinery.

The steady creep of environmental hazards, tightening like the grip of a kudzu vine, spurs some people to action, while others surrender with the rhetorical question, "Well, what can you do?" When people transform that "you" into "I," then the story changes. "What can I do?" is the question the people in these stories asked themselves when confronted by injustice. In answering that question, they recognized the power of converting isolation into community.

A particularly comforting thought is that most of the people in our stories did not consider themselves environmentalists or activists when they started their efforts—some still don't. They had no special training for what they undertook; nobody handed them a blueprint for creating change. A vigorous community network was not a precondition for their success. Rather, these local leaders found and formed community as their campaigns grew and took shape. In many cases, the struggle itself was the incubator that created community. Like many of us, they didn't recognize that community was lacking in their lives, but upon discovering it, they realized that community was the most meaningful reward that came out of their hard-won victories.

What these stories show is that in coming together people find a way to tap into that most important of our renewable resources—human creativity.

Business Unusual: Can We Buy Change?

"The test of a first-rate intelligence," F. Scott Fitzgerald once wrote, "is the ability to hold two opposed ideas in the mind at the same time, and still retain the ability to function. One should, for example, be able to see that things are hopeless and yet be determined to make them otherwise."

If so, then the growth of the green economy marks something of an IQ test for the progressive movement. How can we celebrate companies that implement better practices while noting how much farther they still need to go?

The signs of change are everywhere. General Electric and British Petroleum are ramping up their investments in renewable energy as wind and solar become more price competitive with electricity from coal and natural gas. The market for non-residential green building is at $43 billion a year. More than $2 trillion in assets are invested in socially responsible funds. Sales of organically grown food are increasing at 20 percent a year. Sustainable living has gone from granola fringe to glossy fashion.

This poses a real dilemma for those of us who have long advocated a cleaner, more humane way of doing business. Of course, it's a tangible benefit to reduce the amount of toxins in the air we breathe, the food we eat, the clothes we wear, and the buildings that surround us. But are mega-corporations—the same companies that sold us the toxins in the first place—really the best vehicles for lasting reform?

This quandary proves that victories are rarely clean-cut. Success almost always comes with compromises and contradictions. Progress is, in a word, messy.

Is it a victory when Wal-Mart is the number one seller of organic milk and the largest purchaser of organic cotton? Should we applaud when Ford offers a hybrid SUV? In short: What does success look like? How will an ecologically sustainable and socially responsible economy take shape?

After careful consideration, our response is a cagey "Yes, but." Yes, it's progress when big companies take steps to lessen their environmental impact. But it's not quite victory yet.

There are real advantages to large companies adopting more environmentally sound practices. More organic food and clothing means less poisons in our soil and water. More solar energy means less greenhouse gas emissions. More hybrid vehicles mean fewer gallons of gas burned.

At its most basic, the green economy movement—which has been spearheaded by small entrepreneurs and is only now being embraced by giant corporations—involves the restructuring of the simple act of buying and selling. We all need some amount of stuff, after all: food, clothing, shelter, and maybe an iPod for kicks The trick is how to produce that stuff in a way that doesn't destroy the planet or abuse workers.

For too long we've allowed corporations to co-opt our social movements through greenwashing and phony charities. It's about time that we start co-opting the corporations. Let's use what businesses are good at—marketing, distribution, retail sales—and make it work for us.

Yet the dangers of a big business takeover of the local, green economy movement are equally real. Will transnational corporations use green practices to more effectively wipe out their mom-and-pop competitors? Will organic standards be weakened by the power of large corporations? Will Americans retain the bad habit of over-consumption and just switch to earth-friendly products?

In truth, we are not going to spend our way out of a social and ecological crisis 500 years in the making.

The inherent contradictions in the trend toward more green business need not be overwhelming. Instead of succumbing to an either/or thinking that says we can either have Safeway organic broccoli or we can have local farmers markets, we should adopt a both/and mentality that makes room for each path. Nature abhors monocropping, and so should we, recognizing that there isn't just one way forward. There are many roads to the future, and while some get there by bike, others may choose to carpool or take a biodiesel bus.

In practice we encourage people to take whatever actions they are capable of. Call it smorgasbord politics. For the pioneers and the early adapters, there will continue to be Community Supported Agriculture programs, off-the-grid energy, bike lanes and co-ops. For the newcomers just beginning to think about the impacts of their purchasing decisions, buying organic frozen dinners at Whole Foods is at least a step in the right direction. By all means, buy local. But keep in mind that your neighbor might still need some convincing that the green economy is not a fringe movement anymore.

The idea is to construct a green economy broad enough to accommodate a range of interests, niches for both the deeply committed and the newly curious, while at all times pushing farther and redefining "mainstream" and "normal" and "acceptable."

No, we can't buy the change we wish to see—not when buying too much has gotten us in this pinch in the first place. But we can make a down payment on a future that will have no clear-cut forests, no starving children, no sweatshops, and no endangered species.

Beginning the Conversation

As we explained, our definition of the green economy is a broad one. You'll realize this as you read the stories. Sure, we have chapters about organic businesses, clean energy campaigns, and efforts to stop genetically modified foods. But we also tell tales about youth prisons, the grassroots movement to stop the USA Patriot Act, and community campaigns to redefine the legal standing of corporations. Regardless of the particular issue, all of the stories highlight the principle that creating a sustainable economy will depend on local control and local decision-making. In the absence of national leadership, innovations at the state and local level—the famous "laboratories of democracy"—are essential.

The system for selecting our subjects was basic: We asked some of the best and brightest minds we know which grassroots campaigns they admired most, and then we profiled those. We contacted the people who spearheaded the campaigns and asked them to share their experiences with us. Then we spoke with their colleagues and allies and interviewed them as well. Background research and a little internet sleuthing filled out the rest. All errors and omissions, of course, are our own.

The vast majority of these stories take place in the United States. This is partially our own cultural bias. We live here, and it's our country. The focus, though, is also deliberate, an acknowledgment that U.S. citizens have a unique role to play in creating a more sustainable economy. As the dominant player in the global economy—and the biggest consumer of the planet's resources—the United States has a special responsibility to help redefine human civilization in the 21st century. Leadership abhors a vacuum, and if the United States refuses to contribute to international efforts to reduce greenhouse gas emissions, or to halt unsustainable fishing, or to stop rainforest logging, then other nations will have less incentive to do so. If a global transition to an ecologically sustainable economy is going to occur, a transition must occur here in the United States.

That said, we must note that the movement for a local green economy is an international one. In many ways, grassroots leaders in other countries are far ahead of those in North America. For example, villagers in India were resisting the introduction of genetically modified seeds long before farmers in North Dakota started to do so. The adoption of off-the-grid electricity technologies has been more rapid in some poorer nations, for the simple reason that there wasn't much of a grid to begin with. In a nod to such efforts, we have included stories from Sweden, Cuba, and Brazil, our way of noting that U.S. activists have a great deal to learn from our allies around the world. Although the movement for a green economy must be locally led, it will also require regional, national, and international networking, some kind of global federation that will allow communities to share lessons and celebrate victories.

For the most part, we are the narrators. Yet we also wanted to give others a chance to speak for themselves, so we have included an assortment of "conversations." That title is our way of showing that all change begins with an exchange between two people. Conversation is the wellspring of community, and a fundamental ingredient of democracy.

Choosing the Antidote

Democracy is the common thread that knits our stories together. Much like "community," the word "democracy" is so misused that its true meaning has become muddled. Democracy in its best sense is much more than a mechanism for choosing leaders. At its heart it is a method, a way of living based on the principle that "sovereignty" (ultimate political authority) resides in the people. Government is a derivative institution whose authority comes from the consent of its citizens.

True democracy—if we can achieve it—holds the promise of giving all citizens the power to be the agents of their own destiny. By establishing every person as equal to all others, democracy can be quite unruly. That messiness of democracy is on display in our stories. None of the "victories" we portray are final. Democracy, like sustainability, is not a destination; it is an ongoing process.

Here in the United States, that process is highly contested as there is a culture war underway. No, not a culture war along the conventional lines of "conservative" versus "liberal." Rather, the culture war we perceive goes deeper, for it touches on the question of our place on this planet. It's a values struggle that involves two distinct views of human nature and two different answers to the question, "What kind of a world do we want to hand over to our children?"

One of these cultures—the currently dominant culture of corporate capitalism—argues that nothing has value unless a price tag can be placed on it. The thousand-year-old redwood tree is worthless until someone cuts it down and sells the lumber, or unless someone is willing to pay for the privilege of admiring it. Under this worldview, a person living in Europe or the United States is worth more than a person in Africa, for the simple reason that they have access to more money. This is a value system based on the belief that maximizing profit will lead to maximum human happiness.

The second culture says that every person, every plant, and every animal has intrinsic value, and we have a responsibility to safeguard every living thing. We cannot destroy the planet or debase other people for quick cash. Under this worldview, our personal profit does not form the center of the universe. It is a culture that recognizes that we are merely passing through this place, and we owe it to our descendents to leave the planet in better condition than we found it. It is a value system based on a deep reverence for life.

The culture war is, then, a battle over whether money values or life values will be the most important guiding principle for the human race. The movement for a local green economy is a central part of the effort to ensure that money values will be subordinated to life values.

Here is a simple test for judging whether money values should dominate life values or vice versa. Ask anyone you know, "Which is sacred, commerce or life?", and see what they say. Commerce is just an activity, like sport or sex. It is something we *do*, not who we are. Life, on the other hand, is sacred.

To acknowledge that we are engaged in a cultural contest is to recognize that change will not come from the politicians in Washington. If we are part of a struggle to change the core values of society, then that effort will happen slowly and locally, through millions of individual conversations about the responsibilities we owe to each other and to the planet.

The tug-of-war between the culture of life and the culture of profit holds the possibility of re-aligning U.S. politics. For example, critiques of the media come from both the right and the left, each resenting the media corporations for undermining traditional values of family and community. Efforts to assist the world's poorest people also transcend conventional political labels, as conservatives and progressives come together for debt cancellation and increased aid to poor nations. The growing involvement of Christian evangelicals on environmental issues such as climate change reveals the universality of apprehending the sacred in nature.

Together, these trends suggest that a politics based on life values could overcome the divisions that have long plagued our political discourse. A union of life-values progressives and conservatives could form a powerful democratic majority that would help usher in a more ecologically sustainable and socially just economy. Our optimistic view of human nature tells us that just beneath the veneer of our consumer society, the life-values majority is coalescing, waiting for the opportunity to show itself.

When it does, it will reshape our society and our economy, proving once again that real democracy is the most powerful antidote to the injustices that ail us.

Section One

Toxic Avengers

Mmmm, that new car smell. You know the one—the slightly sharp scent that reaches into the higher registers of the nose, that seems the essence of clean. The smell of a new car is like a whiff of progress. It's the very aroma of modernity.

New car smell may be feel like a balm, but it's an odor of danger. What you're smelling is the "off-gassing" of polyvinyl chloride—or PVC—a common plastic that contains hazardous toxins that can cause cancer, immune system damage, and harm to the reproductive organs. The key word in that sentence is "common." PVCs aren't found just in your car. They are almost everywhere—in the shower curtain in your bathroom, in the desk chair at your office, in the food packaging in your kitchen, in the toys your children play with.

Our world is awash in chemicals. The lawns and shrubs at your neighborhood park, for example, were likely sprayed with pesticides and herbicides containing such things as acephate, dichlorvos malathion, tetrachlorvinphos and trichlorfon, chemicals that have been linked to nervous system disorders. The particleboard and plywood used in construction are held together by formaldehyde, a probable carcinogen that has also been linked to respiratory allergies. Bisphenol A—a chemical used in the lining of food and beverage containers—has been found to cause chromosomal damage in mice that spans generations.

There's a word for these kinds of substances: poison.

It doesn't require a Ph.D. to recognize the hazards of our chemical-based lifestyle. The inherent dangers of our toxic world are obvious. You won't find the CEOs of Dow Chemical or American Plastics living next to their factories. Those places are ugly. They smell bad.

This basic unfairness—in which the poor and, typically, the darker skinned, live and work next to the most dangerous substances—has spurred a movement for environmental justice. The principle behind environmental justice is simple. It says that no community should have to pay a disproportionate health cost for our collective reliance on chemicals. That demand leads to a more radical proposal—we should not produce any material unless it is proven to be safe. This is called the "precautionary principle," and it suggests a common sense approach to how businesses should operate: "First, do no harm."

The stories in this section tell the tales of communities that made that claim and discovered new tools for taking power themselves. The residents of Porter, Pennsylvania, for example, initially wanted to stop the dumping of sewage sludge on nearby fields. They ended up challenging the very nature of corporations. In Norco, Louisiana, neighbors first wanted the local Shell refinery to clean up its operations. They then perfected an easy-to-use system that communities everywhere can employ to test their regional air quality—knowledge that lets them hold local polluters accountable.

These accounts reveal a challenge facing the local green economy: It will have to start with some basic clean-up. Before we can have a sustainable economy, we need to develop a restorative one. The first step in building that restorative economy is to hold the polluters responsible for their actions.

Fortunately, many people are already on that path.

Sick and Tired of Living
Next to (S)hell

Residents Force an Oil Giant
to Pay For Toxic Terror

"When the challenges come ... you must stand up, and start where you are—the street where you are, where you live. We're taught you can't change everything, but I can change my part, and others will follow. Together we can make a difference."
— Margie Richard, former resident of Norco, Louisiana

Sandwiched between a Shell oil refinery and a Shell chemical plant, the tightly knit African-American neighborhood of Diamond—part of the town of Norco, Louisiana—lived in fear of chemical explosions and the effects of 24-hour exposure to toxic emissions. After her sister died of a rare form of cancer linked to chemicals at the plant, Margie Eugene Richard, now called the "Rosa Parks of the environmental justice movement," led Diamond residents in a fight against one of the world's largest corporations, Royal Dutch Shell. Richard and her group succeeded in securing a landmark compensation package from the company, in the process offering hope to other communities living along the fenceline of caustic factories.

Perhaps resistance to injustice resides in our DNA. Maybe there is a gene for struggle, which compels some people to keep fighting for their basic rights. That, at least, seems to be the lesson of the tradition of opposition that exists in Norco, Louisiana.

Deposited in leg irons just north of New Orleans in what was then the French colony of Louisiana, the ancestors of the modern African-American community of Diamond lived as slaves. These unwilling voyagers were forced to carve out a plantation economy in a swampy and harsh environment. In the early 19th century, news of a successful slave rebellion in French Haiti spread to the Mississippi Delta. In 1811, a group of Louisiana slaves, inspired by the events in Haiti, staged one of the largest slave revolts in U.S. history. After three days of fighting, the rebels were captured, tortured and killed; their severed heads were nailed to posts along the river near what is today the town of Norco, as a warning to other potential rebels. Historical records suggest that the modern residents of Old Diamond, the African-American neighborhood of Norco, include the descendants of those freedom fighters.

One of those likely descendants is Margie Richard, retired schoolteacher, grandmother, and church leader who mobilized her neighbors, politicians, celebrities and international environmental organizations to demand that Shell Oil assist those whose homes the company had long poisoned.

During the last 50 years, multinational oil, plastic, and petrochemical companies, drawn to the natural amenities of the broad Mississippi and attracted by Louisiana's lax environmental and health standards, have taken over the waterfront corridor between New Orleans and Baton Rouge. Chemical plants fill the air with ominous and fiery clouds, and thousands of miles of pipelines snake through the marshy terrain. The state has become synonymous with petroleum refining, and by the 1980s Louisiana was producing 200 distinct chemical products with very little regulation.[1] The legacy of Jim Crow followed this growth, as communities of color found themselves to be the ones likely to be living along the perimeters of these industrial behemoths. Such neighborhoods have come to be known as "fenceline communities."

Call it a Diamond in the rough. The fenceline neighborhood of Diamond is a community of 1,500 residents squeezed between two Shell/Motovia facilities, an oil refinery, and a chemical plant. Sickly-sweet smells fill the air day and night, burning the throat and eyes, as children play basketball in the shadow of the factory flares.

Diamond has endured daily exposure to toxic chemical emissions and two major explosions, resulting in deaths and illnesses. Diamond residents felt committed to their community, but they knew that they were living among poisons: the air was toxic, the earth was toxic, and the floorboards of their homes were toxic. No amount of cleanup could make the place safe. Residents knew that leaving the area was essential for their health and safety, but since no one would want to buy their homes, most residents were stuck.

The community sought relief from the source of the problems—the Royal Dutch Shell corporation—but to no avail. The corporate leadership was untroubled by the neighborhood's problems. That was before the community formed the Concerned Citizens of Norco (CCN), and elected the tireless Margie Richard as their president to seek justice from the petrochemical giant. During a 13-year campaign, the community would master political theater, use the most modern data collection technology, develop a bold Internet strategy, involve the international environmental community, and attract celebrities and politicians to their cause. They would ultimately force the Shell corporation to not only relocate residents, but also to make changes at the plant—a victory no other fenceline community had ever accomplished. Margie Richard received national acclaim and honors for her community leadership, and the neighborhood's success set a model for other communities to follow.

By the Light of the Toxic Flares

The town Norco got its name from the first refinery built there in 1916, the New Orleans Refining Company, taken over by Shell in 1929. Norco is part of what has been deemed "petrochemical alley," one of the nation's largest concentrations of oil refineries. The people who lived along the fenceline in Old Diamond use another name: They called it "cancer alley." Old Diamond was the "black part of town"—a remnant of slavery and segregation—and no doubt racism played some part in the decision to build, and later expand, the refinery in the town's black quarter. A thicket of trees 100 yards wide with a ditch running through it still separates Diamond from the rest of Norco.

Over the years, the refinery's expansion created jobs for the white community of Norco, but the corporation employed very few Diamond residents. That fact made the refinery's impact on the Diamond residents even more painful. The chemical plant practically bled into the yards of Diamond. Many had factory pipes running through their property. Soot fell onto eaves and lawns like a soft dusting of black snow; sometimes vapors would creep into homes, forcing residents to breathe through wet towels to keep from choking. The corporation maintained there was nothing unlawful emitting from its Norco facilities.

The Norco plants operate 24 hours a day—lights and flares blazing—and it is almost as if the sun never sets on the residents of Diamond, particularly those who lived closest to the fenceline, like Richard, who lived in a mobile home on Washington Street, on land where her father grew up. As Richard recalled, "Kids would play hopscotch outside, they could draw them in the parking lot in the nighttime. The flares would burn very high at certain times. In our bedrooms, well, you made sure you had good blinds. I could read at night without turning on a light, the flares were so bright out my kitchen window."

Although the community had no way to prove it then, they were certain that the chemicals were causing the high rates of cancer, birth defects, skin disorders, and respiratory diseases that plagued them. There were cases of sarcoidosis, a rare form of cancer associated with chemical exposure. Among the victims was Margie Richard's sister, who died of sarcoidosis at the age of 43.

The EPA would later report that the Shell facilities released some 1.5 million pounds of hazardous chemicals each year. The report stated that half of those emissions were caused by frequent leaks, called "fugitive emissions." Residents were exposed to daily doses of methyl ethyl ketone, benzene, ally chloride, and a host of other deadly chemicals in frightening combinations.

Even before U.S. asthma rates skyrocketed starting in the late 1980s, more than a third of Diamond's children suffered from asthma or bronchitis, and hospital visits for respiratory problems were common. As Diamond resident, Latricia Peoples, told the Refinery Reform Coalition: "My son [is] supposed to be on oxygen for the rest of his life ... It takes a piece of my heart." When Peoples went to visit her pregnant sister in delivery, expectant happiness turned to heartbreak: "I walk in there and see my little nephew, and the doctor says he has a breathing problem and can't be saved. ... I talk boldly like I do 'cause I know there is some kind of justice we deserve."[2]

Life along the Diamond fenceline continued this way for many years—until the first of the fatal explosions.

Sleeping With One Eye Open

On a hot and humid day in 1973, young Leroy Jones walked across Washington Street, just feet away from the Shell chemical factory, and over to Helen Washington's yard, where he earned summer money mowing her lawn. As he

---

How Dangerous Are Refineries?

Texas and Louisiana—where some 50 percent of U.S. refineries are concentrated—have been called "toxic hot spots." But refineries represent a national public health crisis. In thirty-six states and 125 U.S. cities, more than 67 million people breathe air polluted by refineries.

- For years, a majority of the nation's refineries have evaded regulatory scrutiny, including compliance with basic provisions of the Clean Air Act.
- Many refineries are concentrated in heavily populated urban areas and disproportionately impact low-income and minority communities.
- Refineries are the nation's major source of toxic volatile organic compounds, such as cancer-causing benzene, and chemicals that cause asthma and childhood development problems.
- Most refinery air pollution is from product leaks in equipment, not smokestacks. Technology to prevent these leaks has been widely available for decades, but oil companies often resist investing in cleaner technologies.
- Refineries are also a source of large chemical releases during fires, explosions, and spills. During these accidents, thousands of pounds of toxic chemicals can be released in a short time. The spills often dump chemicals into the communities around refineries, causing grave health problems.

Provided by the Refinery Reform Campaign http://www.refineryreform.org/

fired up the lawn mower, a tiny engine spark made fatal contact with gases silently leaking from a Shell pipeline.

In a split second the spark erupted into huge flames that engulfed Leroy as he wildly attempted to extinguish the fire attacking his clothes, hair and body. Helen's home, with her in it, burned to the ground, killing her. Neighbors ran to Leroy's rescue, smothering the flames on his body with a blanket, but it would not be enough to save his life. After two agonizing days in intensive care, he slipped away from a world of pain.

Like all of the residents, Deloris Brown, who lived on Diamond Street, never forgot that day; she would be forever haunted by it. "I just went on living, but we are all still on pins and needles," Brown told the Refinery Reform Campaign over two decades later. "We went to a meeting right after the explosion and the [Shell company] guy said, 'Yes there is something over in the chemical plant. You wouldn't have no chance to escape or nothing.' They come on your mind, you know, they come and go and it's scary."[3]

Richard remembers the day with vivid clarity. "The entire town was in chaos. I heard the explosion and ran over there. Everyone was there. Helen was under a sheet on the ground. A helicopter had picked up [Leroy], but he died from 3rd degree burns." Turning her attention to the company's response, she said, "You know, there was no one to come to talk to people. While I was at [Helen's] funeral, no one from the industry was there. It crossed my mind, how did they feel?"

Shell did little to reach out to the neighborhood. The incident cost the corporation very little: in PR terms the community had little voice and therefore was no threat to the petrochemical titan. By way of financial compensation, Shell awarded Leroy's mother the sum of $500 for her young son's life. The company also purchased Washington's incinerated home from her family for $3,000.

The community started to meet after the explosion to discuss ways of holding Shell accountable for its gross negligence, but Richard says the energy didn't last. The community felt helpless. That would eventually change.

A decade and a half later, in the pre-dawn darkness of May 4, 1988, an explosion so enormous occurred that houses shook or blew off their foundations, windows shattered, ceilings caved in, and debris was strewn for miles. A total of seven Shell workers and residents were killed, another 48 were injured, and 4,500 people had to be evacuated.

A catalytic cracking unit at the refinery was the cause of the explosion. The residents would never again feel safe living so close to the plant. Years later, residents would liken the experience to being—no pun intended—shell shocked.

Latricia Peoples and her children were among those injured. The blast threw her out of bed, violently casting her sleeping body against the night stand. Her family was forced to evacuate their home for three months. She would then be among the large number of residents who would never again sleep in pajamas, but dressed in some fashion. In case of another emergency, they would at least have the clothes on their backs. "Yes, after that we were in fear," Richard told us. "When we would get notice that the flare was going to be high, they'd say, 'don't panic,' but how could you not? It became the talk of the town, to go to sleep a lot of people slept in clothes so you were ready to go."

Living in fear, and knowing that even without the trauma of the next explosion they were exposed to daily doses of unknown chemicals that were killing them slowly, residents wanted to get away from Diamond. They wanted to live in safety, to have their children play without risk, to breathe clean air. But the realities of real estate wouldn't allow it; no buyers were interested in contaminated homes next to an accident-prone refinery. "We didn't have enough money to move. Nobody was buying the houses," Richard said. "The lawyers came in after the explosion to file suits or whatever, but the attorneys seemed to walk away with the bulk of the money. Some people were in a large class action suit, some of them got enough to move, but not everyone."

After years of trauma, the community could not tolerate any further inaction. Despite a connection to the land that went back generations, Diamond residents knew they would never be safe living so close to the oil and chemical facilities. Most residents agreed that they needed to move away from the fenceline, and to force Royal Dutch Shell to pay for it.

The Shell Game

Church had always been a central part of community life in Diamond, and it was there that the campaign to demand relocation compensation from Shell began in 1989. One Sunday after services a group of women from the church organized a meeting to talk about what they could do to change Shell's complacency. The discussion turned to filing a lawsuit against Shell. But none of them had any experience with legal matters, or even knew any lawyers they felt they could trust. The conversation meandered.

Then, near the end of the time scheduled for the meeting, Margie Richard walked in, and a chorus of voices nominated her to lead the effort. Richard had come to the meeting just to listen. A retired teacher, she was well known for her boundless energy and her readiness to speak her mind. She was, quite simply, a natural leader. By the end of the gathering, Richard found herself the president of the newly formed Concerned Citizens of Norco (CCN).

Taking on a company as large as Shell was a bigger task than any of them could have anticipated, but Margie Eugene Richard was ready to lead the way. She accepted the challenge without hesitation, drawing strength from her faith in God and the courage of those who came before her. With her voice taking on the impassioned timbre of a preacher at the pulpit, she explained: "I know where my strength comes from. It's not just being religious, but living what you are taught. I see why people do not speak up or stand up. It's not because they don't want to. It's fear of what others can do, and not knowing who you are that can hinder your progress. I have no problem with that. I know I'm well put together and I know where I come from. I think of my ancestors, and how my race of people were chained and held in slavery and yet they made it. They paved the way with the hardest struggle, and on their shoulders I stand."

It was time, Richard felt, for her community to step up and learn to become activists. They had no direct communication with the executives at the plant, so Richard would change that; members of CCN would attend every public meeting at the plant thereafter. The company had released some "good neighbor policies." The group needed to study those and see if the company was meeting its own promises. Also, the CCN would have to look more closely at state and federal pollution regulations. What laws were being broken at the plant? Where were the air quality monitors? It was time to find out.

Once the group understood the relevant laws and company policies, there was more research to do. How would they prove that the toxics from the plant were making people sick? What did the community need to know about Shell's vulnerabilities, the community's rights, health regulations, environmental clean-up? How would they go about asking for what they needed? What did the community really want from Shell, and how would they pressure the oil giant to respond to this seemingly invisible and disadvantaged community? The list of unknowns was intimidating.

To help find the answers to such questions and chart a course for success, the Concerned Citizens of Norco would enlist the assistance of a range of allies. Ultimately, the Refinery Reform Coalition and the Bucket Brigade, Earthjustice Legal Defense Fund, Greenpeace USA, the Sierra Club, relocation specialists Michael Lithcott Company, Pulitzer Prize-winning author Alice Walker, actors, civil rights leader Dr. Yvonne Scruggs-Leftwich, and a U.S. Congresswoman from California, Maxine Waters, would join the campaign before victory was secured. But the first stop was the Deep South Center for Environmental Justice (DSCEJ) at Xavier University of Louisiana.

DSCEJ had been focusing on the communities of color that were disproportionately impacted by the toxicity of the petrochemical corridor. They had begun teaching residents how to use computers to track pollution, and learn about environmental regulations, permitting rules, and relocation processes.

Diamond residents learned that essentially the Shell corporation was responsible for monitoring itself, and not surprisingly, regularly reported no emissions of toxic gases. They also learned that there were very few enforceable regulations protecting refinery communities. Few fenceline towns were equipped with the monitoring equipment needed to document toxic chemicals leaking into the neighborhood. Richard told us, "There was no air quality monitoring going on. The nearest monitor was in a town 40 miles away across the river."

Over the next couple of years, the Diamond neighbors tried unsuccessfully to get Shell executives to discuss changes at the plant. Community members, now assisted by environmental attorneys, took Shell to court, and again failed. The corporation had no incentive to help the residents relocate. If the Diamond neighbors were going to be successful in pushing their demands, they would need to prove how the plant harmed them. But how?

The First "Gotcha!" Moment

Enter the "Bucket Brigade." Denny Larson, founder of the Refinery Reform Campaign, had seen a contraption that could capture air and identify any toxic elements contained in the sample, but the cost was prohibitive. "The canisters were running up to a thousand dollars, and you needed a technician to set them up, had to have top notch lab to run the tests ... The canisters also measured for one or maybe a couple of gases." It was not a tool ready-made for communities like Diamond.

Larson was convinced that he could fiddle with the design, and come up with something that could be a community-friendly tool. In the early 1990s he did just that.

Larson's bucket is a simple, inexpensive device connected to a five-gallon plastic canister that looks like an ordinary paint bucket. "The bucket is the permanent vessel, the cylinder creates a vacuum to suck the air into the detachable bag inside," Larson explained. "Remove the bag once the sample is taken, ship if off to the lab, and load the next bag." The cost per unit would be as low as $150, and anyone would be able to work the device after a little training. The other innovative thing about Larson's version was that his bucket could test for 86 different gases at the same time.

Larson, working from California, was trying to establish a national refinery reform campaign. He told us, "I contacted the Norco community to see if they wanted to be part of the network. We wanted to exercise the power of networking to bring about bigger policy reform. We also wanted to help them in their community struggle." That was in early 1995. He met Margie Richard on the phone and she convinced him to come to Diamond to take a tour of her neighborhood. "Margie showed me her house, about 25 feet from the plant, and past all the houses where residents had died, all the illnesses," Larson said. "She rattled off the list of those who had cancer, where the explosions took place, everything the community had suffered."

Larson's bucket was new and barely tested, but he had a plan for how to make the contraption a centerpiece of community activism. Diamond would be the first to test it out as part of a national grassroots effort. "We don't just show up and hand folks buckets," Larson told us, "It's a partnership to develop a program. There is a fair amount of investment of time and energy, and it also takes funding—it can run up to $55 a test."

It took more than a year, but CCN worked to develop the capacity to do the testing. The Diamond residents trained with Larson, they got some funding and found a lab that would run the tests.

The CCN members had not been using the buckets that long when they had an emergency opportunity to test the power of this grassroots tool. In early December 1998 Larson happened to be in a nearby community when he heard from Richard that there had been some kind of chemical release. "I said, geez, can you still smell the stuff?" Larson told us, "She said 'yes' and I told her I was only 60 miles up the road. When I got there, we could still smell the chemicals, and proceeded to the stinkiest spot we could find and took our first sample."

Meanwhile, the media team at Shell had released a statement about the explosion, maintaining that it was just an overpressured tank—no cause for alarm. "There were no chemical releases to our neighbors," Shell officials wrote in a "Notice to Neighbors." The crisis was apparently neutralized.

What Shell officials did not know was that their assurances were about to be exploded by clear evidence that dangerous gases had escaped the facility. It usually takes about ten days for a lab to complete an air sample test. But Larson and Richard found a lab that could test an air sample from one of the Bucket Brigades within 24 hours. The tests came back proving that deadly methyl ethyl ketone had been released in large quantities. Larson recalls, "It was the quintessential 'gotcha' moment. The state of Louisiana did not do tests, and [at that time] there was no routine monitoring in the area. There was no way to tell without this bucket. They would have gotten off scot-free."

By coincidence, at that same time federal officials from the Environmental Protection Agency were meeting at an environmental conference at Xavier University, home of the Deep South Center for Environmental Justice, CCN's allies. Richard, Larson and the CCN crew hastily called a press conference to discuss the results from their bucket sampling. Lab readout in hand, Richard was able to explain to reporters and EPA officials how Shell had lied about chemical release. The corporate deception made headlines, and federal officials promised an investigation.

The Bucket Brigade had dramatically changed the dynamic of the struggle against Shell. Equipped with a low-budget, low-tech—yet accurate—way of measuring toxic emissions, the Diamond residents were now equipped with knowledge. And that knowledge conferred on them the ability to directly confront the corporation about the true nature of its practices. The CCN's ability to identify what was lurking in the air put a national spotlight on the tiny community, and Diamond neighbors suddenly found themselves something of a poster child for the environmental justice community, a clear-cut example of those trying to relocate from the shadows of refinery towers.

After the December 1998 incident, the CCN activists kept sampling. The buckets gave residents the opportunity to know exactly what it was they were breathing, and what they were breathing—lab tests confirmed—were more than 20 volatile compounds, including dangerous levels of sulfur. The CCN could now prove that Shell's claims of air quality were false. It was a small, but meaningful, victory. It would not be their last.

The Fenceline Is Worldwide

The CCN's successful uncovering of Shell's deception not only bolstered the community's confidence, it also put the Diamond neighbors in touch with hundreds of other communities in the United States—almost without exception communities of color—that were also the victims of toxic exposure and industrial accidents. The CCN activists learned that Shell Oil was making record profits by disregarding environmental and safety regulations, the cost of which was borne by those on the fenceline, not just in Diamond, and not just in the USA, but all over the world.

Although Richard and her cohorts continued to tirelessly speak out whenever they could, kept attending hearings and meetings, it felt as if the campaign was at a standstill. Margie Richard could see that a victory for Diamond residents would be won only by connecting to others struggling for justice against the Shell corporation around the world, and that a victory for her neighborhood could provide a wedge enabling others to follow.

In an effort to make that connection, Richard joined a fact-finding delegation to Nigeria sponsored by the human rights organization, Global Exchange. Walter Turner, president of the Global Exchange board of directors, led the delegation. "It was a delegation of environmental justice action, the leaders of communities doing work on the ground in impacted communities," Turner told us. "We were there to look at the impact of oil and multinational corporations on Nigeria. We went to Ogoniland, talked with communities, taking photos and testimonies, and we spoke with representatives from the Shell company."

Richard was struck by the similarities she witnessed between the Ogoni people and her own community struggles. "I cried. Here I was in a different part of the world but yet, still on the fenceline. What did I see? People like you and me, people of dignity and pride, yet suffering injustice of every kind, thoroughly exploited."

"There was the pipeline in one area, blackened from oil leaks," Turner told us. "The water was filmy, scummy. That was for drinking, for cooking, for everything."

Richard took her water bottle and scooped it full of the brown and filmy Ogoni water to take home with her. "I put it in my kitchen cabinet at home. I said, 'Lord, one day I'm going to speak up for Nigeria. If I can speak up for my own community I can speak up for them too.'"

For Richard, the visit had a great impact, and she brought home not just the water but also the spirit of the Nigerians she met. "I wanted to get to the owners [of the Shell corporation] to present my case, and Nigeria's case. I thought, if I can do that, I'll be satisfied."

Richard's new resolve prompted her to co-found the New Orleans-based National Black Environmental Justice Network (NBEJN). The connections forged through the network, combined with the media attention from the Bucket Brigade success and the relationships established during her trip to Nigeria, gave Richard a greatly enhanced public profile. She used her modest measure of celebrity to highlight the campaign in Norco.

Adopting a whirlwind schedule, Richard spent an increasing amount of time on the road, sharing with people outside of Louisiana her experience of environmental racism. She testified before the U.S. Congress, where she used the Civil Rights Act of 1964 to demand justice for her neighbors. In May 1999, she traveled to Geneva, where she and seven other African-American leaders spoke before the United Nations' Human Rights Commission. In Geneva, Richard and her colleagues told UN officials that persistent environmental racism represented a human rights abuse. "There must be an end to industry pollution and environmental racism," Richard said to the UN audience. "Even as U.S. citizens, we are not protected from environmental racism in the United States of America by our government ... I am bringing these issues before you to increase international support to end support of these human rights violations by the United States and: 1) to propose actions that protect communities of color from being dumping places for industrial waste, because these deadly toxic substances cause health problems which contribute to poor social and economic conditions; and 2) to change the way human beings are mistreated by multinational corporations worldwide."

Richard's appearance before the UN was a major event in her life and an important turning point in the campaign. She was now ready for an even more challenging audience—the shareholders of Royal Dutch Shell itself.

Offering Execs a Sip of Nigeria's Water

One day Richard heard a knock at her door. "It was people from Communities for a Better Environment," Richard said. They brought good news, that Richard had been selected to travel to The Netherlands as part of a fact finding group going to a Shell Stakeholders meeting. She could hardly contain her glee. Her church group prayed for her, and as she packed, throwing in an air bag sample from Norco and her Nigerian water, she thought to herself, "This is the last thing we can do. May God be with me."

The Stakeholders meeting was packed with Shell executives, financial analysts, even the Dutch queen. As the meeting droned on, Richard feared that she would not have a chance to speak. "They came out and said they had time for only four more public statements. I raised my hand, but so did many others. I was praying not to go home, I didn't come this far not to be heard." She was picked, and she went in, with her air bucket and her water.

Nervous, she told herself, "Keep it simple, keep it clear." She introduced herself, and with an obvious natural flair for political theater, asked the room, "Do you have a mother? Father? Do you have children and grandchildren?" She pulled out the murky looking water bottle and raised it up for the Shell executives, and the media, to see. "Would you drink this? It is from your facility in Nigeria." She then passed around the bag of air. She told those assembled that it was from her neighborhood in Louisiana, that it contained some 20 toxins, and that she and the rest of her community were breathing it everyday. She invited them to take a deep breath of Norco air. Cameras were rolling, flashes were flashing, and there, in a boardroom thousands of miles from Norco, Louisiana, Margie Eugene Richard became a celebrity of sorts.

A "Flare Cam" and a Flair for Victory

Back in Diamond, the campaign for relocation was starting to gain traction. Richards' new media profile had evidently grabbed the Shell executives' attention. Though a resolution was not yet in sight, the oil company officials were giving the CCN organizers more respect. "They were no longer putting us out of their meetings for one thing," Richard told us.

At the same time, the long, arduous organizing in Norco was starting to attract the support of larger, better financed, and more established national environmental groups. In June 2001, GreenpeaceUSA, working with the Diamond neighbors and other community groups in the area, organized a "Toxic Tour" of lower Louisiana. Congresswoman Maxine Waters, a Democrat from California known for her commitment to environmental justice, was joined by Pulitzer Prize-winning author Alice Walker, actor Mike Farrell and many others who visited Diamond, and spoke directly with residents. The celebrity tour brought fresh media attention to the campaign in Norco. In a letter posted on his website, actor Farrell described the situation in Diamond as "virtual imprisonment."

Following the celebrity tour, Representative Waters raised the Norco issue with the EPA, which she encouraged to investigate and document Shell's failure to ensure safety at its facilities. The investigation eventually prompted a Shell whistleblower to confirm that refinery officials had falsified the facility's emissions reporting. Waters also joined Margie Richard in meeting with Shell officials. Explaining her interest, Waters said, "My district is not only in California but also right here in Norco, Louisiana. Environmental struggles are happening all over the world. This is a little light shining through the tunnel saying it's possible to win."

Next, Richard worked with the Sierra Club to outfit her trailer with a 24-hour "Flare Cam" that enabled anyone with Internet access to log on day or night and witness the plant's constant stream of fiery emissions. "That didn't come easy," Richard said. "We still had people opposing us, saying it was just talk. It was a beautiful day when they came to put up the camera. Some were afraid of putting it on their house, I was real bold, I said 'I'd put it on my trailer. This is my land, go ahead!' Everybody saw it, it was up for a whole year."

Media attention continued to build. In late 2001 and early 2002, a PBS film crew came to Diamond to make a one-hour documentary about the Norco struggle titled, "Fenceline: A Company Town Divided."

Then something happened—Shell blinked. The combined political and media pressure had evidently convinced company officials that helping some Diamond residents to relocate was well worth the trouble. The company offered to relocate half of the residents on the four streets that make up the Diamond neighborhood. It was not what residents had demanded. After so many years of providing no offer at all, Shell evidently was betting that the neighbors would feel that something was better than nothing. Once again Shell had underestimated the community and their bond to each other. Refusing the offer, the residents demanded justice for the entire community. Through the spring of 2002, Shell and CCN held a series of negotiations to come up with a solution agreeable to the long-suffering neighbors.

In June 2002, more than a dozen years after Richard started her campaign, Shell made an offer the community felt was fair. The company agreed to pay some $12 million to help relocate about 400 residents living in 170 dwellings closest to the refinery. Homeowners would be given $80,000 for their homes, $50,000 if they lived in a trailer. Additionally, the company would provide a $5,000 moving allowance. If residents decided to stay, they could receive a $25,000 home improvement loan. Additionally, Shell promised to reduce emissions by 30 percent, and to contribute $5 million to a community development fund. All but 15 homeowners decided to leave the neighborhood they had called home.

The victory was always going to be bittersweet. Families that had lived so closely to each other for generations knew they would have to part. Richard says that most residents moved within a half an hour of Diamond, and most still go there to attend church together. "I live 15 minutes away," Richard said. "I didn't want to go far, but it was the lesser of two evils. We couldn't stay there, people were dying. We all still see each other. Oh yes, that was the hardest part when it came to negotiating with Shell company executives."

In 2004 Richard was awarded the Goldman Environmental Prize, often referred to as the Nobel of the environmental movement. Since then, Margie Richard has become an international activist, helping other communities worldwide to step up and create change where they live. The agreement between Shell and the Diamond residents remains the largest settlement of its kind, and the first in the South, where racism has played a strong role in maintaining the social structure of oppression for communities on the fenceline.

"We were the first, but we showed that even a big corporation like that can be forced to change, to operate better," she told us. "But you have to speak up, you must stand up. You must have input and faith to get the job done." Though she is often singled out for her work on behalf of the Diamond community, Richard knows that everyone did their part, and that no one person, no matter how bold, could have achieved the success her community did. She shares the accolades with her neighbors. "When the challenges come … you must stand up, and start where you are—the street where you are, where you live. We're taught you can't change everything, but I can change my part, and others will follow. Together we can make a difference."

CONVERSATION

Lois Gibbs

In 1978, Lois Marie Gibbs was a 27-year-old housewife in the work-ing class town of Niagara Falls, New York. When she learned that her neighborhood had been built on top of 20,000 tons of toxic chemicals, she became an environmental activist overnight, and soon organized her community into the Love Canal Homeowners Association. After a three-year battle, Gibbs and her allies succeeded in relocating 900 families away from the site. The nationally prominent campaign led to the creation of the U.S. EPA Superfund program, which identifies and cleans up toxic sites. For the past 25 years, Gibbs has been the director of the Center for Health and Environmental Justice.

Q: When you first uncovered the Love Canal scandal, you didn't have a history of activism. What was the most challenging leap for you to become a citizen-activist?

LG: The most challenging thing was not understanding how you do that. And actually trusting. There are two levels of trust. One is that if there's a problem, government would do something, all you need to do is ask. It really made me mad when they didn't. And second, I always thought that the cor-porations were responsible. It was a chemical city and a chemical world. They fed our families; they paid for our mortgages. The smell of chemicals meant the smell of a good economy. And we were brainwashed by them. So when I learned that both of them couldn't care less about us—and in fact the govern-ment decided that it was OK to harm us—that was when I got angry. We just took to anger. It wasn't conscious strategic thinking or anything like that. It was like, "How dare they! How dare they say we are not worth saving!"

Q: How did you in that day-to-day work develop your own skills as a leader and an organizer?

LG: I developed them as I went along, by the seat of my pants. I worked with a lot of local community people who also had never organized around any-thing. We were the Vietnam generation, so we knew about campus organizing.

But for the most part, the community itself was not college educated, so we weren't really involved in it; we were at the sidelines of it. One of the things the women did—it was mostly ladies—was we organized like households. We gave different people different responsibilities, like what you do in your household: You cut the grass, you wash the dishes, you set the table. And we held them accountable. We used a lot of our skills as homemakers to run the organization, and it was actually pretty good. What didn't happen was we didn't become a top-heavy organization. I think it really strengthened our organizing in ways that helped us to win this fight.

Q: How did that kind of organizing make you stronger?

LG: I was a spokesperson that was identified in the media. But if I were hit by a bus, the group would still move forward. Every decision that we made was democratic. So we had different groups who would present something and it was either voted up or voted down. It wasn't done in a small little room; it was literally done in a room of 500 people. Everybody had a voice, everybody had a vote. It was disallowed to make fun or mock or to be negative about somebody's idea. … We also knew that communication was really important, so we took something out of the electoral world of organizing. We set up block captains. It was the block captains' job to talk to the community folks on their block, invite them to meetings, collect dues, squelch rumors that were not true. The block captains also made sure that the people got to the meetings. That was kind of cool because we would have smaller meetings with the block captains before we had larger meetings with the community to figure out what's going on out there, what people's concerns are. We really had our fingers on the pulse at all times, and that was pretty remarkable.

Q: What lessons do you think the older, more established environmental groups could learn from that experience?

LG: One of the things they can learn is to stop talking *for* people. Give people the information and give them a voice in the conversation and the debate. They will come along. You just have to trust them. You can't really decide what's best because you are so much smarter than them. People can come up with really strong ideas, and they will make sure the policy gets through in a much easier way because there's many more people and many more voices.

Q: Despite all the successes you have mentioned, I think it's safe to say that most Americans are pretty disengaged from the political process and from grassroots environmental campaigns. Why do you think that is?

LG: I think one of the problems is that people don't think their voice matters. We hear that wherever we go. And if their voice doesn't matter, then why should they bother going out and getting engaged in politics in some fashion … When we come to the table we want you to help us figure out what to do. People are like, "Wow! I have a lot of ideas. You want to hear what I have to say about this?" Yes, you are a really smart person that has a lot of really good ideas about this. A lot of what people call apathetic America, it's about people not really understanding any longer that they can begin from zero and create a policy and create change in different ways. The population has been brainwashed that we can't make a difference.

Q: How do you see the work that you are doing fitting within a larger movement to create a more sustainable and more equitable economy where we don't have these kinds of problems in the first place?

LG: Well, I think it's shifting the market. So for example in the PVC campaign, it's about the life cycle. In Louisiana, in Cancer Alley, you have people getting really sick as a result of the manufacturing of PVC. In the use by consumers, depending upon on what they put in it, a PVC bottle leaks into their product and goes into their body. And then in disposal goes into an incinerator and creates the same dioxins. … So it's not enough just to talk about shutting down a plant or transferring a plant that produces PVC plastic to another type of plastic. So in the PVC campaign, for example, Johnson and Johnson, who were one of our target corporations, rolled over entirely. They're not using PVC in their bottles anymore. They're using bio-based plastics. If we can get enough industries to use bio-based plastics, we have now created a new industry because somebody is going to have to make the bio-based plastics, somebody is going to have to ship the bio-based plastics. People will be using it. And when it gets disposed of, it's actually pretty benign. And so those PVC industries in Louisiana can turn to making bio-based plastics. And you are getting more family farmers involved, so instead of having resource extraction like what happens with PVC, which is petroleum-based plastic, you are having family farmers growing the products that go into the plastics.

Q: What kind of a green economy do we want to reach eventually?

LG: Years ago they said that if you set regulations to protect the wildlife and the rivers, then you will protect all living things. But now you are looking at if you build a green economy, you will protect many, many things. And I think that answer is much more accurate, because you protect the workers in the workplace, you protect the consumers, you protect the water supply, you reduce the greenhouse gases. It will just create a significant change.

Q: If you could share one lesson from your decades of advocacy, what would it be?

LG: That people can make a difference, regardless of their income, regardless of their formal education. People are just remarkable when they join together. If you look at Love Canal, where the people were blue collar, high school graduate families who brought the president of the United States to his knees. And you look at McDonalds rolling over, and you look at Johnson and Johnson rolling over. This is all because people have joined together.

If we all did one little thing—and we don't have to do what Lois Gibbs did and commit her life to this issue—but if we all did one little step, then the world would be a better place tomorrow.

Sludge Busters

Porter, Pennsylvania Sets New Rules for Corporations

"We cannot have democracy when large corporations wield their legal rights against communities to deny the rights of citizens to build sustainable communities. That's what this is about—who is in charge."

— Thomas Linzey, Esq.

Across the country, rural communities face a new danger—giant agribusiness corporations of a scale unseen before the age of industrial food production. The agribusiness assault comes in many forms, including 100,000-head hog factories and mountains of toxic sludge that are spread on farm fields. Following the death of two children from exposure to sludge, several communities in Pennsylvania decided to restrict the activities of waste companies. In doing so, they discovered that corporations had a "secret weapon"—the U.S. Constitution, which guarantees big business the same rights as people. But one community, Porter Township, determined that in their town, the citizens—not corporations—would govern, setting in motion a new organizing model for communities nationwide.

On a crisp fall day in October 1994, 11-year-old Tony Behun woke up and, remembering it was not a school day, charged out of bed. His still-gleaming dirt bike, a birthday present, beckoned. The rural countryside of Osceola Mills, Pennsylvania, was glorious; the autumn leaves were in their splendor, framing the country roads and sloping hills with bright magentas and dazzling hues of orange. Nothing about this pristine day could have foreshadowed what was to come, as Tony cycled for hours through wooded paths and fields, and over the Al Hamilton Mountain Top Mine site.

What was known only to the mine company and one of its business partners, was that the mine site on which Tony rode had been freshly spread with toxic sludge, also called "biosolids." By the time Tony cycled home, he was covered in a black muddy substance emanating a fetid stench. At his mother's instruction, he removed his clothing in the basement and immediately took a bath. His bike, too, had to be hosed down.

Within two days, Tony began complaining of flu-like symptoms, which alone may not have stirred alarm, but which were accompanied by lesions on his arms. After three more days his condition worsened, and he was flown to Pittsburgh, where a medical team attempted to identify and treat the mysterious illness plaguing his body. Had Tony been exposed to anything "out of the ordinary," the doctors wondered?

No one thought to question the safety of the Al Hamilton mountaintop. There had been no signs posted warning Tony or anyone else of the dangers of a "Biosolids Utilization Area." And if the legally requisite signs had been posted, would a young boy have understood the danger implied?

As the doctors struggled to understand what could have caused his condition, Tony slipped into a coma. He never awoke. In the morning hours of October 21, eight days after his jeopardy joyride, Tony died of kidney failure.

In the months and years that followed, news investigations connected Tony's death with the EPA-approved practice of sludge spreading, whereby sewage— including medical and industrial waste that is "treated" to remove some but not all of the deadly pathogens—is applied to farm land.[1] Eventually, miners working near the site of Tony's exposure would come forward to say they had become ill, too, but were afraid to speak out for fear of losing their jobs. People in other communities across the state would also start complaining of illness and livestock loss attributed to sludge.

Tony Behun's death was followed a year later by the sludge-related death of another boy, Daniel Pennock, in Heidelberg Township, Pennsylvania. The two tragedies, combined with a 1997 state law loosening the regulations around sludge application, ignited a grassroots movement in central Pennsylvania to tighten local rules around the practice. When companies profiting from sludge-spreading sued one of the towns that had tried to crack down on the procedure—on the basis that the local rules infringed on the corporation's "personhood rights"—the movement turned into rebellion against the idea of corporate rights.

By seeking to prohibit the application of sludge, communities learned a painful lesson in civics: Under our current legal system, local towns' authority to ban or control hazardous practices has been stripped, and efforts to stop corporations from spreading sludge would violate the corporation's "rights." Citizens throughout rural Pennsylvania were shocked to discover that the sludge corporations possessed more rights than the citizens.

In one such community, Porter Township, shock quickly turned to anger and a resolve to assert the rights of residents—not corporations—over local control. With assistance from a Pennsylvania attorney named Thomas Linzey, the United Mineworkers and other partners, Porter Township made history by becoming the first community in the United States to pass an ordinance stripping corporate constitutional protections within the township. Echoing the Boston Tea Party, a citizens' revolt for real democracy and local control began to sprout across Pennsylvania, and is today spreading across the country.

Sludge and the Corporate "Chilling Effect"

Most of the sludge entering rural Pennsylvania isn't local; it comes from the city of Pittsburgh. With a metropolitan population of about 1.7 million people, Pittsburgh generates tons of waste every day from homes, hospitals, and industry. Dumping it in the landfill has always been an expensive proposition for waste management companies. So, following heavy industry lobbying, legislators in Pennsylvania lowered waste disposal standards in 1997 to accommodate the interests of big business.

The lowering of the statewide standard opened the floodgates for sludge-spreading in rural areas. It also automatically repealed more than 100 existing local regulations that had restricted factory farms from setting up shop. Factory farms had been a problem for rural communities in other states, and many

Toxic Sludge Is Not Good For You

Sludge is everything that passes through the sewage system—not just human waste flushed from toilets—but also industrial waste, much of which is illegally dumped in municipal sewers. In 1991, Congress determined that sludge was too dangerous to continue dumping in oceans. Yet two years later, the EPA approved a Sludge Program, setting out guidelines for sewage "treatment" and enabling the waste to be spread on land. The EPA teamed up with the clean-sounding Water Environment Federation (the sludge industry's lobbying and public relations arm, previously known as the Federation of Sewage Works Associations), to re-brand sludge as environmentally friendly fertilizer. Together they hatched a million-dollar PR campaign to change public perceptions—and dictionary definitions—about toxic sludge. This effort included euphemistically renaming sludge "biosolids," and describing it as a "safe fertilizer product" (www.e_net.org). As a result, millions of tons of sludge are spread each year; some 60 percent of all sludge is now used as fertilizer for marketed crops. Under EPA regulations, sludge only needs to be tested for 10 heavy metals out of a possible 70,000 chemicals and deadly pathogens, before being applied to land or composted and sold.

Pennsylvania towns had taken precautions to keep them out.

The loosened standards for sludge spreading caught the attention of an attorney named Thomas Linzey, who had founded the Community Environmental Legal Defense Fund (CELDF) as a law school graduate in 1995 to assist those who could not afford to challenge companies that were violating regulatory law. Linzey is no slick city lawyer. Bespectacled, blue-eyed, and dressed for comfort in khakis and a fleece jacket, he's right at home in the kitchens and church halls in which he's likely to be found around Pennsylvania, talking to conservative farmers about the U.S. Constitution and the rights of corporations. Despite being a non-local, he's well respected—not because he's a lawyer, or even because he's deeply knowledgeable about the law, but because he's a listener, and because he truly believes local communities have the right to determine the policies that affect their lives.

Linzey explained that a community with a 10,000-head hog farm linked to a cancer cluster had very little ability to effect change. Proving the link between cancer and the corporation is very hard to do under our system of law, and communities have no legal recourse to stop corporations from locating in their area. As Linzey told us: "What communities have been forced to do instead is to go through the regulatory system. Instead of talking about whether or not you want the corporation in your neighborhood, people are channeled into talking about 'parts per million'—about how high the perimeter walls must be, or how deep the waste pools can be, or how many. That is all citizens can do."

Linzey spent the better part of the 1990s in court. He watched communities win small regulatory battles and celebrate their victories: higher walls, smaller and fewer waste pools, hooray! Then he'd witness the corporate attorney's return and threaten to bankrupt towns by appealing rulings and prolonging the battle—hopefully forcing communities to cave in and accept the existing conditions. Linzey says he witnessed legislators eagerly meeting lobbyists and corporate lawyers brazenly seeking to lower environmental and safety standards that impeded profits or conceded any local control over corporate activities. He watched as corporate lawyers and legislators drafted legislation together to benefit the corporations.

Through the years, Linzey began to see a disturbing pattern: The legal system favors the corporation. "We would go to court, time after time," Linzey told us, "and even if we won the day, the corporate boys would be back later."

Linzey's experiences led him to question whether the regulatory system was broken, or whether it was actually working perfectly. Who really was being regulated—the corporations or the people? "The thing about the permitting process is that you are permitting a certain level of toxins in the first place.

Why? And who gets to say how many parts per million are safe? Is it citizens or is it corporations? Who is deciding these things, and for whose benefit?"

When the Pennsylvania legislature lowered the state's waste management standards, CELDF was flooded with calls. Soon Linzey and his understaffed and underfunded team were working with more than 100 communities state-wide to tighten local standards for sludge applications.

As residents in several Pennsylvania townships began investigating the issue, they found that state law required sludge to be tested only once every three months, and only for *E. coli* and heavy metals, not for the spectrum of deadly micro-organisms that can live for months and even years. They also discovered that most batches were never tested at all. Once spread, biosolids were sup-posed to be restricted from human contact for at least 30 days. Yet the state's Department of the Environment (DEP) was not enforcing this regulation.

Residents in a number of townships were determined to protect loved ones and themselves from harm. Rush Township—a community of about 4,000 people in the heart of the state's coal belt—was the first to take action. Tony Behun had grown up near Rush, and locals still held painful memories of his death from sludge exposure. Although many residents wanted to ban sludge spreading entirely, state law prohibited them from going that far. So Rush leaders moved to ensure that every batch of sludge would be thoroughly tested before application. It took some time to get the ordinance in place, but in 1999, Rush approved a law mandating the testing of every batch of sludge that entered the township and passed along the testing costs to the sludge haulers via a $40 per biosolid ton "tipping fee." The idea quickly spread, and within a year, dozens of communities throughout Pennsylvania had adopted similar legislation. It seemed that the regulatory framework was working after all.

Then, in 2000, something happened that sent shockwaves through the net-work of rural communities battling sludge. Synagro corporation, based in Texas and among the largest U.S. sludge haulers, sued Rush Township, alleging that the tipping fee law violated the corporation's civil and constitutional rights. The corporate attorneys went even further, suing Rush supervisors personally for $1 million each. Explaining the effect of this threat on a small-town super-visor, Linzey told us, "These are the folks salting the roads in the winter and patching the roads in the summer. They're the ones sporting the John Deere hats. These are good community folks with families to provide for."

The Synagro lawyers' didn't sue all the towns with tipping fees. They usually came down hard on one town in order to scare the others. As Linzey recalled, "In Clarion County, about half the townships had passed the fee by now. They were all calling us. They were angry, confused, scared."

The Legacy of Daniel Pennock

Daniel Pennock was a teenager with a promising future until he contracted the bacteria staphylococcus aureus and died. Years later, his parents, Russell and Antoinette Pennock, discovered that the cause of Danny's infection was exposure to sludge. They answered these questions together.

What kind of a young man was Daniel?

Daniel turned 17 on January 23, 1995. Danny had light brown hair brown and eyes. He was a nice looking kid. Danny liked hunting, fishing, any outdoor sports. He was a leader; people were drawn to him. If he had a story to tell you, he went on forever, he was very into details. Danny loved history as a kid; he was fascinated with the Civil War. ... His life was just starting; he had just gotten a part-time job at a food market. He talked about going into the Air Force. He had started going out with this girl about a month before he died. She was his first girlfriend. He was happy, and so inexperienced. One night, he was asking me [his mother] for advice about kissing her for the first time. I asked him, "What are you waiting for?"

Tell us about how Daniel got sick.

It was a warm winter evening. Danny had shorts on and was playing basketball outside. He started getting sick right after that. It was so bizarre—on a Thursday evening he was playing basketball, on Sunday he was in the hospital. When we brought him in, he was ashen; it was 13 days of pure hell. They were asking us, "Does he have asthma? Does he smoke?" Danny was healthy. He didn't drink or smoke. Monday morning they did a culture, there was all this hushed conversation, doctors and nurses going in and out of his room. They told us he had a massive staph infection, but that he was young and strong and should pull through, but we knew ... we knew. Nobody this young and strong should get that sick from staph. They intubated him, and he never spoke again after Monday night. A hole had been blown in his lung. The doctors had no clue what to do, they only reacted to his symptoms. Danny died on April 1, 1995. It would be years before we would find out why he really died. Our son, he never got a chance to be in love, he never graduated, and he didn't get to see the world.

Can you tell us about how you traced the cause of his illness?

We blamed ourselves for a long time. We thought it must have been something we had done, so we did everything we could think of to do. Within a week we had our water checked. [Later] the DEP would say it was our water, but we had checked the well and our pool. We started eating differently, buying organic, in case that was it ... It wasn't until 2001, when [we] opened the paper. There was an article, "Raising a Stink: A PA boy dies of sewage sludge." It was Tony Behun. When we read the article, what happened to him, it was all just too familiar ... We hadn't even thought about the farm across the road before that. Then we learned they had been sludging there for years. When we found out that staph is caused by sludge, it was like 2 + 2 = sludge.

Did you understand the danger you were all exposed to?

Spreading Their Story

Among those who were angry and confused were Russell and Antoinette Pennock of Heidelberg Township, Pennsylvania. Their son Daniel—a healthy boy of 17—had died in 1995 from a sudden and inexplicable staph infection.

In 2001, as the Rush case wound its way through the courts, Antoinette was at her kitchen table, quietly drinking coffee and reading the morning paper, when she read a story about sludge exposure and Tony Behun's death. Her mind was racing. She called out to her husband to read the article. The

When Danny died, we didn't know about sludge, that it was dangerous, that the farmer spread it on his property. When we bought the house there was no warning. We found out much later they had been putting that stuff down for years and we were exposed to it—in fact, we had his permission to hunt and cross through his land and had done so for years. We could see when they were spreading it, but at that time we didn't know what it was, we just thought it was fertilizer. [The farmer] certainly must have known. Antoinette called the reporter, and he came and talked to us. He connected us with Dave Lewis [a scientist with the EPA who would lose his job for speaking out about the toxicity of sludge]. Dave Lewis asked us questions like, "Did we have lesions, boils, sore throats, allergies, sinus or ear infections?" We had had a of those things at different times over the years, our visitors too. … After the sludge issue broke, we got many visitors. Two DEP investigators came out, they were very condescending, asking us if we knew what sewage sludge was. They wanted the hospital records, to find out what we knew. At one point Alvin Thomas [Executive Vice President] from Synagro [sludge hauling corporation] wanted to meet to explain why they had settled [another case about sludge] out of court. He thought we were interested in money. You can't put a dollar on your kid; you couldn't pay us enough.

How did you get involved with the Democracy Schools?

We were looking for environmental lawyers. We got an email from someone about Thomas Linzey. It was probably fall of 2001. … With Thomas, we went all the way up [the justice system], we tried. Even the Supreme Court wouldn't hear our case. We didn't want revenge; we wanted justice. We've talked to lots of reporters, and Thomas would call and ask us to come tell our story to a community. [Russ] went the first time, in Bedford County. We told our story over and over. We went to many meetings like that. I know it doesn't sound like a lot, but we know other lives have been saved through the work that has been done. If someone had told us this stuff, maybe things would be different; we would have had an opportunity to act on it. Then Thomas told us about the Democracy Schools that CELDF was doing, that they were going to name them after Daniel. We thought that was great. The schools talk about how the citizen is getting screwed over by the government and the corporations, how the two work together. They tell you what your rights really are, what you can and can't do in this country, in your community. It's a great thing, an important thing that gives people the tools to fight for change.

account of Tony Behun's suffering and death stirred a flood of memories and emotions within the Pennocks. Most striking were the similarities to their own son's painful last days. The Pennocks wondered if Danny had also succumbed to sludge exposure. For years they had unsuccessfully sought clues about his death. Suddenly, it seemed, the answer was there in print. Pieces of their lives that had never made sense began to click: a decade of sinus infections, headaches, lesions, and other maladies, combined with dead livestock and barn cats, and the strange and pungent fertilizer used by a neighboring farmer. They began making calls to newspapers, the DEP, and lawyers.

The Pennocks were soon in touch with Linzey, then in the midst of his campaign to restrict sludge spreading. Although for the Pennocks the two-year statute of limitations for filing a wrongful death suit had expired, Linzey believed justice might be sought another way—by taking Danny's story to other Pennsylvania communities as a way of inspiring people to defend their local tipping fee ordinances.

The Pennocks were ready. They felt that trying to hold the waste companies accountable for their actions was the least they could do to serve their son's memory. Soon the Pennocks, often with Linzey in tow, were traveling the length of the state sharing their experience with townships struggling with the effects of sludge spreading. "We would go to talk to people, and explain how sludging is considered a normal agricultural practice," Russell Pennock told us. "A hundred people could walk across a sludged field, maybe only one would die, but who wants to be that one? If they had seen our son's suffering ... no one should ever die like that."

The Pennsylvania Model in Action

One of the places where the Pennock story took hold was Porter Township in Clarion County. Porter citizens, working with the town's three elected commissioners, had adopted a sludge-tipping fee similar to the one in Rush. In late 2002, the Alcosan Corporation, the sludge haulers operating in Porter, threatened to take legal action as Synagro had in Rush. Linzey was asked by the commissioners to attend a town meeting. He figured it was to discuss retreat. But the town wanted something else.

A Porter town hall meeting was set up, and some 100 of the town's 1,500 citizens turned out. As Linzey recalled: "I never saw anything like it. Farmers came with the Constitution rolled up in their back pockets. They really got to the heart of it, asking what good it was to pass local laws if corporations can use the system against them to nullify what they worked so hard to pass?"

Linzey listened intently as the town's residents engaged in a high-level discussion, not about sludge and tipping fees, but about rights, about democracy. "One supervisor asked, 'What in the hell are corporate personhood rights anyway?' ... The community was asking serious questions about the foundations of this country, and how corporations obtained the rights that were created for natural people," Linzey said.

Linzey explained that while at one time shareholders and executives could be held personally liable for a corporation's actions, they are now protected from such personal responsibility. For example, the First Amendment protecting citizens' right to free speech allows corporations to make campaign contributions; the Fourth Amendment protecting citizens from unlawful police entry also shields corporations from unannounced inspections; the Fifth Amendment to due process protects us against being tried twice for the same crime, but it also ensures a corporation's right to "just compensation" if its profits are hampered by community enacted laws for health and safety—such as a tipping fee for sludge haulers.

After much impassioned conversation, Linzey asked the people of Porter Township the million-dollar question: "What do you want us to do?" Their response stunned him.

"Strategically, they were way ahead of us," Linzey said. "They wanted to refuse to recognize corporations' 'personhood rights'—to make law without being interfered with." What this conservative rural community was proposing was effectively civil disobedience using the legal system. It was radical. And it had never been done before.

What Porter Township wanted was local majority rule, not minority control in the form of a giant corporation. Linzey and the CELDF team, in partnership with Richard Grossman from the Program on Corporations Law and Democracy, put together the first Elimination of Corporate Personhood ordinance in the country. As Linzey recalls, "It was all about who was in control in Porter, about shifting the focus to basic concepts about power."

In Licking Township, Pennsylvania, the community was struggling with the same sludge issues and had passed the tipping fee structure in early 2002. While some might consider Porter a small town, it's practically a metropolis compared to Licking, with a population of 479 people. When the citizens of Licking learned what had happened in Rush and Porter, they too contacted CELDF to learn about their options. Michael J. ("Mik") Robertson, one of three supervisors made the call. Robertson is a busy man: A husband and father, he is also a geologist and town supervisor—patching roads and otherwise governing town affairs—and the chair of the Libertarian Party of Pennsylvania. Despite his many hats, Robertson comes across as serious-minded, a person very little gets by—a man of details.

"We had been aware that the [Porter tipping fee] ordinance was being challenged in court," said Robertson. "Linzey faxed me a copy of the complaint from [the sludge haulers] and told me about the anti-corporate personhood ordinance he was developing for Porter. I asked him to fax me that, too." Robertson and his fellow supervisors met with folks in Porter and held town meetings of their own to discuss the possibility of adopting a similar ordinance. The rights of people were at the center of the discussion, as Robertson told us. "As a Libertarian, it's pretty clear to me that rights are something that only individuals can have. Governments have authority, corporations have a charter filed away somewhere, but neither governments nor corporations can claim the rights of individuals."

This political perspective also speaks to the way in which individuals should have input. As Robertson reflected, "The most direct input citizens can have is at the local level. You can go to your township meeting and as an individual can have a substantial impact on the way things are considered. At the state level, other voices are coming in that may or may not care about the local community. Citizens' rights get drowned out in that larger process. It shouldn't happen, but it does. By the time you get to the federal level, you are way out of influence in decision-making."

Are Corporations People Too?

"The first truth is that the liberty of a democracy is not safe if the people tolerate the growth of private power to a point where it becomes stronger than their democratic state itself. That, in essence, is fascism—ownership of government by an individual, by a group, or by any other controlling power."
— President Franklin Delano Roosevelt

Roosevelt was by no means the first to warn citizens about the dangers of vesting too much power in the legal fiction known as the corporation. Thomas Jefferson vehemently warned against vesting the corporate form with too much power, and the Boston Tea Party was a revolt against the concentrated power of the East India Company, the Wal-Mart of its day.

Corporations are not mentioned in the U.S. Constitution. Yet over the last century and a half, judges have increasingly "found" the corporation in the Bill of Rights and the Commerce Clause. The rights of people represented in the Bill of Rights were won by people's movements and were intended to protect citizens. By fighting against oppression—often with great personal sacrifices—women and African-Americans won their freedoms, now enshrined in Amendments to the Constitution. Through corporate lobbying over many decades, and through a number of decisions by Supreme Court justices sympathetic to moneyed interests, corporations have secured these rights and protections intended for persons and now wield them to keep communities from governing themselves.

As far as local land-control issues went, Robertson and the majority of his fellow conservative constituents agreed—a local-level approach that empowered residents to make critical decisions was the only way to move forward. Using the ordinance drafted for Porter as a guide, they began crafting their own ordinance.

Meanwhile, back in Porter, the ordinance passed unanimously at a public hearing on December 9, 2002. It is a simple three-page document. Its essence is contained in a single paragraph stating that within Porter's limits, "Corporations shall not be considered to be persons protected by the Constitution of the United States or the Constitution of the Commonwealth of Pennsylvania."

News of Porter's Elimination of Corporate Personhood ordinance spread fast and far. Licking's similar ordinance passed a few months later in March 2003, providing added momentum to the model legislation and demonstrating that Porter's action hadn't been a fluke.

Communities throughout the state and around the nation immediately began contacting CELDF to find out how they could enact similar legislation. Model ordinances began popping up on the Internet. As Linzey points out, "Municipalities and community groups are now looking more to passing local laws rather than appealing state agency decisions, because it has become obvious to communities facing these giant corporations that if they don't make their own law, others will do it for them."

Despite the town's radical role as corporate crime fighters, life in otherwise quiet Porter Township remains pretty much unchanged; the special at the diner is still meatloaf on Wednesdays. But the children playing tackle football in the fallow field across the road are not running through toxic sludge. The Alcosan corporation and its attorneys, willing to sue Porter into bankruptcy over a tipping fee, have been reluctant to challenge a law that is framed in the context of corporate rights versus people's rights.

At this writing, more than 100 rights-based ordinances and resolutions based on the Porter framework have been enacted across Pennsylvania and the nation. This type of work is now often referred to as the "Pennsylvania model" of organizing. Other communities are taking the idea a step further and actually rewriting their town charters to include provisions that not only protect against corporate personhood, but also define in the affirmative what they want their town to aspire to—including putting local businesses first and protecting open spaces that affirm the rights of nature.

Though none of the corporations affected has yet challenged a community, Linzey expects to see the issue of corporate personhood before the Supreme Court within a decade, adding that it will take "a very large movement of people, working on a number of issues, to focus on corporate power."

The work begun in Porter has changed CELDF, too. The phones haven't stopped ringing. By way of spreading this work, CELDF has started running three-day, intensive "Democracy Schools" for communities answering the big questions: Why does the corporation have these rights? Where did it get them? And what did past people's movements do to secure their rights? The experience of these schools feels a bit like slowly unpeeling an onion—not just because it is a many-layered conversation about law, democracy, and corporations, but also because it almost makes your eyes water from the sting.

These are not easy questions, and they show that when communities feel cornered by the power of corporations, they are ready to come out swinging. The Democracy School, named after Daniel Pennock, has "graduated" more than 1,600 people in 23 different locations across the country, with more schools being added almost every weekend. As Linzey is fond of saying, "We don't have democracy in this county, and if we don't do something different, we'll never have one."

CONVERSATION

Gopal Dayaneni

Whether he's working with Indigenous communities in North America to oppose oil extraction, partnering with Nigerians to resist human rights abuses, or trying to uncover the modern-day slavery of prison labor, Gopal Dayaneni can be found on the front lines of environmental justice struggles. Friends and colleagues know Dayaneni as an especially thoughtful activist. While he is busy doing his own small part to promote progressive social change, he is also a big-picture thinker, always encouraging those around him to consider the long view of what it takes to create a more sane and humane world. That trait distinguishes Dayaneni as an important resource for communities looking for the strategic, tactical, and imaginative skills necessary to effect change. We caught up with the 37-year-old campaigner at his home in Berkeley, California, where he was busy tending to his young daughter.

Q: You use the term "environmental justice." Can you define that?
GD: Environmental Justice is a term that talks about a movement that developed over the last 20 years to really take on the disproportionate impact of environmental toxics and pollution on poor communities and communities of color. At the heart of that movement is a commitment to bottom-up organizing and grassroots community organizing. Environmental justice is not about a bunch of people trying to lobby for better laws or a bunch of high-level policy people trying to change environmental policy. It's about communities organizing themselves and resisting environmental abuse by industry or government. And because it is grassroots led, and because it is driven by communities directly attempting to make concrete improvements in the quality of their daily lives, it is ripe for an opening to see the intersections between environmental policy, economics, race, class, the war.

Q: You talk about the difference between defending your concrete interests and defending the environment in general. Is it because when the stakes are higher, the passion is greater?
GD: Yeah, I think there's something to be said for the expression, "There's

nothing to lose but your chains." I think there's a greater sense of solidarity. I think people are much more willing to share their successes to work together. I think there's a much greater sense of empowerment because people are actually in control of the campaigns that they are organizing. People are not passive participants watching somebody else try and make things better. They are actively the voice of the issue. People are telling their own stories, they're speaking for themselves.

Changing policy may open up political space to stop the immediate bad things from continuing to happen. But if we're talking about fundamentally transforming our society to be more democratic and more equitable and more humane, the strategy is grassroots community organizing, in my opinion. A good friend of mine once said to me, "Campaigns don't change the world, organizations do." And my response to him was, "Organizations don't change the world, organizing does." That's really for me what's important. For me, that's central to my theory of change.

Q: There is a stereotypical view of U.S. environmentalists as white, middle class, and into bird watching. What do you think of this issue?

GD: Race is a scary thing in America. Race is scary to most white people in America. Race is scary to most people of color in America. Being people of color does not make us smarter, or more revolutionary, or more right, or better. It just makes us oppressed, and there's no great glory in that.

Race is a problem for Americans. It's easy to talk about saving the trees or saving the birds. When you start talking about the relationship between saving the trees and saving the birds and white supremacy in America, you start losing people. It takes a lot of work to help build that consciousness. Just in this conversation, we won't start talking about it by calling it white supremacy. We have to figure out ways of helping people to understand the dynamics of power in this country, and how those attitudes and structures and systems serve the interests of some classes and communities of people over the interests of other communities.

Q: As we try to move toward this whole green economy, what are some of the things you think that these bigger organizations can learn from community-based groups?

GD: The grassroots community-based organizing, I think, is the most important thing that people can learn. I think the other thing is, as people begin to fight for concrete improvements in their daily lives, they also have a taste for what they really want. People start building their own alternatives. People build their own organizations. People start building their own co-ops. People start running their own community farms. It's not enough to get rid of the polluting power plant. People are also building community gardens in those same neighborhoods. It's not enough for them to just say, 'We don't like that there are polluting diesel trucks in our neighborhood.' As you fight that and as you experience victory, your revolutionary imagination is liberated. I think that's where the great promise is.

It's not enough for us to make the oil industry start investing in photovoltaics. There's not a technical solution to our environmental problems. There may be technical things that we can use to help us transition, but the solution is deeply political, and deeply structural and societal. It's about really changing the way we organize our relationship to resources. It shouldn't be mediated by mega-corporations who make a huge amount of money off of it. It should be directly controlled and distributed by communities in their own interest.

Q: What's a vision of what an environmentally justice-informed green economy looks like?
GD: Well, one of the things that we have to open ourselves up to when we embrace the idea that we are going to build from the bottom up is that we don't know exactly what it's going to look like. We can't have this idea that there's this road map. We need the creativity of everybody diving into the mix.

But I think there are a few different pieces that are really important. In terms of the scale at which we currently operate, there's absolutely no question that we're not going to suddenly go from where we are today—where everybody drives a car and the box stores and all of that—to everybody getting their produce from a farmer's market. That's not going to happen overnight. And that may not even be the collective vision of everyone. But given the scale of where we are at right now, one of the places where we need to start is empowering workers and communities to have greater control and input over the resources in their community and in their workplace.

Another big part of it is people working hard to meet their own needs within their local environment. All of the models of urban gardening that have been driven by community needs—not just recreation—really demonstrate the power of that. I think one of the areas where we have been an exception is really looking at the relationship between organized labor and these community-based needs. What does it mean that most people in the United States get their groceries—heavily processed foods and all of the things we know that are terrifying about them—from big chain grocery stores? But let's also not forget that a significant portion of these big chain grocery stores are unionized. And they do have workers who have fought hard to get protections and to protect themselves. And we're not talking about suddenly saying, 'Oh, everyone's going to get their food from community-based gardens.' It's about also figuring out how we're going to integrate the needs of people who are existing in this economy into our meaningful alternatives and into our positive solutions.

Q: Speaking of solutions, we live in a one-size-fits-all, silver-bullet kind of culture. Could you talk about how we're going to have to juggle a number of different things?

GD: I don't know when and how it's going to happen, but I personally believe we have to break the expectation that you can have whatever you want, whenever you want. There's a desire to be able to have every kind of produce year-round. There is this idea that we should have access to everything at any time, like changing your cell phone every six months. And I think we're going to have to break that. Part of breaking that is going to be learning to appreciate the local and regional diversity. The more people have the opportunity to embrace the localism and the value of the localism, I think that will help us break that monoculture and allow us to appreciate diversity.

We have the ability to imagine a different future. It's not about going back in time. It's about going forward in a way in which we are living within our ecological boundaries.

What You Can Do

Neither Paper Nor Plastic

The stories and conversations in this section prove that people can clean up noxious corporate practices. Yet despite all the inspiration they offer, these tales remain "end-of-pipeline" politics. That is, they are cleaning up the waste after it leaves the factory. A more long-term strategy is to prevent the pollution in the first place. And the best way to do that is by making polluting factories obsolete through the coordinated act of refusing to buy what they're selling.

Planning the obsolescence of the industrial economy lies at the center of the local green economy movement. If you don't want to campaign against field applications of sewage sludge, then buy organic food. If you don't want to fight against the pollution of a paper mill, lower the amount of paper you use. Get the PVC out of your house—and fast.

"Live simply so that others may simply live." That bumper sticker wisdom reveals what's required to reduce the toxins that poison us, especially our poorest communities. The way to fulfill that goal is by cutting back on the amount of stuff in our lives and clearly distinguishing between "needs" and "wants."

When it comes to your daily life, the three Rs of environmental sustainability are a helpful checklist for limiting your impact on the environment.

Reduce. Do you really need more clothes? A bigger car? More gadgets to put in the junk drawer? Americans are the biggest consumers on the planet, and research shows that most of what we buy ends up in the trash within just six months. The most effective way to shrink your ecological footprint is by consuming less. Just cut back on the things you buy; it will leave you with more money and more time for your loved ones. At the same time, share. Does every home on your block need its own lawn mower, or can the neighborhood make do with one, fully employed? If we can find a way to use our scarce resources collectively, we won't need to use so much of them in the first place, and we will get to know our neighbors better.

Re-use. Before throwing something into the garbage, take a minute to think about whether you can employ it for some other use. Turn the yogurt container into improvised Tupperware. Rinse out your plastic produce bags, take them back to the grocery story, and use them again. Also, trade, barter, and swap. Surely someone somewhere wants your sweaters and books—and they probably have a novel you've been dying to read or a blouse you'd love to wear. Check out freecycle.org for giving things away. Hold a garage sale or donate to charity. Give your possessions a second life.

Recycle. Sorting your office paper into different recycling bins will not save the ecosystem, but it can save you money. (White paper separated from colored paper can be sold.) A sweeping ethic of recycling that looks at how to extend the cradle-to-grave life cycle of every product is not only possible, it is becoming increasingly necessary. By all means, deposit your cans, plastic bottles, and paper into the right receptacles. At the same time, think about how you can recycle your computer, the batteries you use, the parts in your car. Don't let anything go to waste.

Let's make it part of human culture to pay respect to nature's gifts by not wasting them.

Section Two

Food & Water

What's for dinner?

It's among the most ordinary of questions and seemingly easy to answer: pasta, chicken, enchiladas, whatever. But the response gets trickier if you look at the ingredients listed on the packaged food most Americans eat. Read closely and you'll find polysyllabic curiosities like thiamin mononitrate (used to enrich flours), the all-purpose emulsifier soy lecithin, preservatives such as potassium sorbate, and that bane of nutritionists, high fructose corn syrup. Often you'll see an ingredient so vague as to be automatically suspicious—the all-too-common "flavoring."

Fruits, vegetables, meat, eggs, and milk found at the supermarket can be equally suspect. These "fresh" foods fail to disclose the inputs that went into their production. For example, the pesticides and herbicides that were doused on the produce, or the growth hormones and antibiotics injected into the animals that end up as hamburger and pork chops.

This is food? Yuck.

Fifty years after the TV dinner came to symbolize the industrial food chain, a food revolt is underway in the United States. Shoppers are skipping the boxed goods in favor of whole foods. Sales of organic produce are skyrocketing. Hormone-free and antibiotic-free milk is in such high demand that dairies are struggling to keep up with consumer tastes.

That a growing number of people are seeking to get closer to their food can be witnessed in the explosive popularity of farmers markets, which have doubled in the last 15 years to more than 3,400.

There is also budding interest among people to grow their own food. A good example is Chicago's LaDonna Redmond. She was a typical supermarket shopper until her son developed acute food allergies; then she decided to start an urban farm in the country's third largest city. Redmond is not alone. From Los Angeles to Houston to New York, community activists are planting urban farms in an attempt to seed self-sufficient economies. The drive for local control over local resources can also be seen in the story of Oregon's Applegate watershed, where loggers and conservationists came together to chart a plan for using the area's natural wealth. And as we show in our story about Cuba, the U.S. movement can still go much further.

The re-localization of our food is a central pillar of the emerging green economy for the obvious reason that eating is our most basic need. If we can't find a way to feed ourselves without committing ecological and social crimes, then we're in real trouble.

While communities seek to localize their food, there's also a backlash against the privatization of the planet's water. Fifteen years ago, bottled water was reserved for a Perrier-drinking elite. Now it's as common as, well, rainwater. There may be no clear consensus on what exactly the local, green economy will look like, but it's a pretty sure bet that it won't include shipping water from Fijian aquifers halfway around the world.

The struggles for control over our food and water reveal a movement seeking to reconnect to the biological systems on which we rely. These efforts prove that, to paraphrase organic farming pioneer Sir Albert Howard, humanity—despite all our pretensions and inventions—still depends on six inches of topsoil and the fact that it rains.

Green Acres In
The Windy City

Urban Farming Grows
Food Justice in Chicago

"Every community has the intellect to heal itself."
—LaDonna Redmond

In a largely African-American section of Chicago, one mother found herself struggling to meet the needs of her son, whose food allergies put his life at risk. Seeking nutritious food for her family, she found that healthy food was neither available nor affordable in her neighborhood. So La-Donna Redmond decided to grow organic food in her family's back yard. Over the next four years, she led her neighbors in transforming the way they provide food, jobs and health for the community.

H er eyes were red from hours of watchful worry. She was tired, sleepless. Like any mother standing over her baby lying in intensive care, La-Donna Redmond felt helpless. She was responsible for this tiny life, for taking care of him, yet she could do nothing for him. His little lungs strained to take in air, each breath a struggle for life. Her son Wade suffered from severe food allergies—a long list of everyday ingredients including milk, peanuts, shellfish, and eggs, and harder-to-spot additives and preservatives found in most packaged foods. In that moment, gazing down at her son breathing laboriously through tubes and connected to various machines, LaDonna knew that she and her husband, Tracey, would need to learn everything they could about his food needs. She had no idea how this seemingly simple quest for nutritional knowledge would alter all their lives.

"When Wade was born, it was 1998, my life totally changed," Redmond said. "His allergies were not the point. It was that I was responsible for this human being. I saw my job as protecting him from the evils of the world. I had never looked at myself in that way before." Redmond had been working at a violence prevention center run by the State of Illinois. Now it appeared she

55

would need to quit her job and spend all of her time caring for her son.

Redmond told the doctors she was going to need a treatment plan for Wade, but they didn't seem to know what to feed him. He was allergic to so many things, including milk and ingredients found in most milk substitutes, even soy milk. Most baby foods used binding agents like eggs or other things he couldn't eat, and reading the label didn't always make it easier.

"It was shocking to me what was on those labels, and what wasn't," Redmond told us. "You needed a degree in chemistry to understand what was in there—all these scientific names. And some foods had ingredients that were not listed at all."

Since the doctors couldn't help her, she would need to find her own answers.

A Dangerous Food System

"Then one day, I was reading the newspaper and I read about Greenpeace dumping tons of GMO grain in front of [British Prime Minister] Tony Blair's house, and I thought, 'What's a GMO?'" She read on and found out that it stood for genetically modified organism, food that was scientifically altered at the genetic level. This seemed strange. She had never seen "contains GMOs" on the label of any food product in any store. And why did food need to be altered in the first place? The article didn't explain.

A few weeks later, as she was watching the evening news in December 1999, a story about the "Battle of Seattle" depicted tens of thousands of people shutting down the city's streets at the World Trade Organization (WTO) conference. "We could see they were activists, they were not black. ... But what is the WTO? Why were so many farmers involved? Then the news was over."

Redmond instinctively felt the stories were connected, but she wasn't sure how or why. She spent countless nights researching on the internet. Redmond's research led her to the website of the Organic Consumers Association (OCA), a nonprofit organization that informs consumers about the dangers lurking in our corporate food system.

Redmond started sifting through information about pesticide residue, global food production, food grown in toxic sewer sludge, genetically altered seeds, industrial hog farms, cows injected with growth hormones, corporations policing farmers. The facts were so scary she wondered how it was possible they weren't front-page news.

"I was not prepared for the revelation that I knew very little about where my food came from or who grew it," Redmond once told a writer with the Rodale

Institute's New Farm website. "Prior to this incident with my son, I would not have even considered the fact that healthy and nutritious food has a lot to do with how that food was produced."[1]

The information was troubling. Her priority was feeding her son, but she knew that others were going through the same things she was. She wanted to simply shut off the computer, but she knew that wasn't the answer.

What happened to the natural food chain? When did food stop being about farmers growing good food in the earth? When did it turn into a system defined by weird science and international trade bureaucracies like the WTO? Food was supposed to be about making personal choices, but Redmond realized that nothing in the grocery store was personal anymore. Somewhere along the way to industrial agriculture, food had become political.

By looking beneath the surface of her daily meals, Redmond had stumbled upon a Pandora's lunch box, a vast food system of corporate-controlled, worldwide production and shipment that was more about corporate efficiency than delivering wholesome sustenance. Giant machines rolling among acres of uniform crops had replaced small farms harvesting a variety of local delights; gene scientists had become more important than hometown farmers; and unique local varieties of seasonal produce had been supplanted by uniform, bland-tasting vegetables picked prematurely and transported thousands of miles. It was a system in which most of the food we eat is no longer local, no longer fresh, and no longer natural or healthful.

Redmond struggled to make sense of it all. It was too much information. But she was determined to take control of the food on her family's table.

"Wallowing in the 'industrial agriculture in the country needs to change' mentality did not get the food on the table in my neighborhood," Redmond said. "I needed to gain access to food unpolluted by genetic engineering and free from pesticides. I needed organic food."[2]

The Three Pillars of Food Justice

The Redmonds live in Austin, a working-class, mostly black neighborhood on the west side of Chicago. Austin is the largest borough in Chicago, home to 114,000 residents. Despite the neighborhood's size, only one "midsize" grocery store was in business there when Redmond started her campaign. Many families shopped at the neighborhood's small convenience stores.

The underwhelming shopping options available to Austin residents translate into capital flight from the neighborhood. Of the $134 million Austin residents spent on groceries in 2001, only $34 million was spent in their own neighborhood.[3] The lack of grocery stores also translates into health problems. Like many other low-income neighborhoods, Austin has above average rates of diabetes, heart disease, and obesity.

"Realistically, low-income communities spend three times as much of their household income—or 30 percent on the average—for food, whereas the across-the-board average for all households in the United States is 11 percent," Ronnie Cummins of the Organic Consumers Association, told us. "How would that affect your shopping?"

Given the expense and hassle of shopping locally, convenient fast-food options like White Castle, KFC, and Burger King do a brisk business. Redmond says the lack of options is stark: "In my neighborhood, you can buy Nikes, illegal drugs, weapons and junk food. But we can't get a green salad." As Cummins said, "It's the most unhealthy, damaging food out there, and unlike upscale neighborhoods, there are no options,"

The hardest part for Redmond was actually figuring out where to get organic food. She spent some more time on the Internet and then made the trek to other Chicago neighborhoods where organics were available, only to find that an organic-only diet was costly. "We had to re-do our entire budget in order to shop at Whole Foods." She adds with a laugh, "Or you can call it Whole Paycheck, it was just so expensive."

And there was more to the dilemma than the high price of organics. La-

Where Safeway Won't Tread:
An Inner-City Shopping Experience

In low-income neighborhoods across America, and particularly in communities of color, a strange grocery phenomenon has occurred. Chain supermarkets with produce displayed in dazzling pyramids-of-plenty have fled for more upscale zip codes. Instead, grocers with names like Val-U-Mart and Pete's Discount Food Barn have emerged, promising the full shopping experience for the budget-conscious. Step inside and the differences are immediately obvious. First, notice the security guard sporting an 9-millimeter handgun at the door. To the right, there is no courtesy-banking center; instead there is bullet-proof window for cashing government assistance checks. Unappealing produce lolls around in desolate bins, often shriveled or over-ripe. There are no butchers here, only vacuum-packed trays of lesser-grade cuts, some discolored and risky-looking. Over in the bread aisle, there are no fresh multiseeded baguettes, only bags of airy white bread promising to last forever. And despite the name, these stores are no bargain. Convenience stores, while closer to home, are even more expensive (though beer is on sale) and far more limited in their offerings, which include nothing that isn't packaged, frozen, or canned.

Donna was thinking in a whole new way, considering not just the food in front of her but where it came from and how it was grown. She questioned whether the Whole Foods selection was locally grown, and whether it met the highest standards of sustainability. "I couldn't just say 'organic is the ticket' and that's what we'll buy," Redmond told us. "They were selling me grapes from South Africa! I thought, 'These foods are moving too far.'"

Breaking the industrial food chain meant creating a food justice trifecta: supporting organics, supporting local and regional goods whenever possible, and supporting fairness in food production by ensuring that farmers are getting fair prices for the goods they produce. "I wanted to buy my food from the person who produced it as often as possible, so maybe that means substituting local strawberries for out-of-season grapes from South Africa," Redmond said. "When we move into an environmentally aware market, when we talk about sustainability, we also have to be up on what is socially just. It can't be just about organics. All of these things need to fit together."

So she did some more shopping. She ended up going to farmers markets and considered enrolling in a Community Supported Agriculture (CSA) program. She tried to buy as much of her food as possible from stores that had a connection with producers. There were still frustrations. "The stuff was much cheaper than Whole Foods, but it took all day to get this and that, and in the end, I still had to go to the grocery store."

Standing in the museum-of-food experience that is Whole Foods, LaDonna again contemplated the prices she was paying for produce. Looking at tomatoes that were as much as $5 a pound and expensive lettuce, she thought, "How hard is it to grow lettuce anyway—it practically grows like weeds." She then asked herself the question that would change her life forever: How much work would it be to plant vegetables in the back yard?

Tomatoes That Taste Like … Tomatoes

Tracey and LaDonna Redmond did not have a farming background. Tracey was a senior commodities trader at Lind-Waldock and grew up in nearby Garfield. Born and raised in Chicago, LaDonna majored in economics in college and spent many years working for various community groups before her son was born. The family had what it needed, but they were not rich.

Tracey liked the idea of planting what they called a "micro-farm" in the back yard. LaDonna and Tracey also read a few "farming-by-numbers" books. His parents had rural roots, and acted as technical advisors on what, how, and when to plant. They decided to take over the whole back yard, planting lettuce, brussel sprouts, herbs, tomatoes, squash, and collard greens. "My father-in-law,

Mr. Willie, told me corn wouldn't grow in the back yard," said LaDonna.

That sounded like a challenge to her, so she planted that too. Despite its current status as a metropolis, Chicago is just farm country covered with asphalt and concrete. "The whole state is covered in corn, why couldn't it grow here?" LaDonna asked. "After all, seeds are blind, they only respond to conditions … Mr. Willie was the first person out there telling us the corn was ready!"

They grew about a dozen ears of corn that first year, which was enough for their family. But the rest of the back yard harvest yielded far more than they could eat. The tomatoes came off the vines by the pound, and the sheer number of zucchini overwhelmed them. To cope with all the food, they shared their bounty with neighbors.

To their amazement, the fresh and organic diet had an astonishing effect on their son Wade's health. In fact, the whole family reported feeling better. LaDonna says there were other family benefits too: "My mother had stopped eating tomatoes, she said they tasted like water. She thought she had lost her sense of taste." As they discovered, homegrown tomatoes are naturally delicious, not at all like tomatoes that come from far away. The Redmonds were discovering that tasteless food is one of the disagreeable by-products of market efficiency in an industrialized food system.

Even in Chicago, a city surrounded by agricultural land, just three percent of the produce is local. The vast majority is shipped from California, Florida, Mexico, the Netherlands, and beyond. Even in agricultural states like California, where organics are a booming business and items like tomatoes are a major crop, organic tomatoes are often imported from Europe. No tomatoes, organic or otherwise, can taste fresh, juicy and delicious after traveling 5,000 miles from farm to plate.

The tomato epiphany got the family thinking about other parts of their diet. "Mr. Willie, before he passed on, was having a 'thing' about chickens," LaDonna recalled. He was bothered that chicken breasts seemed unnaturally big and often came with broken bones, strange coloring, and a bland taste. Now that the family had identified the industrial food system as a problem, it seemed worth it to pay extra for an organic chicken that had good color, was the right size, and actually tasted like chicken.

The neighbors soon took great interest in the Redmonds' experiment. Many community elders with agricultural backgrounds were eager to give free advice; others wanted to get their hands dirty. The Redmond's back yard quickly became not only a source of family health, but also a center of conversation, activity, and community.

Another unexpected outcome was that Tracey Redmond had found his true calling. One day he looked around the back yard and announced he wanted to give up the financial world, which he said was "making me sick." What he wanted was to become a full-time farmer.

"Leadership Must Come from Within the Community"

LaDonna was reluctant to make a move to the country. The Redmonds knew farmers, and they knew how tough it was to make a living as a small grower. For starters, land prices are high and equipment is expensive. And while the government does offer assistance to farmers, most federal aid goes to large industrial farms; there is very little assistance for small farmers. The result has been a dramatic decline in the number of farms over time and an equally dramatic increase in the size of farms. Farmers, once one of America's most common occupations, have fallen below one percent of the country's population.

Despite the challenges of converting to farm life, LaDonna was hearing something straight from her husband's heart that she couldn't ignore. As she told us, "At the core of our marriage is understanding; we support each other. We're friends, we've been friends since long before we married. He was telling me he was unhappy. So I'm not happy." The question became: How could the Redmond's make Tracey's dreams come true in a way that made sense for the entire family?

They decided they could all get what they wanted by building a farm right there in Austin. There were several vacant lots just behind the Redmonds' house. They were full of nothing but trash and weeds, all-too-attractive for random gang activity. Because of LaDonna's work in the community, she knew the city had a program to develop vacant lots for community purposes. She laughs, remembering how they got more than they bargained for. "I asked for one lot, they gave me two, so we ended up with a few of them."

The real inspiration, though, wasn't the plants. It was the people in this tough city neighborhood. For LaDonna, that was what made the decision to farm in their community an easy one; the idea of community change was what spoke to her heart. "One of the things I bring with me is this love of people and community," she said. "I really believe in the idea that people can change their community's circumstances."

It was a lesson she grew up with. As a girl, LaDonna remembers the community meetings and the energy around Harold Lee Washington's campaign for Mayor of Chicago. "It was a big thing on the south side of Chicago; everyone pulled for him. Jesse Jackson raised money from black businesses, and there was a massive get out the vote action. Everyone knew what the goal was."

With community organizers registering more than 100,000 new African American voters, Washington won. Watching with child eyes, LaDonna learned that collective action made change possible. "That experience I bring with me always," LaDonna said.

As a young woman, LaDonna was mentored by Leola Spann, an African-American elder who devoted her life to building opportunities for Chicago's West Side. "Mrs. Spann's message was that the community had the capacity to change, in fact the right to change," LaDonna said. "She also taught me that leadership must come from within the community; no outsider can come in and do that."

LaDonna took that message to heart. Looking around at the littered vacant lots, the drug dealers on the corner, the fast food joints, and closed up businesses, LaDonna saw the real promise in her neighborhood. She thought, "Yeah. We can do this."

Eyesores Into Oases

First the family formed a nonprofit organization. Then they got a grant from the Chicago Community Trust, and a consortium of universities led by Loyola provided technical assistance. Other organizations with expertise in such spe-

---

Size Matters: Some Facts About Farms

- Corporate agribusiness profits increased 98 percent during the 1990s. Meanwhile, in 2002, farmers earned their lowest real net cash income since 1940.
- Modern industrial agriculture is making farming unprofitable for many. For more than 60 percent of farm households in 1998, farming actually lowered the household's before tax-income.
- 2002 USDA data show that small farms in the United States are many times more productive (in dollars per acre) than large ones.
- Taxpayers provided $22.9 billion in subsidies during the first three years of the "Freedom to Farm" law (1996-98), but 10 percent of the recipients collected 61 percent of the money.
- Over 80 percent of U.S. farmland is managed by farmers whose operations fall between small-scale direct markets and large agri-business holdings. These farmers are increasingly left out of our food system. If present trends continue, these farms, together with the social and environmental benefits they provide, will likely disappear in the next decade or two. The public good that these farms have provided in the form of land stewardship and community social capital will disappear with them.

Statistics from: http://foodroutes.org/hottopic.jsp?id=4

cialties as composting and raised-bed gardening became part of the growing community the urban farm was building. Tracey traded in his suit and tie for a pair of overalls, and was happy working the fields and supervising the staff.

The farm grew 40,000 pounds of organic produce its first year. As the work grew, it became a news item. Skeptics became converts. LaDonna told us, "We never pressured anyone; we just let folks know it was out there. It was no secret what Tracey was doing out there. It was really his project." In addition to the lots Tracey was supervising, the Redmonds helped start three "Block Clubs," where residents took care of the vacant lots on their own block. "Food would grow, people would watch and begin to think it was something they could do, too," LaDonna said.

At the Block Clubs, each participant received their own plot in a raised 4x20 foot bed. They could plant whatever they wanted: spinach, squash, sunflowers, or dahlias. Tracey and others provided the Block Club gardeners with technical support and information. Vacant lots were turning into organic oases.

Urban Farms
Victory Gardens Get a 21st Century Makeover

Notions of what farming looks like are changing dramatically. You don't need a John Deere hat, miles of open space, or even a tractor. And you definitely don't need pesticides. Urban agriculture is a big trend that is here to stay.

- According to the National Gardening Association, one in five U.S. households grows some produce, which adds up to savings estimated at between $100-$700 per year.

- Urban sprawl has meant an exodus from city centers to the suburbs, leaving tens of thousands of vacant lots and providing opportunities for enterprising gardeners.

- A U.N. report says that 15 percent of the global food supply is produced in urban settings by 800 million urban farmers worldwide, a vastly "overlooked, underestimated and underreported'" resource.

As Ronnie Cummins of the Organic Consumers Association points out, urban farming is not new. "We've seen these phenomena before as recently as the Second World War. Americans were producing more than 40 percent of our produce, fruits, and vegetables in 21 million Victory Gardens across the country. So we've shown the capacity to do in the U.S. what Cubans have been doing for years, which is growing food in urban or semi-urban settings. You can actually start to raise a lot of your food yourself, an important notion in the inner city where local food needs are grossly unmet. Obviously it's a society-wide trend toward healthier, more sustainable living, knowing where your food comes from. It's also cost-effective and gratifying to grow it yourself."

As their production expanded, the Redmonds' organization sold food to restaurants and farmers markets. The Redmonds called their open air stand "Organico's." It wasn't highly organized, but it took on a life of its own. Selling produce to the neighbors was not a problem. There was a deep hunger in the community for fresh, healthful foods. "There seems to be a belief out there that black people won't buy organic food, that all we want is Cheetos, or that we are not concerned about the environment," LaDonna said. "But we need to get folks the information to make a choice."

Suddenly, the nutritionally barren food economy of the West Side was bursting with homegrown energy, good food, and the pride of accomplishment. "People needed to see that it could be done and were inspired to take it wherever they thought it should go," LaDonna told us. "That was the goal, in fact." The Redmonds weren't just growing food; they were cultivating community.

From a Garden to a Grocery

The next year the Redmonds started a black farmers market in Austin, where each Saturday farmers from outside the city and urban gardeners join in selling their locally grown organic fruits, vegetables, preserves, and breads. The market went out of its way to accept electronic food stamps, providing new access to healthy food to low-income families in the neighborhood.

To assist growers and consumers, LaDonna began the Institute for Community Resource Development (ICRD). The group secures vacant lots for community gardens, expands farmers markets, and offers nutrition classes in local schools. With support from the W.K. Kellogg Foundation and several Chicago universities, the ICRD and its partners are now conducting a comprehensive survey of the community's food needs.

LaDonna says the next step is building a community-owned grocery store, where folks in her neighborhood can make healthy choices for their family and keep money in the community at the same time. The Kellogg Foundation recently approved a grant that will leverage financing for the store, and they will break ground soon. The store will operate as a non-profit. There will be some private equity in the store, but the majority of stock will be held by the employees. Food in the store will include content and source labeling, listing all ingredients in plain language so people know what they are eating and where it came from. The commitment to labeling returns to the reason LaDonna got involved in food systems work initially—the desire to find nutritious food for her family.

Tracey and LaDonna's work has inspired others who want to replicate the spirit of community-based food that has taken hold in Austin. Sustain, a Chicago-based environmental organization, is looking at creating a regional infrastructure such as warehouses, trucking services and marketing programs to help bring organic foods to "non-traditional" markets in Chicago. Among her many new posts, LaDonna is part of Chicago Mayor Daley's sustainability task force, whose goal is to make Chicago the "greenest city in the world."

Growing the Next Generation to Be Different

Most of LaDonna's work from the ICRD will be folded into her new job at Chicago State University, where she is responsible for developing the Center for Food Justice. "The idea is to develop leadership capacity in communities of color," Redmond said, "to have policy conversations about inclusion and the capacity of communities." That has implications beyond the food system. It comes back to the philosophy that communities can identify and supply what they most need, food or otherwise.

A large part of letting communities chart their own course involves the next generation, giving youth the choices to do things differently. "We all need to encourage our kids," Redmond said. "They should know how to spend time working with the soil, reconnecting with food and understanding that some people do it for a living." That also means filling in the blanks on the other side, teaching kids about GMOs and how to grow their own food.

"For my son, who is eight now, he eats a lot of fruits and veggies. He chooses to eat them. That has been good for him, good for all of us," Redmond said. She laughs. Even at eight years old, Wade knows how to read a food label like a pro. "He knows that his allergies were not a burden to us, that the way he was born was a blessing for us. I had no idea what I was supposed to do, my role on the planet. Wade reawakened that, and now future generations our family know how to protect the earth, to participate in their community."

The future can be seen in many ways, but the Redmonds have given communities a new way to look at their collective power, and a fresh way to look at cities. From Los Angeles to Chicago to New York City, buried beneath the concrete and steel lies the earth that feeds the planet. It's just waiting to feed the next generation of food activists.

CONVERSATION

Maude Barlow

Maude Barlow is possibly the world's leading expert on water struggles. She is the National Chairperson of the Council of Canadians, that country's largest citizen's advocacy group, with members and chapters across Canada. She is a director with the International Forum on Globalization, a San Francisco research and education institution opposed to corporate globalization. In 2005, she received the prestigious "Right Livelihood Award" given by the Swedish Parliament and widely referred to as "The Alternative Nobel." She has received honorary Ph.D.s from six universities and has authored or co-authored 15 books, including Too Close For Comfort: Canada's Future Within Fortress North America; *and* Blue Gold: The Fight to Stop Corporate Theft of the World's Water *(with Tony Clarke). Her most recent book is* Blue Covenant: The Global Water Crisis and the Fight for the Right to Water.

Q: What are the greatest threats to local water supplies?

MB: First of all, we are creating an ecological crisis by not taking care of our water supplies. Surface waters are being polluted, and we are mining our groundwater at unsustainable rates. At the very time when corporations are privatizing everything, our governments are allowing corporations to move in and take over the ownership of essential resources like water. So we have a double whammy: Our governments are allowing corporations to pollute our water, and then they are signing contracts with corporations to bring in clean-up technology and make billions of dollars cleaning it up. The very sector of society that is polluting our water is turning around and selling our water back to us. And this is going to be more and more of an issue in the future. We'll be increasingly drinking water that has been polluted by corporations, then cleaned up by corporations, then bottled and sold to us by corporations.

Q: What are some success stories of people protecting their water?

MB: The people of Uruguay held a plebiscite and got enough votes for a referendum in the national election in October 2004 in which they called for a constitutional amendment saying that water is a human right, and they won. The government was forced to change its constitution, and Uruguay became the first country in the world to vote on whether people have a human right to water, and the private companies were forced out.

There have been quite a few successful fight-backs across North America. The city of Atlanta allowed a private company to come in to run its water system, and the city kicked them out two-and-a-half years into a 20-year contract. They said, "Get out. You lied. The water coming out of the taps is brown, and you raised the price. Get out." We kept private water companies from taking over the water systems in Toronto and Vancouver. There's a big movement in the heart of France, led by Danielle Mitterand, the widow of the former French president, Francois Mitterand. She is leading this fight to bring water under public control, and many city mayors—not yet Paris—but some good-sized towns and cities are backing her. So even in the belly of the beast, there are some exciting movements.

Q: What about the struggle against Coca-Cola in India?

MB: When you dig deep into Coca-Cola's practices, you see it's really a bad company. They are using military satellite imagery to find clean sources of groundwater and then going in—often in poor tribal communities—and setting up a plant and just helping themselves to the water until the water is gone. I call it water mining. We're working with folks in the state of Kerala, India, who have taken the Coca-Cola company all the way to their Supreme Court to fight the way Coke comes in and sucks up massive amounts of groundwater, pollutes it with sweeteners and chemical additives, and then makes huge profits selling this non-nutritious drink to the public. The Supreme Court of India has ruled largely in the people's favor. Yet Coke is still fighting; they refuse to give up. But these grassroots activists don't give up, either. It's been a real successful fight-back against Coca-Cola.

Q: Does it seem to you that the United States and Canada are more, or less, water conscious than people in other nations?

MB: Individually, we are terrible water-guzzlers. We use a great deal of water per capita through our industrial practices, agriculture, mining, and, in my country, through oil extraction from tar sands. We take a little better care of our groundwater than many third world countries because we citizens have a little more control; the corporations tend to be from our countries, and we can exert greater influence on them. There is serious pollution—I'm not suggesting there isn't—but we don't see the kind of blatant pollution you see in many poor countries. In some countries, the water is foul due to the combination of absolutely no sanitation systems, people using river systems as toilets, to bathe in, to cook in, their garbage dumps, their sewage dumps, everything goes into those open waterways where there's no purification or any kind of water reclamation. As industrial growth and the industrial model moves into the third world, it's bringing massive pollution.

Also, people are being driven off the land. They are moving into urban slums where there's no water, and they create more of a problem because they are adding to the numbers in the cities that are not treating their sewage. About 90 percent of the sewage in the countries of the global south goes untreated back into waterways, rivers, and oceans. It's a cyclical problem that intensifies as we move from rural sustainable living to urban unsustainable living.

We're creating massive water pollution problems. It's lower in the U.S. and Canada because we've got more money for clean-up and slightly better laws for industry. But water pollution is happening just about everywhere. The only societies where water is still treated sacredly are in ancient tribal societies. Many rural communities in India, China, Africa, and Latin America are still living the way that their ancestors did centuries ago; they aren't creating significant levels of pollution.

Q: Who's using the bulk of the water here in North America?

MB: Most of the water is used by industry and agribusiness, which is also an industry. The industrial food production system uses nitrates, chemical fertilizers, and pesticides, which contaminate a lot of water. Intensive livestock operations create horrible pollution. So one of the most important things we can do is to create a more sustainable agricultural system.

Q: Are there any really tough issues that the movement needs to face that you feel we're not confronting adequately?

MB: That's the part of my new book that surprised me the most: the technological takeover of our planet's water system. We have been following very closely the big utility companies like Suez and Vivendi, who run water systems on a for-profit basis. And we have been following the bottled water companies, and those have been the kind of two big ones.

And then we have been worried about major movement of water through pipelines, but we have not been keeping our eye on the whole issue of technology to clean up dirty water, whether that's desalination, water purification, nanotechnology purification. It's going to be the "great white hope," and it's all unregulated and very corporate controlled, and it doesn't surprise me that when you look at the United Nations' millennium development goals on water, nobody is talking about cleaning up polluted water. Because, hey, there's gold in those hills. The more our water becomes polluted, the more precious it becomes. The more desperate people are, the more they will pay for their water, and the more money there is to be made from cleaning it up.

The fastest growing sector of the private water industry is this high technology water clean-up section of this industry, and we must get a better handle on the whole thing. I think that what we are seeing is a cartel of water that is being created like the cartel that has been created for energy. For a long time now, when there was a find of a new field of oil or gas, some large corporation owned it even before it was out of the ground. I see them doing this now with water, and I call them water hunters. These water hunters move in with one goal: to monopolize control over a precious resource in order to make money.

Q: Are you noticing a greater receptivity to your message about the coming water crisis?

MB: Most definitely. I was in down in Lubbock, Texas, on a local radio station, and this guy called in and said, "I'm a right-wing, diehard, Republican, red meat, conservative businessman. And I think the little lady's right. Water is different. You can't have anyone monopolize it." It was fascinating; he totally had my argument. We didn't agree on anything else, but we agreed on the importance of retaining public control over this vital resource. So that is hopeful.

Seeds of Change

Dakota Farmers Give
Monsanto the Boot

"When we saw how our institutions could be warped by the power of big industry, it felt like a blow against our common life as a people. But when we talk about coming together—organizing—we're talking about power, and what is power but the ability to do something?"
—Mark Trechock, Director, Dakota Resource Council

Genetically engineered (GE) foods have been touted as the path to feeding a hungry world. Yet public concern about safety has prompted much of the world to reject GE foods. When the biotechnology corporation Monsanto decided to test its GE variety of wheat seed in North Dakota—a major exporter of wheat—farmers worried it would spell economic disaster. Once introduced, there would be no way to stop the spread of GE seeds. What the wind didn't carry, the bees would. No farmer could be confident they were not growing GE wheat, whether they planted it or not. When farmers joined together to fight Monsanto's plans, they hoped for a victory at the state capital. In the end, what proved more powerful was a classic form of direct action: simply opting out.

Marking the state's centennial, the North Dakota Historical Society summarized the state's history with an odd combination of pride and melancholy: "When North Dakota entered the Federal Union in 1889, its leaders prophesied a glorious future for the Northern Prairie State. Great cities and prosperous farms, said the promoters, would make Dakota the "jewel" in the crown of Democracy. The ensuing century has proven the "boomers" both right and wrong. North Dakota has enjoyed prosperity, but it has also seen devastatingly hard times. As it was in 1889, North Dakota remains a social, cultural, and economic colony, a producer of raw materials, a consumer of manufactures and capital, and an exporter of educated young people."

Seeing itself as both a colony and a democracy is a key irony in this politically conservative Great Plains state. In the city of Grand Forks, about 70 country miles north of Fargo, stands an unassuming testament to this irony—the only state-owned grain mill and elevator in the United States. Erected in the 1920s by the Non Partisan League (one of the most successful state-level reform organizations in U.S. history), the mill remains vital to a local economy in which wheat has always been king. Still, looking at the mill now, in the midst of the Red River Valley of singing cowboy lore, it would be easy to miss what is special about it.

The mill was built in response to the control of North Dakota's economy by the "outside forces", of its day—namely, corporations—that were bleeding the state's farming community of livelihood and autonomy. Dakota farmers have always produced a variety of grains and legumes for far-away tables. In particular, North Dakota conditions are perfect for growing the most coveted of wheat varieties: Hard Red Spring wheat, used for moist yet crusty breads worldwide.

In the early part of the 20th century, Dakota wheat was largely sold as a primary commodity. Producing raw materials meant farmers had no control over the market in which they sold their goods. Wheat was hauled away to markets in Minneapolis via a series of middlemen and subjected to the railroad's extortionate shipping costs. Banks and insurance companies took their cut, and in the end, farmers were often left with little or no profit for a year's harvest.

"The state-owned mill was basically a farmers' rebellion against the colonization of farms by banks, railroads, free haulers, granaries, and other corporations," Mark Trechock, staff director of the Dakota Resource Council (DRC), a partnership of local groups safeguarding farming families and natural resources, told us. "They made a great movie about it in 1978 called 'Northern Lights.'"

The movie tells the real-life tale of the forming of the Non Partisan League, which had taken up the fight against finance, transportation and manufacturing magnates. Before its demise during the Great Depression, the League had racked up impressive reforms, including a state-owned bank, crop insurance and, of course, the mill. Its final victory, in 1932, was to enact what remains today the oldest corporate farming law in the country, preventing corporations from owning and operating farms in the state and helping farmers hold onto their land.

Of all of these reforms, the mill still stands as a physical testament to the democratic spirit that continues to thrive in this self-proclaimed "colony." Nearly a century later, in 2001, wheat farmers would chose the mill as the symbolic site to launch a modern-day revolt against a new breed of corporate power seeking to control their destiny.

This time it was not a rebellion against banks and railroads, but against the heavy-handed Monsanto, a biotechnology and seed corporation. This Fortune 500 company was determined to sell its genetically engineered (GE) Hard Red Spring wheat, which it was planning to field test and release in North Dakota. Through a variety of means—intimidation of farmers, unscrupulous investigations, legal threats, and manipulation of the legislative process—Monsanto tried to compel Dakota wheat farmers to buy its seed, despite widespread international market rejection of GE crops. In response, farmers fought back with the best tools they had: town-by-town organizing, coordinated media campaigns, and grassroots lobbying and testifying at the state capital in Bismarck.

These efforts proved less than successful. The farmers, as you shall see, lost the battle in the halls of power. But they won the war over GE seeds. How? Through an old-fashioned form of direct action: refusal. The farmers simply refused to buy what Monsanto was selling, and ultimately the biotechnology giant had no choice but to retreat.

Gone With the Wind

"I guess we consider ourselves the spiritual descendants of the Non Partisan League," reflected Mark Trechock. "You could say that the purpose of erecting the mill and elevator was to save our wheat farmers. I guess we felt like the [anti-GE wheat] campaign was also to save our farms We thought it was appropriate to launch the campaign to ban Monsanto's GE Hard Red Spring wheat from the steps of the mill ... The corporate structures promoting things like biotech foods don't want you to have choices about what you eat. They want to make those decisions for you. It feels very anti-democratic; it feels despotic and authoritarian."

Indeed. On the surface, the Dakota GE fight was a contest over a single variety of wheat. But beneath that issue lay the much more important question of whether one company's drive for profits would be allowed to trump personal choice and the functioning of the democratic process.

Montana and the Dakotas grow 70 percent of the country's Hard Red Spring wheat. Export sales account for 60 percent of the state's wheat sales. When Monsanto announced, in 1998, that it was developing a line of genetically engineered Hard Red Spring wheat, North Dakota farmers were at first curious. Then they became concerned.

Already, other GE crops—sometimes called Genetically Modified Organisms (GM or GMO)—had been banned from key export markets on which Dakota farmers depend. Japan, Brazil, the European Union, and much of

Africa were refusing to buy any genetically engineered corn or soy products. Some farmers began to fear that if Monsanto were allowed to sell or even field test GE wheat in North Dakota, it could spell financial disaster for the Great Plains wheat farmer, since it put at risk some of the state's most important overseas markets.

The financial risk hinged on basic biology. Between the wind, bees, birds and other seed-dispersing critters and pollinators, it would not take long for GE wheat to cross-pollinate with traditional wheat, jeopardizing the integrity of all wheat farms across North Dakota. Organic farmers could not protect the purity of their crops from the invasion, and conventional farmers would also find that artificially engineered genes had entered their wheat. It was almost inevitable; Monsanto's wheat variety would be impossible to contain. This had already occurred with other crops. Traces of GE canola and soy had been found in fields that were planted with traditional, non-modified seeds. Much of the country's corn has also been affected. Due to the virulent spread of GE corn in the last decade, very little corn in the United States can be sold as organic, or even GE-free.

"The problem is the pollen from GE spring wheat will cross pollinate with all the other wheat varieties," warned Todd Leake, a veteran spring wheat farmer. Along with his brother, Leake farms 2,500 acres in Central Grand Forks, in the heart of the Red River Valley. "Within five years, all commercial supply would be contaminated throughout the wheat-growing region. No farmer and no farm would be safe."

To complicate matters, the wheat being engineered by Monsanto would be sold as part of a package deal. The GE wheat would resist the herbicide glyphosate. Sold under the brand name Roundup, glyphosate is Monsanto's most popular farm product. Resistance to Roundup means that farmers planting Monsanto's GE seeds can spray Roundup directly onto crops, killing weeds but not the crop itself. To many farmers, including Todd Leake, the prospect sounded like a useful and time saving innovation.

As Rebecca Spector, West Coast Director for the Center for Food Safety (CFS) explained, the problem with the selling point is that "the weeds that are not killed by the Roundup bear generations of super-resistant weeds, so the next year farmers will need much more Roundup." The science confirms that in the first nine years of commercial GE crops (which were introduced in 1996), 122 million more pounds of pesticides have been used on GE crops than on conventional ones.[3] And there was still more troubling news.

What the Monsanto corporation was selling was patented biotechnology. When farmers bought GE corn, soy, canola, or cotton seeds, they were forced to sign a "technology agreement" contractually binding them to forgo the oldest practice in farming: seed saving. Such a requirement conflicted with farmers' basic instincts of frugality and neighborliness. Farmers save seeds not only to save themselves money, but also to trade with each other, as a way of maintaining varietal vigor. As Leake said: "Saving seeds is what we do. It's been done for thousands of years. We save seeds to replant the next year; they maintain themselves for about five years."

North Dakota farmers who had started to buy GE canola had to promise not to save seed and to buy more of the corporation's seeds each year. (All generations of seeds belong to Monsanto, not the farmer.) The Monsanto corporation was also busy buying up all the seed companies it could, thus controlling the seed supply.

What is Monsanto?
What is Genetic Engineering?

The multinational corporation Monsanto—based in St. Louis, Missouri—is the world's largest supplier of herbicides, bio-engineered seeds, and hormones to increase milk production. You won't find its name on any label in your pantry, but as one of the most powerful forces in the global food chain, its products are found in nearly every kitchen in America. Monsanto began as a chemical corporation, producing the deadly Agent Orange for the military, as well as manufacturing PCBs and DDT. Its best-known products in the United States are Aspartame sweetener and Roundup, an herbicide relative of Agent Orange used by farmers to control weeds.

Farmers, governments, and consumers worldwide are facing tremendous pressure to accept genetic engineering as an innovation in food production. Genetic engineering is the process of inserting genes from one species into a wholly different species to create an entirely new organism that is then patented by the company for which it was developed. Beginning in 1996, Monsanto led the biotech revolution by genetically engineering seeds that work specifically with Monsanto's herbicides and pesticides. Its patented seeds are either insect-resistant or herbicide-tolerant.

Ryan Zinn, an organizer for the Organic Consumers Association, told us: "Monsanto has led the way in terms of genetic engineering, which is the peak of the corporate life science movement. Because they have gobbled up the seed market, if you want cotton or soy, or alfalfa, or corn or rice, you have to go to them—pretty ingenious. Now they have everything rolled into one package deal: the patenting of existing life forms such as rice, or even pigs, genetically engineering crops that are dependent on their chemical inputs. Monsanto has led this charge, looking to create an integrated supply chain from top to bottom. They are in a position to tell farmers what to grow, what we'll eat, and how much the seeds and chemicals will cost. And you probably never heard of them."

Contractually binding farmers to the GE seeds has consequences on those who purchase them and for those who do not. For those who buy Monsanto's seeds, signing the technology agreement is the first step in losing control over their farming practices. Included in the fine print of the contract is a consent agreement allowing Monsanto agents to inspect crops at any time to guard against the criminal act of "seed theft." For those who did not plant Monsanto's seeds, but fell victim to GE cross pollination and contamination drift, the result was the same; they were breaking the law, whether they knew it or not. And the Monsanto corporation was ready to pounce.

Farmers Face the Men in Black

"These men in black jackets were at my sidewalk one day," Todd Leake told us. "First they ask you if you grow Roundup-ready crops. They were accusing me of planting GE crops without purchasing. All they need to do is accuse you and take you to court. They have an endless supply of money. The plan is to intimidate you and break you."[4]

Todd Leake is a farmer down to his roots. His family has been farming the same land since the pioneer days, before statehood. His parents, in their eighties, still help out on the place, as do his two sons. The Leake clan is part of an extended family of farmers, a close-knit bunch who rely on each other in hard times and celebrate with each other in times of plenty. "All our neighbors, we come together. When one of us is stuck in the mud, we help each other out."

Speaking softly, Leake said, "I guess I take a little bit of pride in my heritage. I'm one of what used to be tens of thousands of farmers in the Northern Plains." Farming, once the country's most popular occupation, now accounts for less than 1 percent of U.S. jobs. Pausing thoughtfully, Leake added, "My colleagues and I are people who are in charge of the tradition, whether we're small or large. Along with that tradition comes the responsibility of caring for the crops that are part of our human heritage going back 10,000 years. Our generation will be handing this most valuable resource to the next generation."

For Leake and like-minded neighbors, the business arrangements surrounding GE crops—the tight control by a single corporation—contradicted those sentiments of stewardship. The Monsanto intimidation, asking whether he had illegally planted GE crops, felt like an attack on Leake's way of life.

Leake and his fellow farmers knew that the Monsanto corporation didn't make hollow threats. Farmers in the Dakotas had heard about the Canadian canola farmer Percy Schmeiser, who was sued by Monsanto lawyers for patent infringement when some GE seeds blew into a ditch on his property line. Spector of CFS, who has reported extensively on Monsanto's practices of farmer intimidation and litigation, told us, "Essentially, when Monsanto's patented seeds find their way onto a non-engineered crop—no matter how innocently it happens—that crop effectively becomes the property of Monsanto."

Percy famously fought Monsanto in court, and farmers around the world took up his cause. But eventually he lost his case. According to the *St. Louis Post-Dispatch*, the litigious Monsanto corporation has an annual legal budget of $10 million, including a staff of 75 lawyers solely for the purpose of prosecuting farmers for patent infringement.[5]

When the men in black started showing up in North Dakota, farmers began taking a closer look at the GMO controversy. As the sales of various GMO seeds grew, so did the presence of the black jacket gang, creating an atmosphere of fear and mistrust among neighbors. As Spector told us, "What we find is that Monsanto is also trespassing on farmers' land who have not signed technology agreements and illegally testing for patent infringement. They are also asking farmers to track their neighbors, to find out what they are growing. Some farmers who have paid for the GE seeds want to be sure that his neighbor is paying too. It sets up a negative relationship, pitting farmers against each other. They begin acting in competition instead of cooperation, which is the basis of the whole farming social structure."

As Leake said: "What I noticed, folks don't talk about it openly, but when it's brought up at the elevator where the farmers hang out, you can tell that they've had the black jacket guys at their places, too. It's almost a violent reaction you have to it."

Many Dakota farmers were coming to the conclusion that there really wasn't a need for Roundup Ready wheat. Farmers began looking at the costs and lack of benefits. The math certainly didn't work, and the buzz was out about the black jacket crew—only trouble and lawsuits could be coming the farmers' way. "Roundup Ready was more of a corn-belt kind of a thing, I didn't see it coming," Leake told us. "Meantime, we saw the market for GE corn drop off the face of the earth in Japan and Europe." The prospect of engineered wheat for North America was not good from a wheat producer's standpoint, as clearly consumers in many countries were rejecting it.

But more importantly, once Roundup Ready wheat was released, there would be no more choice in the matter. As soon as cross pollination and contamination drift occurred, no farmer could decide if they wanted to plant it. It would just arrive one way or another, and yet they would be liable for stealing it if they didn't buy it. It was a question of local autonomy versus colonization, and that was a familiar theme to the Dakota farmer.

A Bottle of Whiskey for the Monsanto Lobbyist

"I certainly had never done anything like this before, and my brother said this wasn't going to be good for us," Leake said of his decision to try to put a stop to the GE invasion. He had spoken to some of his neighbors, and many of them were with him. But no one knew quite what to do. There was no point in trying to ban Roundup Ready wheat locally, in the county—that much they knew. The solution would have to be bigger than that.

Todd Leake knew of the Dakota Resource Council (DRC), and thought perhaps they might help organize a fight. "So I went over there and told them this was going to be the most devastating thing that could happen to us," Leake said. That was January 2000. The DRC told Leake they would back the farmers, devote staff time, and help campaign to stop the introduction of the wheat. "But it fell on me to push it forward," Leake said.

Leake also went to the North Dakota Grain Growers Association and found it had a policy that amounted to "no new varieties grown until there is acceptance from major purchasers." That was good news.

Next, Leake and the staff from the DRC went to visit state Senator Kenneth Kroeplin, a Democrat. Kroeplin listened intently and asked Leake to present his case before a group of farmers at a meeting he was holding. "It was mostly new to them, but they were unanimous in their agreement that it shouldn't go forward," Leake said.

Meanwhile, the U.S. PIRGs (Public Interest Research Groups) had issued a report detailing the dangers of genetically engineered crops, which spoke to the same fears the Dakota farmers were experiencing. As the DRC's Trechock told us: "The report also demonstrated that Monsanto couldn't even prevent contamination from field trials, so we knew that farmers would already be affected before the wheat even went onto the market. We were all very concerned."

Leake continued to speak with farmers across the state, and it seemed that given the fears of the farming community, the widespread rejection abroad, the PIRG report, the policies of the Grain Growers Association, the support from the State Senator and the DRC, a statewide moratorium on GE wheat before it could be introduced commercially was a natural next step.

A radical strategy? Perhaps. But given the facts, only a radical approach would suffice. The wheat farmers felt that their very way of life was at stake. They feared that if GE wheat became widespread in North Dakota, they would lose control over their most important natural resources—their wheat seed bank.

It was September 2000. Not even a year had elapsed from the time Todd Leake had shared his concerns with the DRC, and things were moving quickly. The farmers and their allies launched the campaign against GE wheat with a press conference from the steps of the state-owned mill, highlighting the CFS report about contamination drift. Senator Kroeplin said he would take the farmers' proposal to the next legislative session.

In January 2001, in the midst of a cold North Dakota winter, farmers from across the state drove their pick-up trucks to the state capital in Bismarck. The idea was to pack legislative hearings on the proposed moratorium and on another bill (referred to as the Nelson bill) that made it illegal for corporate representatives to inspect farmers' crops without prior notice and due cause.

The moratorium bill sought to create a regulatory panel of farm groups that, based on market acceptance, would determine if and under what conditions it would be safe to open the door for GE wheat. "We wanted the State to say we don't think this is responsible," Trechock said. "We're thinking of markets and wanted to use market-based triggers."

There was electricity in the air during the hearings, a sense among the farmers that they were shaping their own destiny. Todd Leake was one of many farmers who gave testimony that day before the House Agriculture Committee, and when he was finished—so the lore goes—the room fell silent. It was clear that the legislators in the room had already sided with the farmers. When the Monsanto lobbyist stood to testify, Leake told us, "The chairman of the committee handed him a bottle, whiskey or something, and told the guy, 'You'd better take this, I think you're going to need it.'"

The Monsanto team seemed ill prepared for the tone of the hearing. They argued on the grounds of safety and the environment, when the only argument being lodged by the farmers was on the grounds of international market rejection. By focusing on the health and environmental risks posed by GE foods, Trechock recalled, the Monsanto team badly misjudged the character of the opposition.

The Monsanto executives were well practiced at battling environmental groups, but they were not ready to face off against farmers. "They seemed to think we were all a bunch of greenies. That wasn't where our argument was coming from at all … It was the first farmer-led revolt against the introduction of a biotech crop. Monsanto didn't know how to handle it. They couldn't believe their eyes."

Then the Monsanto lobbyists argued that rejection was nothing more than protectionism from the other countries. "We got a good laugh out of that one," Trechock said. "I mean, how much wheat do you think they grow in Japan, anyway?"

Both houses of the state legislature passed the Nelson bill with a near unanimous vote. On the moratorium bill, the State Senate committee returned with a 14-0 vote in favor. Within days the House of Representatives concurred; Democrats and Republicans agreed that GE wheat was bad for business.

The farmers were ready to celebrate, feeling that they had won the day. All that was left was to send the moratorium bill to the full Senate for confirmation in a few weeks. With the kind of wide and bipartisan support that the bill enjoyed, it seemed only a matter of formality before the bill became law.

In a functioning democracy, that would have been that. The people had spoken to their legislators about policies based on science, markets and on-the-ground experience, and they had prevailed. But then something happened—President George W. Bush came to town.

Did Bush Come to Monsanto's Rescue?

Todd Leake does not come across as a cynic, or even particularly partisan. Yet you won't convince him—nor many of the other farmers that roamed the halls of the Capitol building in January 2001—that President George W. Bush didn't influence what happened next. In the two months between legislative sessions, before the bill was to cross over to the Senate side, something definitely shifted.

As Leake remembers it: "President Bush was flying around the country then promoting his agenda, a campaign on taxes or something. He was visiting every state and came to Fargo. He met with Republicans at the airport; met with the leaders of the House and Senate; met with Gary Nelson, the house majority leader; he met with everyone. The next thing you know, everything changed."

There was a sudden, inexplicable shift in attitude on the moratorium bill. Legislators who had initially supported the bill began trying to kill it. "Could be coincidental," Leake said. "But it was abrupt, I mean a really abrupt change of attitude. Suddenly there was open hostility on the part of the committee members toward our side. Monsanto's team had more time to testify, there was quite an effort suddenly to accommodate these guys." He added: "Legislators that had been on our side just quit fighting against it. They just receded into the background like children that had been scolded."

In March 2001, the Senate reduced the moratorium to a mere study. The farmers felt like their moment had passed, and yet they were still convinced that only an outright ban would protect their crops, their export markets, and their heritage. Out for a meal, several farmers spotted a group of legislators dining with Monsanto's lobbyists. "They were unabashed," Leake said incredulously "We sent them drinks."

While the speculation about Bush's involvement can't be confirmed, there is reason for suspicion. President George W. Bush has strongly supported genetic engineering since taking office. He has spoken out against European resistance to genetic modification on several occasions. In 2006, he mandated that Iraqi farmers purchase only biotech seeds. The Bush Administration's connections to Monsanto have raised eyebrows. For example, Bush's first Attorney General, John Ashcroft, was the top recipient of Monsanto campaign contributions during his 2000 U.S. Senate re-election bid. Ann Veneman, Bush's one-time Agriculture Secretary, was on the board of directors of Calgene Pharmaceuticals, a Monsanto affiliate. One of Monsanto's former chief lobbyists was nominated to be second-in-command at the Environmental Protection Agency.

All these connections are part of a problem identified as the personnel "revolving door" between big business and government. As Ryan Zinn, campaigner with the Organic Consumers Association points out, it's not just about job swapping. There is a real agenda going on behind closed doors that allows big

Monsanto and the Revolving Door

An example of the revolving door is the case of the FDA approval of Monsanto's rBGH (bovine growth hormone). Sold to farmers under the brand name Posilac, rBGH is a genetically engineered hormone injected into cows, increasing milk production 10-15 percent. Dairy cows treated with rBGH suffer a bevy of painful and life-shortening effects and are subjected to constant udder infections requiring heavy doses of antibiotics. These genetically engineered hormones and antibiotics are found in milk that contains rBGH. How this alarming biotechnology won FDA approval reveals the corruption inherent in the revolving door.

In 1992, Monsanto researcher Margaret Miller was tasked with determining the safety of rBGH. Shortly before her report was issued, Miller left Monsanto for the FDA, becoming the Deputy Director of the Office of New Animal Drugs. Her first assignment? Approving rBGH, based on the report she wrote for Monsanto. When rBGH-treated cows became increasingly sick, Miller approved a change to the antibiotics standard, an increase of 100 times the previous allowable level. About one-third of the nation's dairy cows are treated with rBGH and the accompanying high doses of antibiotics.

Studies show that antibiotic-resistant strains of salmonella are the direct result of overdosing farm animals. Public outcry resulted in consumer campaigns calling for "contains rBGH" labeling and an organic dairy industry self-labeling campaign "Contains No rBGH." These efforts have been thwarted by Monsanto's legal team, which claims the corporation's protection under the 1st Amendment guarantees it the right not to inform the public about rBGH. Monsanto has also pursued legal action against organic milk producers for unfairly hampering its profits.

business access to our government that plain folks just don't have. "Monsanto and its subsiciaries go in the door at the FDA, the EPA, and USDA, promote loose regulation around biotech, and provide subsidies to these companies for research and development using taxpayers' money," Zinn said. "But at the end of the day, the corporation is the sole proprietor of the technology. The people have no real say."

Seed Saving Is a Basic Human Right

The farmers' coalition had two years to wait until the next legislative session opened in 2003. Feeling like they had barely missed their big chance, they were determined not to give up. Their strategy was to take the two years to recruit more farm families into the debate.

During this time, a Jamestown farmer and avid seed saver, Tom Wiley, decided to sell some soybeans through a broker, who performed tests on his beans. To Wiley's surprise, they were contaminated with genetically modified seeds. He lost the contract he was vying for, at a personal cost of $10,000. Trechock recalled, "At that time, we were trying to win on the floor of the Senate the right to go back to the original moratorium bill. So we did this action where we put a clear bag of wheat seeds on every legislator's desk. We counted out a few in each bag and painted them red—those represented the GMO seeds—to show them the quantity of GMO seeds that cost Wiley his contract. Just a few seeds were all it took to contaminate a crop and lose our markets."

Wiley, Leake, and other farmers began canvassing the state, putting on town meetings and talking about their experiences. Over the next two years, they visited almost every county, passed out fact-sheets, and mailed information to organic farmers. They spoke with researchers in Canada who had been studying the patterns of contamination on organic canola crops. They confirmed that even field trials couldn't be contained. They brought those voices to the legislative table.

Trechock said, "We were making the argument again about the loss of market to state representative Gene Nicholas of Cando, who had helped us move through the House in 2001. He sat back in his chair and told us that the market for Hard Red Spring wheat is in the U.S. farm program. In other words, price doesn't matter because the federal government is going to cover the cost of production."

It was quite a turnaround from his previous position in 2001. What he was offhandedly proposing was a federal handout that the wheat growers were *not* interested in. More worrisome, it demonstrated a subordination of the farmers to the financial interests of biotech companies. Trechock asked Nicholas,

"Wouldn't we like to achieve a market system where people are paying for the product in the marketplace, rather than cut off your world market and rely on the government?"

Such objections didn't seem to resonate with state lawmakers. In the 2003 legislative session, the farmers' coalition lost again. Farmers like Leake and Wiley felt crushed.

But while the legislature in North Dakota had seemingly turned a deaf ear to the plight of the farmers, there were others who were listening, and evidence around the GE contamination was mounting. For example, in Arkansas, Monsanto was testing GE rice grown under controlled test plots at Louisiana State University. Despite the fact that it had never been commercialized, rice farmers were testing positive for GE rice and losing big markets as a result. A researcher with the Western Resources Council and professor of agriculture at Iowa State, Bob Wisner, analyzed the repercussions and estimated that the rice growers would lose about $175 million a year, according to Trechock. "Monsanto didn't have an answer for that," Trechock said.

The farmers had never diverged from their market-based strategy. Despite the mounting evidence about the dangers of GE to people, animals, and the planet, those points were debatable; Monsanto could provide counter-evidence to refute the argument. But on the basis of the market acceptance, there was no question. As early as 2001, the Dakota farmers started collecting market rejection letters from EU nations and from Japan. Those letters were concrete proof that they were right; the market wasn't buying GE.

The DRC invited Japanese government representatives to explain that they wouldn't buy any wheat from North Dakota. Japanese media came too, and at a press conference, the DRC presented the signatures of over 500 consumer's groups opposing GE wheat. The DRC hosted millers and consumer's associations from other countries to talk to legislators. Over and over again, the legislature and Monsanto were offered hard evidence about the market rejections.

Farmers like Tom Wiley and Todd Leake applied for passports and headed overseas to talk to officials, farmers, and consumers, fortifying their positions on the controversy. Speaking to a radio audience in Torun, Poland, Wiley said: "You fought hard for your independence. Don't give up your freedom to the biotech corporations. Saving seed is a basic human right."

Through it all, two things seemed clear: The farmers knew they had to keep fighting, and Monsanto knew, or was coming to recognize, that though it had the upper hand politically, the farmers had the upper hand economically. The Dakota farmers would not support GE wheat. They wouldn't order the seeds, they wouldn't plant them, and they weren't going to have it. No matter what the legislature voted on the ban, the farmers had already banned it themselves by simply promising not to buy the seeds if they ever were offered for sale.

In a move that was a stunning surprise to most of the farmers involved in the campaign, on May 10, 2004, Monsanto issued a press release announcing it would not seek regulatory applications for Roundup Ready wheat, citing "a lack of widespread wheat industry alignment." And that was that. The hard-fought battle ended—not with a bang but a whimper. As Trechock said: "Clearly we won this not on our legislative performance. We did win it because of the hard market issues we raised, and kept raising, and kept raising. We were right."

The farmers and their allies celebrated in Jamestown with a big picnic that brought families together from across the state. It had been a long road.

As anyone connected with the campaign will tell you, the battle over GE wheat was a fight for democracy and against corporate colonization. "One conclusion that folks came away with was the sense that corporations have too much power," Trechock said, "They are not people, but in fact have more power than we do. That's just wrong. That Monsanto was able to defy the facts, bring the entire state to huge risk just because they have clout and money, seems very anti-democratic."

The deliberative process of the legislature had been disrupted in 2001 simply because Monsanto didn't like the answers democracy had come up with. "Seed saving and the right to grow what you want goes deeper than democracy," reckoned Trechock. "It goes to the basic drive of initiative and human autonomy. Farmers already feel like an endangered species. They don't have a word for how this injustice felt to us."

But despite the odds, they never gave up. Together, they were more than the sum of their parts, strong enough to override a corporate giant and the government that seemed to be protecting the interests of corporations over the people.

"When we saw how our institutions could be warped by the power of big industry, it felt like a blow against our common life as a people," Trechock said. "But when we talk about coming together—organizing—we're talking about power, and what is power but the ability to do something?"

CONVERSATION

Anuradha Mittal

Anuradha Mittal is Founder and Executive Director of the Oakland Institute, a non-profit research and advocacy organization in Oakland, California, that works to ensure public participation and democratic debate on crucial economic and social policy issues. A native of India, Anuradha is an internationally renowned expert on trade, development, human rights, democracy, food security, and agriculture issues.

Q: What are the biggest problems with the food system in the United States?

AM: I think the biggest problem in the United States is that food, instead of being about communities, is now about commodities. It is controlled, not by the family farm, growing food for families and communities, while maintaining bio-diversity; it has come to mean large corporate industrial agriculture farms, where machines have replaced farmers, where monocultures have replaced biodiversity, where corporate agribusiness has replaced family farms. What we see as a result is a disconnect between us and the food system where we have been reduced to mere consumers. So we have to rethink our relationship with the food system before we can effectively challenge that.

One of the biggest myths about hunger is that people are hungry because we are not producing enough food, and therefore technological solutions and genetic engineering is put forward as a solution. There is no shortage of food production. If you look at the figures compiled by the UN's Food and Agriculture Organization (FAO), there is enough food to provide over 2,720 calories per person per day around the world. If the problem was a shortage of food production, you would not have hunger in a country like the United States.

The real problem is the absence of living-wage jobs. Many people have to choose between putting food on the table or having a roof over their heads or having medical insurance for their families. There is a real deficit in governance of the food system, as a result of which today we have nearly 60 percent of the processed food that we eat in the U.S. has genetically modified organisms in it. There was no democratic process whereby people of this country could determine for themselves what kind of food they would eat, how it is grown, and who grows it. So while we have regulatory agencies asleep at the wheel, we have seen genetic contamination—we don't even know the health impacts of this dangerous technology—and we have seen negative impacts on the livelihoods of farmers.

Basically we have been turned into guinea pigs. We have been reduced to people who think freedom is about choosing from 40 different brands of toothpaste, but we have really forgotten what true freedom looks like, what true democracy looks like.

Q: Defenders of the system say that through supply and demand people get the food they want because they choose to buy it in the marketplace. Is there democracy in the marketplace?

AM: It's a big mess. According to a recent poll, 90 percent of Americans want their food labeled. Right now our food does not say it contains GMOs. So when you are drinking your "all natural" Minute Maid orange juice, it doesn't have to say it's not really natural, that it contains GMOs because of the high fructose corn syrup in it. The system is not very democratic.

We are living in a world where corporations are taking so much control of our food system that they are creating monopolies. Less than four companies control 80 percent of pork production, and two grain companies control the majority of the world's grain trade. So we don't really have a choice. What we have are monopolies—Cargill, ADM, Conagra are monopolies, controlling our food system and dictating prices. The biggest brunt of this system has been borne by the farmers, so when U.S. government officials talk about promoting trade agreements to benefit farmers, it's a joke because we have an agricultural system that is destroying our farmers. In 1925, 30 percent of the U.S. population was in agriculture. Today less than 2 percent of the population remains in agriculture. We have more people behind bars than behind the wheel of a tractor. The average age of a farmer in the United States is 55 years or older. An increasing number of farmers get their income from a second or a third job at the gas station or a Wal-Mart. So we are starving our food producers. But the most shocking fact is that the number one cause of death among farmers in the U.S. is suicide. The rates of alcoholism and depression are very high among farmers. And this is the model of agriculture that has been exported around the world by the U.S. government.

Q: Why are so many countries rejecting GMOs, including nations facing food insecurity?

AM: Genetic engineering is a symptom of the larger problem we are all facing: the corporate control of our food system. We are losing food democracy, food sovereignty. And the biggest example of that is the United States. Most countries—Japan, Philippines, South Korea, most of Europe—have set regulations for genetic engineering. But here in the United States, there is a revolving door between the regulatory agencies that approve these crops and the corporations producing the technology, and so we have seen a demise of food democracy. I think that is the root of the issue.

The second thing is that the corporations are also taking over our airwaves. There is a steady flow of myths. "We need this technology to feed the world; we need the technology because it is friendly to the farmers; we need this technology because it is environmentally friendly." But now the truth is beginning to come out ... countries like Romania, which had been growing GMOs, started in 2007 a decontamination process. Brazil was facing GM crops being smuggled in and last year denied the approval of GM crops. Right here in the U.S., we have seen counties in California, including Mendocino, Marin, and others, adopt resolutions declaring themselves to be GMO-free and banning the growing of GM crops. So even in the U.S., we are beginning to see this widespread resistance because food democracy is absolutely essential for any kind of democracy that we envision for ourselves.

Q: Tell us about GMOs and U.S. foreign aid.

AM: Our foreign food aid is mainly about securing new markets. It is about finding new places to dispose of surpluses. Within this context, we have to look at one of the impacts of GMOs on the food system that has deeply impacted livelihoods of U.S. farmers; regulations around the world against GMOs have negatively impacted U.S. exports. For example, the EU does not want genetically modified corn. That results in a loss of over $300 million for the U.S. farmers each year. So the U.S. government has insisted on shipping GM food aid as a way of getting rid of surpluses that it can't sell elsewhere.

In 2002, we saw Zambia stand up and say no to GM food aid, and there was such an uproar here. One U.S. spokesperson on food issues, Congressman Tony Hall, even said that Zambia should be brought to the International Criminal Court (ICC) for starving its own people. Of course, somebody needed to remind Mr. Hall that the U.S. does not participate in the ICC. But when Zambia said no to GM food aid, offers of non-GM food aid came in from other countries including Kenya, Tanzania, India, and China.

Q: In this country, organic food is expanding rapidly. But it seems like it is being taken over by giants like Wal-Mart and Safeway. What do you make of this?

AM: I think just focusing on the labeling of organic is not enough. We have to look at where this food is coming from. If you have organic food traveling lots of miles to get to our table, that's a real issue because you are lowering organic standards. Local is more important, sustainable is very important. This is one of the few countries where organic farmers have to pay to get the labeling that they are organic, but the chemical farmers who pollute earth, air, and water get away scot-free so they can provide so-called cheap food. It's not cheap food. The cost will be paid by each one of us and by future generations with the pollution that has been caused, and the greenhouse gases that result from industrial agriculture. So it is important to emphasize that organic in itself is not organic until we are challenging who benefits and who is harmed by the system. While the large corporations have been lowering organic standards, the small family farmers have been the best tillers of the land.

Q: Can you talk about this lowering of organic standards?

AM: There are great groups that have done excellent work on this issue: the Center for Food Safety, the Organic Consumers Association, and the California Alliance for Family Farmers. One important component of organic is who grows it. Is it large plantations? It's usually on small farms where farmers know every inch of land and they can take care of the crops they are growing. When you grow on large, corporate, industrial levels you are talking about monocultures. On a typical small farm, you will have biodiversity, with a whole bunch of vegetables that are seasonal with some fruits and some chickens and eggs and fish and goats. On a large, industrial, monoculture farm, they will be just growing one crop, and that is not natural. Nature does not do mono-cropping.

Q: You and I live in California, and many people say it's easy for you to buy organic, you live in the biggest agricultural state. How do we do that on the other side of the Sierra Nevadas?

AM: Yes, we are fortunate to live in California. But it is shocking that you can go into the shops that sell local grapes from California and you also find grapes from Chile. You have avocados from here and you also have avocados that have traveled thousands of mile from Chile or wherever. You have melons from here and then you have melons from Mexico. Again, the whole myth of cheap food; it cannot be truly cheap, given the miles it travels.

Today 20 percent of California table grapes go to China, while China is the world's largest producer of table grapes. Half of all California's processed tomatoes go to Canada, and the U.S. imports $36 million worth of Canadian processed tomatoes yearly. California exports brussel sprouts to Canada while California imports brussel sprouts from Belgium. This food system is upside down and backwards. We are exporting what we are also importing because it is profitable for the companies doing it, not because it is good for the nation or the environment.

One of my colleagues did a study showing that if we were to start spending a small percentage or our budget each year on buying food locally, we could have a big impact. If just an additional $85 per person per year of California food expenditures were spent on food produced within the state it would result in $848 million dollars in additional income for the farmers in California. It would result in $1.38 billion being injected into California's overall economy. It would result in $188 million in additional state tax revenue. And nearly 6,000 new jobs would be created. So it's a win-win situation for all of us if you make this one small change.

Q: If you are faced with the choice of buying local or buying organic, which do you choose? Which has a smaller ecological footprint?

AM: I would encourage everyone to look at the label to see where your produce came from. You can buy directly from your own state. I would encourage people to search out local grocery markets so we are not dependent on the big supermarkets such as Albertsons and Safeway and Wal-Mart.

At the Oakland Institute we issued a report showing the impact of these supermarkets' consolidating control of our food system and the impact on low-income communities, the environment, and labor. If we support the independent local grocery stores we can have a relationship with them and tell them what kind of food we want to eat. The local, independent stores are better able to buy directly from small farmers than the supermarkets such as Albertsons and Safeway. And there are amazing websites. There is the True Food Network (truefoodnow.org), where you can find out which products have GMOs.

The key thing to remember is that food is not a privilege, it is a human right. We need to take back the power and get control of our food system.

Loggers & Lizards Find
Common Ground

Saving an Oregon Watershed

"People tend to approach the world as either all black or all white, when the lion's share of what we do is in the gray zone. We've got more in common with each other than not."
— Jack Shipley, co-founder of the Applegate Watershed Partnership

The fight between environmentalists and loggers in southwest Oregon grew so ugly that by the early 1990s many on both sides were carrying guns. The vast, once-pristine Applegate River watershed had been over-logged, over-mined, and over-grazed, leaving forests clear-cut and stumpy, tributaries muddy, and fish populations struggling. Government agencies seemed paralyzed to protect the area until an unlikely dynamic duo, a logger and a conservationist, tried something new—they talked to each other. Together they started a nationally acclaimed partnership that has revitalized the watershed and established trust among enemy camps, thus creating a sense of real community.

I believe we met at Denny's." Jack Shipley pauses, thinking back more than a decade. "We had breakfast. That's where it all started." Shipley calls himself an avid conservationist. Jim Neal, his breakfast date, considers himself a long-time logger. Jack Shipley sports a thinning gray ponytail. Jim Neal ... well, does not. The two had never met before, and each reckoned they had very little in common, outside of a fondness for coffee and early morning pancakes.

"I had written a letter to the *Medford Tribune*," Shipley recalled. "It was something about how, despite the available wisdom of traditional Indian practices such as intentional fire setting—which protects against catastrophic wildfire—society had decided any fire was bad and excluded it as a tool for ecosystem protection."

Soon after the letter was published, Jack Shipley's phone rang. It was Jim Neal. Shipley laughs, remembering their first encounter. "He said it was the first letter he'd ever read from an environmentalist that he agreed with. So we met for coffee and became fast friends."

Jim Neal's recollection of events is slightly different, but the outcome was the same. "So I was in Medford, Oregon, when I turned on the TV, and this guy Jack Shipley was on the news. He was obviously an environmentalist, he wanted to save the forest."

Thinking back, Neal recalls the palpable bitterness that so divided the people of the region. "Of course, at that time you were considered to be either a redneck logger or a tree-hugging environmentalist. Jack was saying stuff that made sense to me about cooperating with each other and utilizing natural resources. So I called the TV station and found out how to get in touch with him. We met the next day."

More than just the start of a beautiful friendship, something bigger was brewing that crisp morning in 1992. Together, these two men determined to chart a new and innovative course for community-led resource management based on principals many thought were incompatible: promotion of locally-based economic opportunity and ecosystem health. Even more challenging was where they chose to experiment—the Applegate River watershed in southern Oregon, a place many called ground zero for the destructive and combative Timber Wars of the late 1980s.

Together, Shipley and Neal committed themselves to establishing common ground among folks who were deeply mistrustful of each other's intentions, lifestyles, and actions. These former enemies—loggers, environmentalists, ranchers, and even government agencies—would find a way protect this watershed and become a thriving community. In the process, they not only safeguarded their own home territory, but also established a national model for maintaining local resources. Their experience proved that, when it comes administering scarce resources, neighbors often know best.

The Jim and Jack Show

Jack Shipley the conservationist grew up in Texas, went to Texas Tech, and received an advanced degree in resource planning in Oregon. He eventually became the parks and recreation director for Grants Pass, Oregon, where he was in charge of public works. "I left the city and was raising some cows, sheep, and horses, worked in Mexico doing medical aid, and built some houses in Nicaragua during the Contra war," Shipley said. "When I met Jim, I was the Vice President of Headwaters [a conservation organization] in Ashland, Oregon."

Jim Neal was born and raised in a logging camp in Midwestern Oregon, about 15 miles outside of a town of 400 people. At Oregon State he got a degree to become a forest engineer. "Then I decided it'd be fun to build dams, so I bought some more books, and got a civil engineering certificate. Then I met my wife."

One day Neal got a call from a friend who was starting a helicopter logging business. "I threw away everything because I thought pulling logs up straight into the air sounded so cool. So I became a choker setter, a basic laborer." He loved the adrenaline rush he got from the danger of helicopter logging. "We were young and out there and nobody else could do it. I thought if you can't go to war, the next best thing was helicopter logging." A natural leader, Neal was soon running things. "So then in the late 1980s or early 90s all these timber people got together and said, 'We need to clean you up and send you to town to be our spokesperson.'" Off he went to Medford, where he met up with Shipley at Denny's.

In between java refills that auspicious morning, they really opened up to each other. Shipley explained that in his work as a conservationist, despite winning some small battles, he was tired of losing the war. "We'd stop a timber sale here and there, but in the big picture, we were hemorrhaging to death."

All throughout the state and across the country, the timber wars had been heating up, with extremists on both sides turning to violence. Meanwhile the environment was degrading, and fast. "Whether it was the spotted owl or other crises, the media had made our camps into enemies," Neal told us. "It was so polarizing it made me sick."

Both men expressed exasperation at the futility of the jobs-versus-environment, logger-versus-lizards debate, a zero-sum game with nothing in between.

"We sat there talking about this for a good long time. We both felt there had to be a middle ground, a way to maintain habitat without destroying the timber business," Shipley said. "After all, it's just stuff we learned in the sandbox, isn't it? You steal some kid's toy, you spend time in the corner, so you learn to share and compromise. Then we grow up and throw these lessons aside, everything becomes all win or lose."

Shipley also confided in his new friend a sense that something else was missing. "My wife and I were considering moving to Mexico. There was just no sense of community in the Applegate watershed." By the time they picked up the check, Shipley and Neal determined that if *they* could find common ground, there was more to find between their respective communities.

For a year, Shipley and Neal worked on that premise. Each took the other to meetings to open dialogue about building a stable local economy and a healthy ecosystem.

"I had friends in environmental circles, so I suggested we make a presentation to Audubon to try and share our ideas on how both sides could work together and find a middle ground," Shipley said. They selected the Olympia, Washington, chapter, some distance away from where either of them lived— "In case we screwed it up."

When they arrived at the meeting, they drew straws to see who would talk first. Jim Neal won, but it was no prize. "No one wanted to hear from me, a logger, and they made no bones about it," he said. "In fact, an older gent stood up and actually asked me to sit down, saying they wanted to hear from the environmentalist."

So Shipley stood up and gave the same presentation Neal had intended to give, only this time people listened. It seemed that the messenger was as important as the message.

Not long after, they went to a Timber Association meeting in Ashland, where it was the same sort of thing in reverse. There was no love and certainly no trust for the environmentalist. As Shipley recalls, "Here we had so much in common, and so many ideas of how both sides could benefit, but with so much distrust, no one could get past it to hear it."

The two became the Jim and Jack show, traveling around Southern Oregon spreading the gospel of finding a place in the middle that worked for everyone. Shipley admits he sometimes found it easier to sit with loggers than with environmentalists. "It was fascinating to me—I had imaginations about how they were, but once I sat in there, talking about kids and families, real common ground stuff, the focal point about them working for the industry became less important. You begin to see people as folks who are just doing something else for a living, maybe they are really okay." Shipley and Neal discovered that both camps wanted the same things for themselves and their families—health, security, and a comfortable home in a naturally beautiful place.

They Are Us

After all the talk, it was time to put thoughts into action. Shipley and Neal looked around for a place to experiment to see if they could actually protect an ecosystem without sacrificing economic opportunity. "One day it just hit me," Shipley said. "What about where I live, the Applegate watershed?" The Applegate is a big place, but they were undeterred. "We started looking at it, got some maps out. I lived here but still I had no idea how big it was—500,000 acres. Jim thought it looked good, too. That is how we came to focus here."

Simply defined, a watershed is the area where rainfall makes its way to the river. As they go, the Applegate River watershed is large. A 30-mile vista boasts soft green meadows and year-round frosty peaks. Of course, a river runs through it, delicately veined with streams and creeks. Endangered species such as bald eagles and peregrine falcon inhabit this place, as do wolverines and spotted owls. Equally breathtaking are naked hills where the damage from clear-cutting, a drought, wildfires, cattle grazing, and development can't be missed. The ground is barren, littered with rotting vegetation alongside stagnant muddy tracks of tree-removal equipment, miles of stumps where graceful giants once pierced the sky. The damage is even visible from 5,000 feet up in the air, where Jack Shipley spends a good deal of time flying his Cessna and surveying the sins and failures modern life ravages on nature.

A hodge-podge of residents live in the Applegate: retirees, ranchers, farmers, loggers, the odd celebrity, entrepreneurs, small business owners, off-the-grid survivalists, government detractors, and a garden variety of enviro-types. Complicating a sense of community, the Applegate includes several unincorporated towns and even crosses state lines into northern California. Timber has been the largest industry by far. Over 70 percent of the Applegate is public land, yet government agencies seemed to be failing to protect the land from the mélange of interests so clearly killing it and dividing those who lived there.

To start their plan, Shipley and Neal asked a variety of experts, scientists, and professors from Oregon State University and University of Washington what they should do.

"We told them we had no preconceived notions about what should be done," Neal said. "We don't care. You tell us from a hydrology or geology or science or forestry standpoint." The experts all agreed; the forest needed to be thinned. The practice of tree thinning has multiple benefits for the forest, wildlife, and the watershed as a whole. Jim Neal also asked loggers what they thought should be done. "Privately, they all told us that it should be thinned, but publicly, they'd be up against it to say that, because they'd profit more by clear-cutting."

With consensus in hand, Shipley and Neal felt it was time to make their move. The next step was to call a meeting of all their friends with interests in the Applegate. A gathering of about 65 people showed up at Jack Shipley's house, including loggers, official agency folks, and environmentalists. Shipley and Neal asked for volunteers to create a board of directors who would lead the process of guiding the array of interests in the watershed.

"There was no name for it yet," Shipley recalled, "It was just people willing to put aside their personal interests, who could commit the time and were eager to work together."

The group selected nine people who would meet three times a week for the next few months to start building community consensus. Meetings focused on coming up with a name, a vision, objectives and goals.

"In that group we had at-large members, special interests, forest service, and the Bureau of Land Management," Neal said. "We were a dedicated group of peacemakers who were willing to work toward common ground solutions. We gave the group seven years. We thought we'd have it licked in that time." He laughs. "That's how naive we were, not wanting to create long term structures."

The Applegate Partnership was born, rooted in community and cooperation among industry, natural resource agencies, conservationists and residents. The vision was simple: finding a way to manage all land and water within the watershed in way that would please everyone.

"This stuff isn't rocket science," Shipley told us. "It's about managing public and private lands as a habitat for critters, meeting the timber need without clear-cutting, reducing fires, and creating healthy forests and waterways while allowing for the needs of ranchers too. It's pretty simple, but it brings us face to face with diametrically opposed interests."

First, there was a lot of public education to be done. "When we started talking about our watershed, people who lived here had no idea what we were talking about," Shipley said. "They didn't know that they are connected to people at other end of the water." It was as if those who lived around the water's edges and throughout the hills believed they lived in a separate world. There was no realization that they were intimately connected by the water's course. Shipley and Neal knew they would need to create a common language of the watershed among residents if they were to create change. They also knew that it would take time and hard work.

"If we're really going to take care of salmon in the creek," Shipley said, "we have to take responsibility for those communities along the waterways. We sink or swim together—we needed time to reach out to people."

Among many other community outreach tools, they Partnership began mailing a bimonthly newsletter, *The Applegator*, to all 12,000 residents of the watershed. Still published today, the newsletter contains information about ongoing projects, while helping to build community by celebrating birthdays, offering opinion columns, and publishing announcements. Each issue brings in $2,000 in advertising revenue. Educational, colorful and chatty, *The Applegator* helps cultivate a sense of neighborliness.

The Biggest Challenge

Creating the kind of trust that is at the heart of any healthy neighborhood, no matter how spread out, was the biggest challenge. Some of those at the early meetings were bitter enemies whose only previous encounters had been in a courtroom. Forest and other official agency representatives were also there. A third-generation farmer, Connie Young, only attended the meetings to keep a watchful eye on the environmentalists, whom she deeply mistrusted.

She was not alone. Remembering the timber wars, she knew many loggers who carried guns, fearful of being shot themselves by radical environmentalists while simply trying to do their jobs "I was very suspicious," Young told a reporter from *High Country News*. "I said they're probably going to take over our property and water rights. They have changed my mind on a few things, like conserving water and being more frugal."[1] Now Young, along with most everyone else believes that the trust established is itself a victory.

In those early days, board members wore buttons that read, "Practice Trust—Them Is Us," a hard-won motto. They spent a long time learning how to communicate, even bringing in facilitators for some meetings. It wasn't easy. They had to learn how to disagree peacefully. They had to find ways of debating that didn't involve accusations. But after so much time spent together, over potlucks, good times and personal crises, it was hard not to feel like a family.

"We began to see that watershed protection wasn't just about the land and the water, it was about the people, our neighbors," Shipley said. "Along with the water and the trees, we had to help the ranchers and the loggers and the homeowners. It's part of the big picture in the watershed."

They had some early successes (see next box), and with them came national acclaim. Just prior to the Clinton Administration's Northwest Forest Conference, Interior Secretary Bruce Babbitt visited the Applegate to learn about the partnership's philosophy. At a press conference Babbitt proclaimed: "I may be witness today to a very important beginning. It's important to know there are a few places on this battlefield where people have put down their weapons and started talking to each other." Clinton's Northwest Forest Plan would propose Applegate-style partnerships as a management plan for guiding experimental forest practices in 10 "Adaptive Management Areas (AMAs)" covering over 1.1 million acres of federal land. More than 100 research and monitoring projects were undertaken in partnership with federal and state agencies and regional and local groups, ranging from studying the effects of intentional fire setting to water quality monitoring to impact assessments of innovative harvest methods on bird populations.

Defending Community Wisdom

Despite the accolades, trouble was brewing. Timber companies soon challenged the Northwest Forest Plan, and the administration was forced to remove all federal employees from the Plan and also take them out of the Partnership. A model whose success had been based on close communication between private and public stakeholders living in the community was suddenly at-risk.

Success the AP Way

The Applegate Partnership is volunteer-based and non-hierarchical. AP has many ambitious projects involving many partners and the community at large. Among its accomplishments:

Innovative logging plan: Overcrowded timberland poses a fire risk, but is also home to scores of wildlife species. Companies demonstrating non-intrusive logging techniques (such as good ground-based operations and helicopter tree-removal) win rights to harvest dead and young trees, reducing fire hazards while preserving old-growth forests. Over 250,000 trees have been planted on 300 parcels of private land.

Elimination of clear-cutting: Since AP began, there has been no clear-cutting in the watershed. Companies clear-cutting in other areas are encouraged to observe best-practices in the Applegate, illustrating that local communities can influence corporate behavior.

Farms and fish: Perhaps the biggest undertaking on private land was the ditch restructuring project providing irrigation for more than 40 ranches. One of two small dams that was killing fish and cutting off access to spawning grounds was removed. Farmers gained irrigation water and pumps in return, which were funded by state and federal grants, private foundations, sporting goods companies, and environmental groups such as Oregon Water Trust and the World Wildlife Federation.

Wildfire reduction: In 2001, AP completed the first citizen-developed fire plan in the U.S. providing a menu of prevention options. Neighbors work together to thin trees and shrubs in common areas (such as driveways and around homes) funded by the National Fire Plan's cost-share incentive plan. Each year 300-400 landowners help shield their homes and community space against wildfire through this comprehensive plan.

Private land management: In 1994 the State of Oregon selected AP as the official Watershed Council for the Applegate Valley. A subcommittee, the Applegate River Watershed Council (ARWC), was formed to implement restoration on private lands. They have taken on numerous projects since then, and been successful in helping shift management approaches on private lands.

Community oneness: Many successes have created a sense of community in the valley. Bumper stickers boasting "THEY" with red circle-slash are common. Cooperation between private landowners and government agencies, once unheard of, are commonplace.

Outside forces, rather than serving as constructive mediators, were behaving like counterproductive meddlers. In the face of this challenge, the Partnership decided to maintain its commitment to local decision-making. The partners agreed that only a management plan deeply rooted in community and based on hard-won trust would meet their needs and protect all the interests in the watershed.

The federal agencies' resistance to the Applegate Partnership's closely considered plan provided a harsh lesson about how government bureaus work. Says Shipley, "What we didn't know then was that policies drive what occurs in our backyard—policies set in Washington, D.C." Policy wonks living 3,000 miles away were making decisions about how local resources were to be used. And yet those who were in the positions of power and influence had very little knowledge about the reality in the watershed.

"We found out that in D.C., every few years when the administration changes, there is all this hustling going on," Shipley said. "Special interests are lobbying politicians that don't have the interests of the community in mind, just their narrow piece, and you can't change anyone's mind back there with your perspective of living here. They just aren't interested."

Allowing impersonal, uninformed federal policies to control what happened in this now close-knit community was no longer acceptable. A hard-won community consensus was in place in the Applegate, and those who had struggled for that consensus were not prepared to surrender their fate to faraway powers. After all, didn't leaving decision-making in the hands of others lead to the timber wars in the first place?

"We found a way to work around it," Shipley said. "In the end, it just took some creativity." Essentially, the Partnership invited the agencies to attend meetings as "unofficial observers." Agency observers also reported on what they were doing, which enabled everyone to make informed decisions. As Shipley said, the system "has worked well ever since."

The partnership's actions were also criticized by some national environmental groups, such as the Sierra Club, which accused the Applegate Partnership of pandering to logging interests: "The timber industry thinks its odds are better in these forums. It believes it can dominate them over time and relieve itself from the burden of tough national rules." But for the Applegate Partnership, a no-cut policy as advocated by national environmental organizations was untenable. Again, it came back to thoughtful local wisdom as the guiding force for decision-making.

Local control didn't mean discounting the involvement of green groups, but the partnership did find that local environmental groups—as opposed to the national organizations whose policies are also usually formulated in Washington—could relate better to the Applegate's situation. As Jim Neal put it, "National environmental organizations may simply not have the time to be involved in the planning stages. Local environmental organizations can be more interactive."

The success of the partnership's approach is evident in the watershed today. Through creative management, there has been more timber harvested in the Applegate than other nearby areas. But the clear-cutting and old growth removal that once plagued the Applegate has ceased, and a quarter of a million new trees have been planted on private lands. The agencies awarded limited timber contracts based on the community principles rooted in ecosystem protection. Trees are selected for harvesting based on principles of natural fire-reduction and the overall health of the forest. Most trees are also removed by helicopter, a far less intrusive practice than by ground machinery.

It's not just the trees that are being protected. Because the Partnership found state funding to install 3,000 feet of fencing, Billy Joe Hunter's cattle no longer foul the stream that runs through his property, and he's pleased to be a part of the solution. Local sort yards are being considered to meet local lumber needs, a concept that was once foreign. The "Apple Core" program looks out for innovative ideas that strengthen the local economy from within the community. Even with a brag sheet as long as the Applegate community's, there is always more that can be done to strengthen the ecosystem. By safeguarding its environment, this once-fractured community has also discovered itself.

These days, Jack Shipley is reducing his involvement to make room for new leadership. His new goal is to see uncontrolled housing development halted in the Valley—not through legislation—but by giving the farm community incentives to hold on to its land. "If we function by competition, there will always be those who win and those who lose. It's a zero sum game. If we work together we can all win. We can have our cake and eat it too."

Green Revolution

Urban Organic Agriculture in Cuba

"In 25 years of working with farmers, these are the happiest, most optimistic, and best paid farmers I have ever met."
— Joe Kovach, Ohio State University

Necessity is indeed the mother of invention. When the Soviet Union collapsed, the island nation of Cuba was cut off from the chemicals, petroleum-based fertilizers, and other inputs on which its agriculture system depended. Food scarcities became acute, and hunger skyrocketed. Then Cubans got to work and established a system of local, organic agriculture that has been recognized as an international model. If climate change or peak oil seriously disrupt industrial food systems, the Cuban experience will provide a valuable road map for survival.

The Alamar district in eastern Havana is a typical example of Soviet-style housing. Perfectly rectangular apartment blocks march in formation, one after another. The plazas between the buildings are spacious, yet somehow eerie in their geometric severity. The uniform architecture is meant to erase class distinctions, but the effect—as in the public housing complexes of the United States—serves mostly to erase creativity and liveliness. The monotony of the layout seems to weaken morale.

Until, that is, one discovers Vivero Alamar—Alamar Gardens. Surrounded on all sides by seven-story apartment buildings, Vivero Alamar is a kind of oasis, a 27-acre working farm set right in the middle of a bustling city of two million people. The farm is everything that the surrounding architecture is not—polyform, versatile, organic.

Founded in 1994 on a smaller nine-acre parcel of land, Vivero Alamar today is a 140-person venture growing a wide range of fruits and vegetables. A patchwork quilt of orchards, shade houses, and row crops provides a steady harvest of bright green lettuces, sweet carrots, fresh tomatoes, avocados, culinary and medicinal herbs, chard, and cucumbers. The crops are healthy-looking, well tended, and grown without the use of chemical fertilizers, pesticides, or herbicides. Vivero Alamar is a completely organic operation.

Upon harvest, the produce is sold to the neighbors at a colorful farm stand. Vivero Alamar also sells a range of organic composts and mulches for family use as well as a broad selection of patio plants—propagated on site—for homes. In 2005, this neighborhood-managed, worker-owned cooperative earned approximately $180,000. After capital improvements and operating expenses are taken into account, that translates to about $500 per worker annually; not bad, considering that the Cuban minimum wage is about $10/month.

Noel Peña, the 41-year-old production manager of Vivero Alamar, is quick to describe the farm's benefits. "First, it's a job opportunity for the people. Second, it provides a fresh food supply to the community. Third, it has many economic benefits for the families. And I could mention a fourth, which is that an ugly place in the city has been turned into a beautiful garden."

Vivero Alamar is just one example of a revolution in food production that swept Cuba in the early 1990s and continues today. From Santiago de Cuba in the east to Pinar del Rio in the west, thousands of urban gardens like Vivero Alamar are blossoming. In community food parks, backyard patios, and large urban farms like the one in Alamar, some 300,000 Cubans are growing their own fruits and vegetables and then selling the surplus to their neighbors.

"We have all kinds of gardeners—artists, doctors, teachers," Fernando Morel, president of the Cuban Association of Agronomists, told us during a visit to the island's farms and gardens.

This innovative system has distinguished Cuba as a model of urban, organic agriculture; the Cuban government and community groups have won numerous international awards for their agriculture system. While the experience of this tropical nation of 11 million people is not entirely replicable in U.S. communities, the Cuban experiment nevertheless offers important lessons. Their recent history proves that, if driven by necessity, people can and will organize grassroots, community-based ways to feed themselves. At the same time, the Cuban experience shows that even a modest amount of government support and investment can greatly amplify community efforts. If—as a growing number of scientists warn—industrial nations ever face food supply disruptions due to climate change or peak oil, such lessons will be vital.

Things Fall Apart

The Cubans didn't become organic pioneers through a benevolent ecological epiphany. Their conversion to organic agriculture was the result of scarcity.

They ran out of money and oil, and then they started to run out of food.

During the Cold War, the Cuban economy relied heavily on support from the Soviet Union and the other members of the Socialist Bloc. The Cubans sent sugar to the U.S.S.R. and in return received oil and a range of industrial products, including chemical fertilizers, pesticides, herbicides, and tractors. The Soviets also sold cattle to the Cubans and provided animal feed and antibiotics. Approximately 50 percent of Cuba's food came from abroad. The USSR provided Cuba with a security shield against U.S. aggression, but it also left the island dangerously insecure when it came to food.

When the U.S.S.R. collapsed, Cuba ground to a halt. From 1989 to 1993, the Cuban economy contracted by 35 percent; foreign trade dropped a precipitous 75 percent. Without Soviet oil, city streets were emptied of cars and, more ominously, tractors were idled in the fields; domestic agriculture production fell by half. Millions of hogs, cattle, and goats died as the processed forage and antibiotics they depended on evaporated. Imported essentials such as vegetable oil and wheat flour were difficult to come by.

During this time, which Cuban officials euphemistically called the "Special Period," food scarcities became acute. The average per-capita calorie intake fell from 2,900 a day in 1989 to 1,800 calories in 1995. Protein consumption plummeted 40 percent. As Cubans lost weight, cats disappeared from the streets of Havana, destined for family soup pots.

Then the Cubans went to work, proving that necessity is, in fact, the mother of invention. Without government direction or urging—an important point, given the state-run nature of Cuban society—people began to spontaneously grow their own food. In the cities, residents took over garbage dumps, parking lots, and abandoned corners and started to plant gardens and build chicken coops. In the countryside, the old-timers went back to the fields and showed people how they could make do with oxen and hand labor.

"We started this with no money," said Vilda Figueroa, who built one of the first urban gardens in Havana and who now hosts a nutrition education program on television with her husband, Pepe. "We knew that the most valuable thing was the support of the community. So we started training volunteers who could horizontally spread the knowledge among their neighbors. We wanted something grassroots so we could popularize this idea of small scale production."

While urban residents built community gardens to meet their own needs, the government undertook sweeping agrarian reforms. The large, Soviet-model state farms were broken into smaller, farmer-run cooperatives to meet local needs. The state set up an infrastructure of organic compost and organic pest and plant disease control centers to help farmers make the transition away from chemical inputs. To give farmers incentives, the government allowed the creation of farmers markets in the cities, a break from the formerly state-dominated food system.

Today, Cuban agriculture is on the mend. Vegetable production doubled from 1994 to 1998, and then doubled again in 1999. Harvest totals for key crops such as potatoes and plantains have tripled. Cereal and bean yields are up, as are numbers for meat and egg production. Perhaps most significantly, daily caloric intake is back to its 1989 level and, in a sign of restored prosperity, some Cubans are beginning to worry about obesity.

And all of it has occurred using just a fraction of the chemicals that agriculture in the "developed" world depends on. Before the crisis hit, Cuba used more than one million tons of synthetic fertilizers a year; today it uses about 90,000 tons. During the Soviet period, Cuba applied up to 35,000 tons of herbicides and pesticides a year; today the number is about 1,000 tons. The country is a living example of how to grow food on a large, national scale without being reliant on petroleum-based inputs.

"It's very simple. We've moved to organics, not because we're Greenpeace members, but because we can't afford chemicals," Juan Jose Leon, an official at the Cuban Ministry of Agriculture, told us. "Everything we have gained, all the experience we have gained, we are not going to leave that behind."

Growing Community

Like many small, poor countries, Cuba relies on export-oriented agriculture to earn hard currency. The island is a robust exporter of sugar, tobacco, coffee and citrus, and is selling a significant amount of its agricultural products as organically certified. Foreign investment in such ventures is on the rise.

When it comes to sustainable agriculture, Cuba's most impressive innovation is its network of urban farms and gardens. According to the country's Ministry of Agriculture, some 150,000 acres of land are being cultivated in urban and suburban settings. That represents thousands of community farms, ranging from modest courtyards to production sites that fill entire city blocks.

These urban farms and gardens—*organoponicos* in Spanish—offer an inspiring example of community organizing and empowerment. An unusual mix of private initiative and public investment, the *organoponicos* show how a combination of grassroots effort and government support can result in sweeping change. They illustrate, in a very real and tangible way, how neighbors can come together to fulfill that most basic of needs—feeding ourselves.

When the food crisis hit, the *organoponicos* were an ad hoc response by local communities to increase the amount of food. No government official from on-high had to tell the people that they needed more to eat. But as the potency of the community farming movement became obvious, the Cuban government stepped in to provide key infrastructure support and to assist with information dissemination and skills sharing.

At most *organoponicos*, the government provides community farmers with land and water. The gardens can buy from the government key materials such as organic composts, seeds, and irrigation parts. Especially important in organic systems, the government sells "biocontrols" such as beneficial insects (predatory bugs like lacewings that eat pests such as aphids); bacterial agents that suppress plant diseases; and plant-based oils (such as Neem oil) that work as pesticides. These biological pest and disease controls are produced in some 200 government centers, deliberately small scale and spread out to increase access to local farms and decrease the need for transportation and fuel use.

What the people provide is labor. Since most of the *organoponicos* are built on land unsuitable for cultivation, they rely on raised planter beds to grow their crops: planter beds built with lot of muscle-power. No matter what city or town you find them in, the *organoponicos* have a signature look: 4 feet wide by 2 1/2 feet deep white-washed planter beds dominate the scene. The length depends on the size of the lot. Some beds are 10 feet long. Others are closer to 300 feet long: A football field sized vegetable bed—in the middle of a city.

Once the *organoponicos* are laid out, the work remains labor-intensive. All of the planting and weeding is done by hand, as is the harvesting. Soil fertility is maintained through a complex system of worm composting. The farms feed their excess plant materials and manure from nearby rural farms to worms that then produce a nutrient-rich fertilizer. Crews spread a kilogram of compost per square meter on the bed tops before each new planting.

Despite the tropical heat, it doesn't look like drudgery. Among *organoponico* employees, there is a palpable pride in their creation. The atmosphere is cooperative and congenial: There is no boss in sight, and each person seems to understand well their role and what's expected of them. The work occurs fluidly, with a quiet grace.

"It's amazing," Fernando Morel of the agronomists' association said. "When we had more resources in the 80s, oil and everything, the system was less efficient than it is today."

Indeed, the hybrid public-private partnership appears to work well. In return for providing the land, the government receives a portion of the produce—usually about one-fifth of the harvest—to use at state-run day-care centers, schools, and hospitals. The workers get to keep the rest to sell at produce stands located right at the farm. It seems a fair trade.

Progress You Can Taste

By statistical measures, the Cuban experiment with urban agriculture is a success. For example, Havana produces enough food for each resident to receive a daily serving of 280 grams of fruits and vegetables. The United Nation's Food Program recommends 305 grams of fruits and vegetables a day. There are few other cities in the world that could say as much.

But, beyond the government press releases and brochure-friendly images of gardens next to highways, does it really work for ordinary Cubans? The answer is yes, at least as measured by the good cheer of the farmers and the gratitude of the shoppers.

Joe Kovach, an entomologist from Ohio State University who visited Cuba on a 2006 research delegation, summed up the situation: "In 25 years of working with farmers, these are the happiest, most optimistic, and best paid farmers I have ever met."

The workers at the five-acre "Celia Sanchez Manguley" *organoponico* in the provincial city of Sancti Spíritus prove the point. "This is beautiful work," a woman named Aymara said as she harvested tomatoes. "It's great to be able to reclaim the production for ourselves."

"I like working here," said another worker, cigar clamped firmly in his teeth, as he helped with the tomatoes. "It's close to home. I can go home for lunch. And if I want to work a Saturday or a Sunday and then take off a Monday, I can."

The other proof is the lines of people that every day stretch past the *organoponico* produce stands. People are hungry for the local, fresh produce, which is cheaper than the food available at the farmers markets and government stores. Questioned about why they shop at the *organoponicos*, Cubans almost always give the same response: quality.

"It's good quality, it's good quantity, and it's good price," a woman shopping at the largest urban farm in the central city of Santa Clara told a foreign visitor. "It's fresh. Look, look at it. They're harvesting it right now." She points, and indeed they are. As each customer places an order at the farm stand, farm workers fulfill the request, a system that prevents waste. It's incredible: harvest-on-demand.

This is a stellar example of the kind of direct marketing small farmers in the United States hope to achieve through sales at local farmers' markets. By eliminating the middleman, the farmers get a better price for their product. And by bringing the consumer closer to the point of production, people get fresher, tastier, healthier foods. It's local food production at its best, and everyone wins.

Exporting Revolution?

Of course, it's important to acknowledge that Cuba's green revolution—as impressive as it may be—is not entirely replicable in other countries. After all, Cuba remains a state-dominated society. The question is whether a more liberal society without that kind of central command structure could respond as effectively to a sudden breakdown in the food system.

Perhaps the answer can be glimpsed in the resilience of the experiment. For people in other countries, the lessons of the Cuban success come through the average Cuban citizen's commitment to the ideal of local food production.

The case of bicycling in Havana helps make the case. During the Special Period, bikes became a common site throughout Cuba as the country grasped for fossil fuel-free transportation. Recently, however, Venezuela's ideologically sympathetic president, Hugo Chavez, has given some $2 billion a year in subsidized oil to Cuba. Not surprisingly, perhaps, most people in Havana have given up their bikes and returned to their cars. But while the bikes have disappeared, the urban farms and gardens have not. That's because they provide a direct source of jobs and healthy food to the community. Nothing sharpens the attention quite like hunger.

Even as Cuba finds increased opportunities to return to a chemical-based, long distance food system, the country is sticking with its *organoponicos*.

Urban farmer Israel Hernandez says that he would not give up managing his half-acre *organoponico*. A wiry and intense old-timer, he has the leathery hands and wrinkled features of someone who has spent most of his years in the sun. When he talks about his garden—the work he does there with children, and how he provides vegetables to a local day-care center—his pride is obvious. In his commitment to growing food for his neighborhood, one hears the persistence of nature, the yearning that we feel to be connected to the biological systems on which our very lives depend.

"I used to live in the mountains, and I fought in the mountains with the Revolution, and I worked on a dairy," Hernandez said. "I became a history teacher, and later I worked for the government in the Interior Ministry. I was retired. I stopped working. And then I came back to run this garden. I love it, I love it. We have a saying here in Cuba: 'The wild animal returns to the wild.' … I am that wild animal."

Street Beets

Urban Farmers Get
Hip to Growing

"As the cheap fuels dry up, metro areas are at huge risk. We're looking at huge potential problems if we don't make changes."
—Bob Randall, Urban Harvest

It's a chilly December day in Oakland, California—overcast and gray, the first real bite of winter—and most folks are staying indoors and warm. But behind a modest bungalow on the city's impoverished West Side, three young women volunteers are busy building a backyard garden for a local resident. The team works with practiced precision, and as the wheelbarrow loads of dark, rich soil pile up, a three-foot by eight-foot planter bed begins to take shape. A selection of fruit and vegetable seedlings offers a glimpse of harvests to come—strawberries and chard, lettuce, herbs and shelling peas.

The backyard garden construction is a project of City Slicker Farms, a local non-profit that provides fresh food to a neighborhood better known for its rail yards and warehouses than its green spaces. In just seven years, City Slicker has become a vital part of the West Oakland landscape. Its six market gardens grow a range of organic fruit, vegetables, eggs and honey for sale at a neighborhood produce stand. An environmental education program gives children and adults opportunities to learn more about where their food comes from. The backyard vegetable garden construction service is so popular that there is a months-long waiting list.

Judging by the reception from neighborhood residents, the program is a success. "I buy all my vegetables here, and so does my wife," said Tony Lejones, a local truck driver, as he perused the offerings at the City Slicker stand. "The whole neighborhood comes here—black, white, and brown. They do a fine job. It's fantastic work."

City Slicker Farms is not alone in doing fantastic work. Across the United States, an urban agriculture movement is flowering as a growing number of people get interested in growing their own food. Urban farms and gardens are taking root in areas where previously there was only concrete and asphalt.

In Birmingham, Alabama, Jones Valley Urban Farm is reclaiming abandoned lots and using them to grow organic produce and flowers for sale to restaurants. Chicago's Ken Dunn does similar work as he takes over unused parking lots, piles on tons of soil, and uses the sites to grow heirloom tomatoes. Fairview Gardens in Santa Barbara, California flourishes even as the city has surrounded it on all sides. In St. Louis, a housing developer, Whittaker Homes, is setting up an organic farm within a new subdivision in an effort to make residents feel more at home. Even in chilly Alaska, community gardens are thriving in places such as the town of Homer, where residents have formed a network to encourage local food production.

Neighborhood gardening is as old as the first planted seed. As recently as World War II, Americans' connection to their food remained strong when thousands of "Victory Gardens" produced nearly half of all household produce as part of the war effort. But in the last few generations local food production has become scarce. Until, that is, the last decade, when urban farming began to sprout again.

Veteran environmental activists and community organizers say the recent increase in urban food production marks a real change.

"Whether it's the Food Project or Redhook Farm or countless other projects, urban agriculture is definitely increasing," Betsy Johnson, executive director of the American Community Gardening Association (ACGA), said. "I think the trend is very positive."

Longtime observers of the U.S. food system say there are several concerns propelling the renaissance in city agriculture. One is the country's obesity epidemic and the need to provide more healthful foods. Another is the drive for more sustainable economies as worries about climate change and peak oil spur demand for enterprises grounded in ecological principles. A third is the simple fact that horticulture—with its regular, seasonal rewards—is an ideal vehicle for community organizing, especially when it comes to youth.

"The drivers come from the public health community and the urban planning community that wants to green cities," Tom Forster, policy director of the Community Food Security Coalition, said. "And I think the other big driver is preparedness and homeland security, which now embraces food production at the local level, whether that's a fear of climate change or a fear of disruption in the food distribution chain."

Such worries are motivating new food production in Houston, according to Bob Randall, who directs an organization there called Urban Harvest. The group sponsors a series of vegetable growing classes, as well as a permaculture design course. Urban Harvest also launched Houston's first farmers market, and organizes a yearly fruit tree sale that earns nearly $50,000 in the course of a weekend. Randall says increased interest in his group's programs has been noticeable in just the past few years—and he says that anxiety about eventual petroleum scarcities, and the promise of petroleum-free local food production, are part of the reason.

"This being the oil capital, people here are more aware than most that oil prices are going to rise faster than inflation," Randall said. "As the cheap fuels dry up, metro areas are at huge risk. We're looking at huge potential problems if we don't make changes."

While some of the new urban farmers are worried about the future challenges of a contraction in the national food system, many are driven by a more immediate problem—the country's obesity epidemic. Across the country rates of heart disease and diabetes are skyrocketing as the population becomes heavier. Obesity hits low-income communities hardest, since the foods that are starchiest and highest in fat are also the cheapest. Poor neighborhoods also grapple with a lack of options, since many grocery chains have abandoned the inner city for the more lucrative suburbs.

Many urban food projects, then, are driven by a desire to provide poor and people-of-color communities with healthier eating options. That's the idea behind Mill Creek Farm in Philadelphia. Started two years ago by a pair of twenty-something nutrition educators-turned farmers, Mill Creek Farm has converted a vacant lot into a 1.5-acre garden full of carrots, squash, tomatoes, okra, garlic, lettuces, and greens. At the height of summer, the farm's produce stand regularly sells out of goods.

"People don't have the option to get fresh, affordable, good quality, organic food in their neighborhood, and that's really sad," said Johanna Rosen, one of the co-founders of Mill Creek Farm. "The food access issue is really important to me. We are producing food in the city to increase access in low-income neighborhoods, and trying to involve the community as much as we can."

Community involvement is vital for urban agriculture projects to succeed. Since the available vacant properties in cities are usually in poorer neighborhoods, today's urban farmers have to find ways of showing that growing one's own food is not just good for the planet or good for your health, but also a real economic benefit. Which is exactly what Redhook Farm in Brooklyn is all about. A three-acre farm built on an abandoned baseball field, Redhook Farm uses organic farming and marketing as a way to grow economic opportunities for disadvantaged youth. The very act of taking a plant from seed to sale builds empowerment for teens, according to farm staff.

"We want to have a 21st century park that is training teens for 21st century citizenship," Ian Marvey, a co-founder of Redhook Farm, said. "Which means hands-on training to build a sustainable economy, whether that means learning how to grow food, or how to build a greenhouse, or how to grow compost."

At the core of urban farming is the desire to put the culture back into agriculture. It's an effort that goes beyond organic to place communities at the center of our food system. Sure, you can get your produce from an organic farmer located somewhere in your state—but wouldn't you rather buy it from your neighbor if you could? For those involved in the new urban farms, it's the people—not the plants—that make the change.

At least, that's what motivates Liz Monk, a 26-year-old from Ithaca, New York. Back at the City Slicker garden in Oakland, a cold rain has started to fall, but Monk and the other volunteers keep working. As she shovels compost out of an old pickup truck, Monk tells a visitor that she spent a summer working on a farm out in the country, but says she finds urban farming more rewarding because she is able to have a deeper relationship with the people she is growing for.

"Just making connections with people, just having face to face contact—that's something that's very positive," Monk said. "It's the kind of thing that feeds your soul."

What You Can Do

Get It Fresh From the Farm

K now your farmer, know your food. That slogan of the local food movement can be your guide as you try to navigate closer to a dinner you can trust.

The best way to create a relationship with your farmer is to join a Community Supported Agriculture (CSA) program. Some 100,000 households are enrolled in these systems, whereby your family receives a weekly box of seasonal fruits and vegetables (and sometimes eggs and cheese) straight from a particular farm. It's a great way to support farmers and let them know they will have a dependable market.

If a CSA doesn't work for your household, then head to the farmers market. Learn the names of the farmers there, and ask them if they use chemical-free methods. You can find a national directory of CSAs and farmers markets at www.localharvest.org.

For your other food needs, seek out locally owned and operated markets. Get your grains, beans, and nuts from the bulk bins instead of the processed stuff manufactured by giant corporations. Search out local butchers and fish sellers, and ask if they sell cage-free chicken, grass-fed beef, and wild-caught fish.

When it comes to that other staff of life—water—the answer is right at your kitchen tap. As Maude Barlow points out, about 85 percent of U.S. water is safe to drink. To make sure you aren't ingesting any extra hormones, put a water purifier on the tap. If you live in that other 15 percent of cities with unreliable tap water, order a home delivery service with a water cooler company. The large 2.5-gallon jugs are a more efficient use of resources than buying several new 16-ounce bottles daily.

These steps shouldn't feel burdensome. Remember, until recently people only ate food that was local and organic and went about their day without having to carry a few sips of water wrapped in plastic. Reconnecting with our food means reconnecting to the seasons, to the natural systems of which we are a part. It means putting some of the taste back in life.

Section Three

From Mean Streets to Green Streets

Across the country, grassroots organizations and ad-hoc citizen groups are expanding the definition of democracy. They are pushing the concept beyond the limited political realm of elections, politicians, and legislation toward the broader definition embodied in the word's Greek roots: *demos,* meaning people, and *kratos,* meaning rule. The people—not corporations—are supposed to rule in a real democracy.

In fact, corporations are not even mentioned in the U.S. Constitution. Ultimate authority derives from the citizenry. The United States was the first nation to ensnarine the principle that government is a derivative institution, drawing its authority from the informed consent of the citizens. It's why the U.S. Constitution starts with those three magic words: We the People.

That principle has not always been honored in practice. At the republic's founding, the definition of people did not include women, slaves, or Native Americans. The country's founders were at times acutely afraid of "They the People" and dreaded the prospect of "mob rule." Still, if the founders feared open and direct democracy, some of them also feared the power of concentrated wealth. The third president of the United States, Thomas Jefferson, seeing how the concentration of money had taken England in an imperial direction, said, "I hope we shall take warning from the example of England and crush in its birth the aristocracy of our moneyed corporations which dare already to challenge our Government to trial and bid defiance to the laws of our country."

More than 200 years later, that tension between wealth and democracy still exists. Today grassroots groups are waging struggles on a wide range of fronts that all share a common ideal: to have local people control their institutions, whether it be how we define corporate responsibilities, the way we discipline youth accused of crimes, or the way we define national security.

Jefferson's warning seems an especially precise prediction of events in Humboldt County, California, where a local district attorney had the nerve to challenge the way a giant corporation was clear-cutting the local forests. Maxxam

Corporation didn't appreciate how the district attorney was seeking to enforce the law, and so the company sought to remove him from office. The resulting battle led to path-breaking legislation challenging the power of large corporations in their community.

The Humboldt County story illustrates a fundamental contradiction between transnational corporations and local political institutions. Mayors, town councils, and state legislators have authority based on specific geographical boundaries. Transnational corporations don't like boundaries; they are rootless. They want to be able to move their capital across borders at will.

As more people wake up to this contradiction, they are realizing that they must take control of their local institutions and shape them to meet *local* needs, not those of distant institutions with narrow interests. Local and state officials are often caught in the middle of this contradiction. They are pulled to one side by the large corporations that can write big campaign checks, and pulled to the other side by voters who have the power to remove officials from office. In the Humboldt case, the people won the tug-of-war.

The ideal of "We the People" also can be found in the story of Tallulah, Louisiana, which was once the site of an infamously brutal youth prison. When the prison was built, the local residents were hardly consulted, and one of the key promises of the prison construction—providing jobs—never materialized. So when parents of the incarcerated minors launched a campaign to close the prison, the residents joined them. The coalition proved that people united in a common cause can decide what will form the base of the local economy.

The power of unusual political alliances is also on display in our story about the national movement against the Patriot Act. Since 2002, Americans in hundreds of communities across the country have rejected the legitimacy of a complicated piece of federal legislation written prior to the events of September 11, 2001, but rushed through Congress soon thereafter. The robust political energy of the local Bill of Rights Defense Committees is a great example of the American tradition of the masses inserting themselves into a political process that is usually the preserve of elites.

To create a globally sustainable economy, we must have local networks exerting effective control over local conditions. Sometimes this local control will have an obvious green element, and sometimes it will not. A key challenge confronting this movement is to build links between struggles focused solely on green issues and those focused solely on local control, and getting both sides to realize that they need each other. The fate of the planet is directly related to whether or not we can merge these movements.

Breaking the Chains

Parents and Locals
Transform a Juvenile Prison

"People said it could never happen—but people underestimate the power of compassion and a commitment to justice."
            —Grace Bauer, mother of an incarcerated youth

In 1994, the state of Louisiana, with the highest incarceration rate in the world and a reputation for some of the toughest prisons in the country, opened a juvenile correctional facility in the impoverished town of Tallulah. Parents began complaining that their children were regularly abused and "warehoused" in deplorable conditions, and before long the prison was considered the nation's most corrupt and dangerous youth facility. Then an unlikely coalition of local Tallulah residents, parents, lawyers, legislators and child advocates linked arms to successfully shut down the prison and pass the most radical reconstruction of the juvenile justice system in the state's history.

Tallulah. Over the years, the name has meant many different things to people living around northeastern Louisiana. Folklore has it that the town of Tallulah got its name in the 1850s, when a local woman used her wiles to persuade the chief engineer to re-route the railroad through her land. Alas, by the time construction was underway, she had tired of him. Alone, brokenhearted and not without resentment, he named the station—and by de facto, the town—Tallulah, after another sweetheart.

A hundred years later, this predominantly African-American community became a civil rights stronghold, led by black veterans returning from World War II and determined to create change at home. By the 1960s, Tallulah was still segregated but was also a trendy hotspot, attracting fun seekers for jazz, blues, and nightlife; B.B. King was a regular at Tallulah clubs. After the lumber mill closed in the late 1980s, the fun seemed to be over and forgotten, replaced by the economic hardship of its 9,000 residents. Today, Tallulah is so economically depressed it ranks among the poorest communities in the nation. With

50 percent of residents living below the poverty line, and 40 percent of adults without a high school diploma, Tallulah became a place few visited.

Then in 1994, following what many called a shady deal made in the governor's office, Tallulah was back on the map, becoming not so much famous as infamous—as the home of a juvenile prison *The New York Times* warned was "so rife with brutality, cronyism, and neglect that many legal experts say it is the worst in the nation." The Tallulah Correctional Center for Youth (TCCY)—known simply as "Tallulah"—marked the entire town with an indelible stamp of child abuse and corruption. Within a month of opening, the media were outside the gates, eagerly reporting as federal judge Frank Polozola called a state of emergency there "due to riots and an inability of the staff to control and protect youth."

Riots notwithstanding, daily conditions were so violent it was estimated that 25 percent of the prison's incarcerated youth required medical treatment each month. In 1995, a Human Rights Watch report singled out TCCY, finding that many children were warehoused in unsanitary isolation cells for up to 23 hours a day without adequate education, exercise, counseling, or any kind of rehabilitative programming. The U.S. Department of Justice investigated the

Corporations Cash in on Prisons

It seems that crime—or at least punishment—does pay. Prisons are built and operated at taxpayers' expense as a matter of public interest. They house offenders, ostensibly to rehabilitate them and return them to society. Now the privatization of prisons has become big business—among the most profitable of all industries—but at what cost?

- In the 1800s, private prisons were common, but due to slave-labor practices and brutal conditions, the practice was phased out. By 1990, there were only five privately run prisons in the United States, accounting for 2,000 inmates. In 2007, there are nearly 100,000 prisoners housed in private facilities.

- In 1992, the stock price of the industry leader, Corrections Corporation of America (CCA), was $8. In 2007, shares were $52 and climbing. In 2005, CCA netted a profit of $70.9 million, a 22.9 percent increase over 2004, with revenues of $1.19 billion.

- Private prisons say they are more efficient than state or federally run facilities. According to Corp Watch, in 1985 one company attempted to site a prison on a toxic dump it had purchased for $1. According to a federal investigation, a 1994 riot at a private immigration detention center was the result of prison management reducing spending on food, building repairs, and guard salaries. Companies have also cut corners on drug rehabilitation, counseling, and literacy programs, all of which make it more likely that inmates will re-offend.

facility in 1996, finding that over a period of just 20 days in August of that year, 28 youth were treated in hospital for serious injuries inflicted by guards or other inmates.

By 1998, parents of the youths held at the Tallulah facility began a campaign to close down the prison. They ran into stiff political opposition founded on the argument that the prison was a benefit to the depressed local economy. Eventually, the parents reached out to the locals and were surprised to discover that the community was not benefiting from the prison. In the end, the alliance between parents and residents led to the facility's closure as a juvenile incarceration unit.

In a nation where incarceration is big business—a supposed economic boon for poor towns—the Tallulah story reveals that few communities want to bet their fiscal future on an industry based on repression. By uniting locals and parents, the Tallulah reformers showed that there is a deep hunger for creating the kind of economy that's more optimistic than opportunistic. "The time spent working next to the folks of that community, fighting so hard to save what they and their families before them had built, gave me a whole new respect for these beautiful folks," said Grace Bauer, whose son, Corey, had been held at TCCY. "In so many ways they too were victims of the prison."

A Dangerous Place

In an atmosphere indistinguishable from high security adult prisons, the Tallulah Correctional Center for Youth was institutionalizing crime in the state

Corrections, Corruption, and Corporations

Private prison deals are rife with corruption, and Tallulah was no different. The prison functioned quite well as a cash cow for the private for-profit corporation who won the state contract to open and operate the facility back in 1994. In May 2001, the state's legislative auditor found that between January 1995 and April 2001, three members of Trans-American Development Associates, cronies of then-Governor Edwin Edwards, pocketed $8.7 million dollars from the deal. Even after lawsuits forced the state to seize control of the facility in 1999, the three continued to put away up to $600,000 each fiscal year until the legislature finally ceased all payments, except those which covered the lease of the facility. These annual lease payments by the state are scheduled to continue until construction bonds for the facility are paid off in 2012, after which the three men—not the state, parish or town—will retain ownership of the physical plant.

From Xochitl Bervera, "The Death of Tallulah Prison," Colorlines, June 24, 2004.

by taking in mostly nonviolent youth—overwhelmingly youth of color—and churning out repeat offenders and future adult felons. The facility's recidivism rate—the rate at which the incarcerated re-offend—was as high as 90 percent, compared with only 7 percent in Missouri's education and counseling-based facilities.

Most of the 400 Tallulah inmates were classified as nonviolent, often transferred from other faraway facilities for behavioral problems, most stemming from a lack of treatment for existing mental health problems that were exacerbated by isolation and abuse. Parents and grandparents often faced drives as long as 400 miles to visit their children. But not all were transfers, as Xochitl Bervera, co-director of Families and Friends of Louisiana's Incarcerated Children (FFLIC), points out. Many of the children were unwittingly placed there by the parents of troubled youth. "The facility also ran a Boot Camp for troubled teens, which some parents thought might be a good experience for their kids," Bervera told us. "What parents did not understand was that once they sent these kids to Boot Camp, they had effectively lost custody of their own children, who were transferred straight from Boot Camp to prison." Very few youth ever "graduated" from Boot Camp.

Once kids were transferred to the "prison side," they were in for a much longer stay than the Boot Camp had called for. It was a shocking transition for kids and their parents. As Bervera recalled, "Once inside the facility, it was a dangerous place. Youth-on-youth violence, guard-on-youth violence, sex was rampant between guards and youth. There was never even any denial of those facts. That level of corruption was well known."

Calling for Juvenile Justice

A fledgling legal advocacy group, the Juvenile Justice Project of Louisiana (JJPL), was determined to make changes at TCCY. Director David Utter started JJPL, along with Shannon Wight and Gabriella Celeste, in 1998. As he said, "We wanted to put pressure on the defender's system, the way they were so poorly represented. We wanted to get better advocates, better treatment, better facilities and ultimately, to shrink the system and the number of kids in secure care. That was our mission statement. The facility at Tallulah was bad, but in fact all the youth facilities were bad." JJPL filed a class action suit on behalf of the children incarcerated at the Tallulah facility, in an attempt to improve conditions.

The group's steady work chipped away at the brutal conditions, though bringing to justice those responsible for conditions there proved far more difficult. The organization helped obtain early release for those inappropriately incarcerated, and reduced those held in isolation cells by 66 percent. Soon after filing the class action lawsuit, the DOJ also filed legal action over the conditions, making Louisiana the first state ever to be sued by the federal government on the basis of their juvenile justice system.

The attorneys' work put them in touch with parents of children incarcerated at Tallulah. Gina Womack, the office administrator, spent a good part of her days fielding a steady stream of calls from scared, confused and outraged family members. Many parents wanted to do something more than just challenge conditions, and in 2000, with help from Womack and others at JJPL, a small group of parents gathered at the home of Earnestine Williams in Baton Rouge. The gathering determined to be as much a political advocacy organization as a support group. Over the next year or so, its members would come from across the state, eventually settling on the name Families and Friends of Louisiana's Incarcerated Children.

The parents' goal in 2000 was not just to change the conditions at Tallulah, but to shut it down forever. "That was fascinating," Utter recalled with a smile. "The best part about the 'Close Tallulah' story is the fact that the idea to close came from parents. It wasn't the lawyers that did it."

A Jazz Funeral

The parents group understood they needed to attract some attention to their campaign. Xochitl Bervera, who began as an intern working with FFLIC, remembers, "It was Avis Brock, granddaughter of a local civil rights leader, who brought the idea to the group, saying, 'This is New Orleans, let's do something truly New Orleans.' And what better than a traditional jazz funeral, with a brass band, coffin, hearse, horse-drawn carriage, all of it?"

Rooted in African cultures, jazz funerals are a specialized New Orleans tradition, a celebration of life that accompanies death. Brass bands mournfully lead the funeral procession to the grave, but once the casket is laid to rest, rousing Ragtime or Dixieland jazz tunes such as "When the Saints Go Marching In" are played.

In September 2001—gathering more than 150 marchers, including the staff of the Juvenile Justice Project, the chair of the Senate Judiciary Committee, and Juvenile Court Judge Mark Doherty—the FFLIC used this symbolic tradition to mourn the untold losses of childhood suffered by their incarcerated children and to "bury" the prison itself. The march led all the way to Orleans Parish Juvenile Court. It was the leading story in many news outlets around the state, officially setting off the campaign to "Close Tallulah Now!"

Over the next two years, the work continued. There were dozens of legal hearings that attempted to close the prison from a variety of angles, includ-

Locked Up At Tallulah: A Mother's Tale

Grace Bauer's son Corey was incarcerated at the Tallulah facility in 2001. She became active in the fight to close the prison and now directs the Lake Charles chapter of Friends and Families of Louisiana's Incarcerated Children (FFLIC). This is her story.

Q. Please describe the first time you went to see your son at the Tallulah Facility.

Tallulah was so far away, it took 10 hours round trip to visit him for less than 2 hours. We did not know Tallulah was a prison; we were told it was a place where our son would get the help he needed. Our first look at the place scared us beyond words. Driving up to the high locked gates the first time, I remember thinking we must be in the wrong place. When guards were physically searching us, including our daughters, I remember thinking, "This is all a mistake, because this is a prison for bad people and our son isn't bad, just sick." Corey was a skinny kid, weighing less than 90 pounds when he arrived. My first trip to see him inside Tallulah, he was beaten so badly he was in the infirmary. His face was bruised and swollen, one eye swollen shut. An imprint of a guard's ring was tattooed on the right temple of his head. The guard's size 9 shoe imprint still bruised into his rib cage.

Q. What led to Corey's incarceration at Tallulah?

On January 5, 1998, my mother passed away. This set off a series of events that put us on a direct path into the juvenile justice system. We were a family of six, including myself, my husband, Robert, my son, my two daughters, Robyn, 7, and Caroline, 5, and my mother, who lived right next door. We were all very close to Momma. Corey, then 11, had just entered into middle school. He was already having a difficult time adjusting to the move into a new school environment. He had trouble getting his locker open, keeping track of all of his books and belongings and getting to so many different classrooms. He had never been in trouble. He was an honor roll student and, according to his teachers, was very bright and an excellent reader.

The night my mother died, Corey had nightmares and wet the bed. A month later he was suspended for smoking on the school campus. From then until Corey was taken into custody of the state in March of 2001, we did everything that we could think of to hold onto him. After numerous suspensions and several expulsions—all for smoking or possession of tobacco—the school system refused to let him back in. He picked up a couple of petty charges for shoplifting and possession of tobacco by a minor, which brought him to the attention of the juvenile justice system.

All the while, his attitude and behavior became more erratic and troubling. He was now drinking and using marijuana. I know now he was extremely depressed and much of what we did during this time only seemed to make the problems worse for him instead of giving him what he needed. There were counselors that were provided for him with military backgrounds, unlikely to ever serve the needs of a child labeled with Oppositional Defiant Disorder.

During the next two years, I became accustomed to sleeping on the floor in his room to keep him from leaving the house during the night. There were many days sat in school with him to keep him from being suspended. Some days he would just take off from school and be gone for hours, eventually being brought home by his friends who would drop him off at the end of driveway, passed out. There were too many nights to remember being afraid to fall asleep for fear of him vomiting in his sleep and choking to death. It was an agonizing time for him, he felt so alone and felt awful for the trouble he was having and bringing to the family.

Q. What happened to Corey once inside the Tallulah Facility?

Inside, he was beaten repeatedly, bullied, sexually assaulted, and neglected. Corey ceased being the little boy we raised during his time there. He became terrified and his daily function in life was about survival. He learned to sleep in the daytime when there were more guards on duty and less chance of being attacked. He learned to steal food and protect with his fists what he was given. His beloved books were taken from him and education was nonexistent. Eventually, Corey refused to come out of isolation. Although I did not know it at the time, I suspect this was after the rape he endured. In isolation, he began to have a mental breakdown. When the guards would try to force him out of the isolation cell, he would spit on them, curse and physically fight them. This behavior would earn him more time in the "hole". This served his purpose of staying safe. With tickets for such behavior he would have never earned release.

Q. When did you begin to work to change what was going on at TCCY?

I naively believed in the system and folks that said they were going to help our boy. Within a month of Corey's arrival at Tallulah I began looking for help. My first stop was a private attorney, who at least had the decency to tell me the truth. It would be 4 months before I came to realize the full extent of what was happening there and how many children it was happening to. By September of 2001, I knew about the fight going on within the state to shut Tallulah down and went to New Orleans to meet with the folks that were pushing for the closure and became involved.

Q. Where is Corey now?

Today, Corey is 20 and sits in the Franklin Parish Detention Center in Winnsboro, Louisiana. He is still as handsome as ever and still loves to read. He reads to his cellmates that can't read and writes letters for those that can't. He has four months to do on a three-year sentence for stealing quarters out of a soda machine. This was his third simple burglary charge in two years. He steals to support his addiction to drugs. His addiction began after his release from Tallulah in 2002. In three years of incarceration inside an adult facility, beginning when he was barely 17, he has grown up a lot. He no longer believes he will ever have a childhood or do the things that teenagers do and he has given up on his childhood dream of becoming a veterinarian. Despite all he has witnessed, experienced, and lived through, he still has hope that he can do something good with his life.

Interview by Tamara Wattnem

ing trying to get the legislature to strip the facility's funding from the state's finance bill. Despite coming close to victory more than once, the coalition was unable to find the right hook to shutter TCCY. Meanwhile, FFLIC continued to expand its statewide outreach to build the coalition's numbers and to keep the issue in the media, often linking the hearings with media-friendly actions.

The coalition's work ignited a media firestorm before the May 2, 2002 Senate Judiciary hearing. The hearing, originally set up to be an educational session about the prison, quickly became much more than that. "Our legislative champion, Donald Cravins, led the fight before the Judiciary committee," Utter said. "He turned it into a fight to get the facility de-funded."

On that day, parents from all over the state were bussed in, and packed the hearing room and the overflow room. Impassioned testimony from parents helped facilitate a legislative field trip to Missouri to examine the much-touted education-based juvenile justice system there—which was not only cheaper to operate, but far more effective at rehabilitation.

When the delegation returned from Missouri, coalition members were shocked to hear one conservative legislator tell the media that Louisiana must "close all of its secure-care facilities" in favor of the Missouri-style model. It was a high point in a campaign that was gaining momentum. The coalition even managed to make the closure a key issue in the governor's race that year. As Utter recalled, "It became an education campaign in June and July of 2003. We started working with all the gubernatorial candidates to close Tallulah before the date proposed in the Bill." All of the candidates pledged to do so.

Meanwhile, local residents of Tallulah had been offended by the campaign's slogan, "Close Tallulah Now!," believing it reinforced the notion that Tallulah was only a torturous prison, not a community of proud people. Through all of the media frenzy, the image of the Tallulah residents had been painted with the same evil brush as the facility that shared its name. After all, didn't the cruel guards come from the local population? Wasn't it the town that allowed the facility to exist at all, and didn't locals thrive on the well-paying jobs that came at the expense of children's suffering?

As Tallulah resident Moses Williams told us, "Parents were against Tallulah folks, thinking it was Tallulah folks that treated their kids that way, and we took offense to the way they painted our town. It was just natural animosity." Grace Bauer thinks back to the long journeys to visit her son in Tallulah, and remembers hating the whole town. "Back then I would cross the Mississippi state line and buy food and gas there rather than patronize their businesses," she told us. "To me, Tallulah, Louisiana and the Tallulah Correctional Facility for Youth were one and the same."

Despite the parents' testimonies and media attention, the hard working advocates, the handful of sympathetic judges and legislators and DOJ charges leveled against the facility, those who lobbied in defense of the prison could always fall back on one familiar refrain—the fragile Tallulah economy needed those jobs. But no one among the anti-prison campaigners had thought to ask residents what they felt about the effort to close the facility, or about the jobs. No one had asked the residents of Tallulah if they wanted a prison in the first place, nor how once the deal was done, construction occurred on the African-American side of town—an echo of Jim Crow.

A booming prison economy including new jobs had been promised, but in the end, the positions required educational degrees or special skills not in large supply in the community. The jobs that did materialize for the locals were mostly low paying. As Moses Williams recalled, "When the prison came, it did provide some jobs, but they weren't the best. Because it was privately run, there was no thought to who they hired, how they hired. There were no true benefits for the community. The company was just trying to make a profit. They weren't concerned with juvenile justice. They were just warehousing kids and making money doing it."

Even after 18 correctional officers walked out in protest of their $6-per-hour pay, leading the state to wrest control of the facility and increase salaries, the staff turnover rate remained at a staggering 84 percent. Pay increased for those that retained their jobs, but state qualifications were also instituted that did not benefit the community. "So the state took over and began changing things. Suddenly workers had to be this and that, have that degree or that certification, and the locals were replaced by more people from the region," Williams told us. "In addition to job loss, it affected our schools. There was an out-migration of certified teachers from the local school system to the prison. The prison boasted a 97 percent certification rate, bringing our public schools below 50 percent." An already poor school system began deteriorating rapidly.

Over time it was as if the physical presence of the barbed wire and cement had imprinted on the town itself, weighing heavily on the community like invisible leg irons of shame. Although the parents didn't know it, the advocates didn't know it, and the legislators didn't know it, Tallulah locals wanted something different too. They were also ready to fight for change.

Inside, Outside, We're All On the Same Side

The young FFLIC organizer Xochitl Bervera was instrumental in bridging the locals with the advocates and parents, a step that would prove key to the campaign's success. Xochitl, now FFLIC's co-director with Gina Womack, recalled the scene: "Tallulah officials were opposed to the closure idea, so was

121

Senator Jones, on the basis of preserving jobs. We began to reach out to the community to see what our options were." They were surprised at what they learned.

By the spring of 2003, the existing coalition of parents and advocates discovered that while many residents were initially opposed to the closure based on the jobs issue, others were now ready to talk. Thinking back, Bervera said, "They talked about how the prison was just dropped on their black community, just two blocks from the junior high, and how it had drained the good teachers from the local school with the lure of better pay. They talked about how they felt slandered by the campaign slogan and media, and about how becoming a prison town had resulted in lost businesses. They wanted to make sure that they could have say in what happened next."

Despite the poverty of the community, the residents knew firsthand that the promises of the prison industrial complex were empty. Like most prison economies, nothing of community value was gained, just the gloomy pall of barbed wire and cinder blocks.

The locals had some better ideas for local economic development. They proposed that an educational facility replace the prison, one that would provide jobs with dignity. The Tallulah residents also suggested using some of the savings from this transformation to fund educational, community-based programs.

No other prison community had ever proposed such a plan. But then again, it's rare for anyone to ask prison towns how they would deliver change, or to have a community such as Tallulah so ready with an answer. The locals brought a powerful new dimension to the discussion. Their opinions immediately removed from the debate the pro-prison argument that maintaining the facility was about helping the local economy. Residents were rejecting that notion, but beyond just saying "no" they were ready to explain what they wanted.

Meanwhile, the coalition's many-pronged approach for the 2003 legislative session was developed, and though it was led by the JJPL lawyers, particularly David Utter, everyone had a role to play. Bervera explained what was essentially an "inside-outside" approach this way: "What we learned was that you need to have more than one way to go about it even in a legislative strategy. We had several different bills, so if one died you could move on another." They also cultivated allies within both political parties and on both the Senate and the House floors, "because although there are times you can control what happens in a hearing, once it reaches the floor, outsiders have no voice, so you need champions there who believe in your cause."

That was the inside work. Outside of the legislative process, the grassroots were also busy. "We spoke to our own legislators, while others made drops of information packets regularly to key legislators," Grace Bauer said. "We spoke to media folks and others wrote articles that laid a foundation. In many direct action activities, parents were the key because of our sheer numbers and our ability to tell what was happening to our children from a place that made the public identify with us." Tallulah residents, although they were not part of the hearings, were beginning to tell the community's story—that despite living in a poor community, they rejected the prison. That view was something no one expected.

The Tallulah locals formed the Louisiana Delta Coalition for Education and Economic Development and named Moses Williams as president. As Williams said, "We just started having meetings with local officials, community leaders, different folks, just talking things through. We tried to be positive about what we wanted to do. We were frank about where we were as a community and what we needed." Within a couple of months, the group had encouraged the Tallulah city council, mayors from many surrounding communities, and the local school board to pass resolutions in support of the closure campaign. Most stunningly, they convinced Senator Jones to not only reverse his position on the prison closure, but to sponsor legislation creating the learning center. The residents were on the move to take back their community from the prison they too felt trapped in.

Change Replaces Chains

Ultimately, there were seven legislative vehicles devised that could have closed the prison. The bill that did the job was a fairly complex 52-page document. As Bervera explained, "The bill included provisions for creating a culture that moved away from the punitive model toward rehabilitation. It created some bodies to oversee reform, and created a pot of money for community-based programs. It mandated studies, things like that. So it doesn't just end when the Governor signs the bill."

The bill passed one year after being introduced. Thanks to the combined efforts of the parents and the local residents in the year that followed its introduction, the bill also set aside 40 percent of the savings from the prison's conversion to an educational facility. That money would be used for community programs, with input from residents themselves directing its distribution. Even though some tensions still existed on both sides, the Tallulah residents and parent advocates began to work together to formulate a common plan for transforming the prison into something that supported the economy and the values of the community. "We brought a group of these folks together and had a strategy session that gave rise to a pretty comprehensive strategy that everyone felt ownership of," Bervera said.

That money has gone back into the community to develop alternative juvenile counseling programs in lieu of incarceration. The Juvenile Justice Reform Act of 2003 stands unquestionably as the most comprehensive and radical juvenile justice reconstruction in the state's history.[1]

On June 4, 2004, with the assistance of the governor's office, the Tallulah youth prison closed its doors to children—ahead of schedule.

On that day, the coalition members gathered across the street from the gates of the closed juvenile facility to hold a press conference. For the first time, large numbers of parents and residents came together, as Bervera recalled, "to make peace and support one another." A lot of changes had taken place since

Who Pays for Inequality?

- Incarcerated youth are five times more likely to be sexually assaulted, and eight times as likely to commit suicide while confined.

- Seventy percent of confined youth are rearrested within two years of release. Alternatively, rehabilitation models including counseling, education, group homes, and day reporting centers have far lower re-arrest (recidivism) rates.[2]

- Only 4 percent of youth arrested in 2003 were arrested for violent crimes. There were 109 times as many juvenile arrests for running away as for homicide.

- Incarceration, particularly for juveniles, is an expensive proposition. Building costs average $100,000 per cell and annual operating costs typically exceed $60,000 per cell. In comparison, more effective community options such as drug treatment or counseling rarely exceed $15,000 and often cost less than $5,000 per year.[3]

- Black and Latino youth are three times more likely to live in poverty than are whites and statistically receive harsher sentencing for comparable crimes. For violent offenses, whites are incarcerated an average of 200 days, African-Americans an average of 250 days, and Latinos around 300 days. For drug offenses, African-Americans are almost 50 times more likely to be imprisoned.[4]

- Youth of color are over-represented in the juvenile justice system. They are more likely to be locked up than white youth, even when charged with the same types of offenses. While they represent about one-third of the adolescent population in the country, youth of color make up two-thirds of the juvenile inmate population.

- Louisiana has the highest incarceration rate in the nation, juveniles included. Approximately 800 of every 100,000 Louisianans are in jail. Even though African-Americans constitute barely one-third of the state's population, they represent around 78 percent of juveniles behind bars.[5]

Statistics compiled By Tamara Wattnem

the campaign's beginning, and it had taken an emotional toll on parents and local residents.

Grace Bauer shook her head in disbelief, recalling, "In 2001, if someone would have told me I had common ground with the community folks in Tallulah, I would not have believed it. Working side by side in this campaign helped me to see the things we shared, and that made all the difference." Pausing, she added, "For the first time, I came to see the bigger picture and saw how much hurt, loss and devastation this prison had brought to our sons and our communities. Before the trip, I had lots of self-doubt and anger; anger that often served little purpose. After that trip, that anger became resolve, and it continues to serve a purpose today in my work."

Today, much has changed for youth in the state of Louisiana. Instead of having five facilities holding 2,000 kids behind bars, there are only three facilities and 500 children in detention. The change wrought by the coalition will not stop youth from getting into trouble. But now, those that do will have a second chance at a life after incarceration: a chance that Grace Bauer's son, Corey, was not given, but one that she has helped create for the next generation. Bauer, who now directs the Lake Charles chapter of FFLIC, told us, "The Juvenile Justice Reform Act of 2003 made a tremendous difference in the system. It is not that all is right with the world, but there was a definite attitude shift in leadership toward our children. Children are more likely to receive an education and be given services that make a difference. Children are less likely to be removed from their homes and communities."

The campaign's successes have also had an impact on the conditions in the state's remaining secure care facilities, which in the old days were often comparable to those at TCCY. "Sure, there are still problems, but it's very different now," Bervera said. "When I go to the other facilities at Swanson and Angola, kids talk about how the food sucks and school is lame, but not about having their jaws wired shut, not about black eyes."

Bervera reflected on the campaign's successes and shortcomings, "The bill certainly had flaws, but it is one of the most impressive wins in criminal justice organizing that this country has seen in years."

Van Jones, a national civil rights and juvenile justice reform leader, agrees: "This was probably the biggest win that we've had. Subsequent events have diminished it somewhat, but this was a truly significant victory."

Green Jobs and Community Vigilance

Back in Tallulah, the struggle continues. The fight to transform the prison into a community-based project has been undermined, at least temporarily, by the corporate interests profiting from the facility at the state's expense. As Bervera told us, "Currently, the TCCY site is housing adult DUI offenders, but there is movement toward transferring ownership of the facility to the state."

With a shake of his head, Moses Williams explained how the complicated corporate ownership and state partnership scheme is to blame for the red tape that seems to have developed into a very expensive venture for taxpayers. "Supposedly, now it's a substance abuse treatment facility for the Department of Corrections. That is what we're told: that if the state did not continue to operate some kind of facility there, the property would default to a bond. So while they are still figuring out what the future use of the property should be, the state has spent $13 to 20 million a year to maintain a facility that supposedly has 150 staff for only 200 inmates. Of course, you can't count 20 people from the community that work there."

Yet the community remains hopeful—as well as vigilant. "Education and workforce training is the cornerstone of [the governor's] plan to eradicate poverty. What we're doing is right in line with that," Williams said. "We're hoping [the governor] will stay true to what she has been talking about, what she campaigned on, her promises to convert the facility."

Given the current staff-to-inmate ratio, the residents' 2006 feasibility study on converting the prison into a learning center looks to be a winner. Built into the plans is a move toward cleaner, greener jobs with the opportunity to build skills along the way, and the development of a community foundation.

While the media spotlight is no longer on the facility, the community does have help with keeping up the pressure. A national funders' collaborative of a dozen or so major philanthropic foundations picked up on the issue, and are underwriting work in the community. "They made our project one of only five 'demonstration sites' they selected across the country," Williams said, "The number one strategy of the collaborative is the diversion of this facility to an educational facility."

Part of the Tallulah plan includes helping victims of Hurricane Katrina. "Out of tragedy arises opportunity," Williams said. "We have a plan to build modular homes up here, to bring people up from southern Louisiana to do the training. We can build the homes that can be transported to the Gulf, where they have a shortage of construction. We can help them get back in the game, and get some economic benefit and training up here."

That kind of thinking shows how the Tallulah residents are looking to the next economic wave: green building and creating triple-bottom-line enterprises. Moses Williams explains it this way: "It's the future. We want to make it a part of our plan to experiment with green building, using more affordable recycled materials, building the modular homes using the latest in energy efficiency. It's good for the environment, and good for people too."

The community has also considered their social values as part of the economic package. "We don't have to make a huge profit," Williams told us. "We won't be driven by pure money values. We can keep costs down, and because it is a training program, folks can get skills to take with them to other jobs. Those folks will build the new school, and it is all tied into the success of the learning center."

Now residents have an opportunity to define what they want for their community. It seems that Tallulah, whose name has meant so many things over the years, may now stand for innovation and community-driven prosperity: a model for others to follow.

CONVERSATION

Van Jones

Van Jones is a passionate civil rights and human rights advocate. He combines practical solutions to problems of social inequality and environmental destruction, focusing on green economic opportunities for urban America. Jones grew up in rural Tennessee, graduated from Yale Law School, and works and lives in Oakland, California. He is the Co-Founder and President of the Ella Baker Center for Human Rights, which seeks to replace the U.S. incarceration industry with community-based solutions.

Q. For the first time in human history, more than 50 percent of people now live in urban areas. Where does the city fit in your conception of environmental sustainability?

VJ: Cities have the capacity to sink or save the planet. The future of all humanity, and most species and systems, will be determined by what we choose to do with cities. The idea that the environment is about critters and creeks is a thing of the past. We have to be thinking about these things in terms of consumption and disposal processes of mega-cities.

Q. Sprawl has a negative impact not only on farmland and open space but on life in urban areas. How did this pattern of sprawl and gentrification develop? Who wins and loses?

VJ: Sprawl is a response to racial fear and anxiety on the part of white elites. The 'burbs were designed as a vehicle to get away from people of color, investing more in the white infrastructure as they moved away from the city, and the neighborhoods where people of color live. The other side of that is the disinvestment for the communities that remain behind; the money follows the new suburban development. Those that remain in the inner city continue to lose in this scenario.

Q. You've talked about cities and land use as issues that interest many groups: the suburbanites, environmentalists, and inner-city residents. If both environmentalists and inner-city residents have an interest in stop-

ping sprawl, what's preventing them from working together?

VJ: Racism. It is the reason that people move away from each other. People don't want to talk about why people call this a "good" neighborhood or that one a "bad" neighborhood, but often it has to do with the race of the people that live there. White people divorce themselves from the bad neighborhoods and move to the suburbs. The black community has a lot of built-up feelings about our history, about the racism we experience. There is some healing that needs to take place there, so these communities have some issues, and don't want to work with each other, necessarily. There are a lot of feelings there.

Q. Many environmentalists genuinely want to work with other communities to address these issues of common interest. What is thwarting those efforts?

VJ: Those folks often speak about working together through "outreach"—outreach in the sense of "outreaching *to*" these people or those people. Outreaching to the black community: "Well, we outreached to them so 'they' could hear our agenda and get onboard with what we are saying." This, as opposed to saying "let's go make some friends," building relationships, creating relationships. Figuring things out from a place where everyone's views are included. Relationships are give and take, mutual aid and help. Outreaching is the white thing, it's about bringing folks into what you are doing, and does not necessarily convey understanding.

Q. What is the effect of the prison industrial complex (especially juvenile prisons) on communities, particularly communities of color, and how does that system impede progress toward a green city revolution?

VJ: The incarceration industry is the new Jim Crow; you don't have to call him the "N word" if you just call him a felon. There are the same amount of drug problems in the 'burbs that there are in the inner city, but in the 'burbs the white kids get counseling, they don't go to prison. Generally speaking, they only call the police in the 'hood. The system has responded with compassion to white kids. Again, the new Jim Crow is incarceration. This is the barrier that separates people from the lives they want to live. You go to the back of the line as a felon. You lose your voting rights, can't get a good job, you're denied student loans. It is devastating. We spend less money on public schools than on locking people up; it's far easier to go to prison than to get a scholarship.

This distorts economic development. The current economic strategy is to take poor black kids, put them in jail in rural areas, and give poor white kids jobs as guards in that prison. That is the economic strategy. Rural towns can't compete with industry, farms are all going away, so prison is an economic boon for rural communities. Come on, we can't come up with a better strategy than that? In California, for example, nearly 10 percent of the state budget goes to the prison system, and that could grow to 15 percent or even higher. When you lock up a state budget like that, where is the money to retrofit buildings for energy efficiency?

California is supposed to be a leader in terms of being clean and energy efficient. So now, put these two together. If you take guards and prisoners and send them all home, then give them green city jobs instead. We could be retrofitting urban America instead of lives laying to waste. Send them home with good work, with a mission, and real job skills, and provide them with opportunity.

We can have a Gulag or a green economy. But we can't have both. If we train former prisoners and guards to put up solar panels, they are already on their way to becoming electrical engineers. If we train them to double pane glass, they are on their way to be a glazer: a good union job and green path out of poverty. Bamboo, it's so different than timber, you can cut it and it grows back quickly. If we can train folks to do the green thing, they can then walk to the front of the line in an economy based on green jobs instead of an economy from pollution-based jobs. That is where these issues connect. What we need is a green wave that can lift all boats, that can lift folks out of poverty.

Q. How important is it to nurture efforts at grassroots democracy? How can larger groups—national groups—help without taking over?

VJ: It's all got to come together, but it's not easy. The national groups don't mean to take over and the local groups can sometimes be schizophrenic: They want and need the help from the big players, but can also resent it. The national groups can find that having the grassroots connections gives their work legitimacy—it's sexy these days to have the grassroots contacts, sexy and cool—but they also have some contempt for the grassroots groups at the same time. Everyone just has to figure it out, make it work. Case by case.

Q. You have said that "We are the heroes we've been waiting for." Can you discuss what "going local" means in terms of creating big change?

VJ: I believe it's a both/and. I believe in both "bottom up" and "top down." Focusing on the local is great, but you need federal government on your side to make the big changes; we learned that in the civil rights movement. The federal government has got to be provoked into action. The local economy can't solve the problems by itself, and some problems are too big to solve by local action alone. Change is bottom up and top down. The grassroots have to push, and the top needs to push. It's sort of an inside-outside strategy. Everybody is going to have to do some work. There is no magic answer, no silver bullet. It's going to be a group effort, cross-organizational. We need to share and play well with others; be flexible and learn from each other. The big change is going to take 20, 30, 40 years. Hopefully, in terms of ecological collapse, we'll get it together enough in the next 10 years to buy us the time we need to do the work that will take longer. But we're going to have to do it together.

Participatory Budgeting
& Direct Democracy

The people of the Brazilian city of Porto Alegre manage their affairs somewhat differently than do the folks in your hometown. Like citizens of any democracy, the residents of this largely middle-class, waterfront city elect leaders to oversee city affairs. But when it comes time to decide how to manage the city's budget, the residents of Porto Alegre put a twist on things. Instead of leaving all the decisions to their elected officials, the citizens are key players in the process, directing how the city budget will be allocated. Through an intricate series of town hall meetings and community councils, the residents decide for themselves how to spend the city's resources.

If you've ever complained about how your tax dollars are being used, you should keep reading.

The Porto Alegre system is called "Participatory Budgeting." The idea got its start in 1989, when the members of the left-of-center Workers' Party were elected to the city's leadership. In an effort to dispel the atmosphere of autocracy that dominated Brazil during the country's dictatorship, the mayor and city council decided to give local residents a greater say in how the city's revenues would be spent. The city established a system of neighborhood assemblies that would set priorities on how the city should use its money.

The pioneering system rested on a very basic principle of democracy: If the primary function of government is to equitably distribute community resources, then the citizens should play a central role in deciding the use of those resources.

"The citizen's participation is not limited to the act of voting to elect the executive or the legislators, but also decides on spending priorities and controls the management of the government," Ubiratan de Souza, one of the co-founders of the Participatory Budgeting process, has written. "[The citizen] ceases to be an enabler of traditional politics and becomes a permanent protagonist of the public administration."

The Porto Alegre experiment has since spread to communities around the globe. Today, approximately 200 local governments worldwide have some sort of participatory budgeting system in place, from Montevideo, the capital of Uruguay, to Cordoba, Spain, to the Andean town of Cotacachi, Ecuador. The concept is largely unknown in the United States, but a few local jurisdictions—such as Seattle and Prince William County in Virginia—have experimented with increasing citizen involvement in the budgeting process.

This system of grassroots decision-making has gained international recognition as an important mechanism for promoting transparency, accountability and citizen participation—all cornerstones of democratic governance.

"By giving a voice to citizens, particularly the urban poor, in defining their needs, participatory planning reinforces ownership in decision-making processes and promotes social cohesion and citizenship," Angelique Habils, a United Nations officer at the UN's Nairobi office, told us. "Most participants of Participatory Budgets agree that one of the most important benefits is the deepening of the exercise of democracy."

Because Participatory Budgeting rests on the ideal of community control, the particulars of each city's system vary widely. Many cities, like Porto Alegre, identify priorities by geography; each neighborhood holds an assembly to discuss and agree upon community needs, and then elects delegates to a municipal level budget council that sifts through all of the proposals.

Other places, such as the Brazilian coastal city of Icapui, divide the budget thematically—there are separate community meetings to discuss healthcare, education, the physical environment, and the needs of youth and the elderly. While most Participatory Budgets rely on individual citizen involvement, others engage people via existing non-governmental organizations such as unions and community centers. Some European cities select budget delegates by lottery in order to involve people who are normally excluded.

The amount of money at stake also varies. Most citizen assemblies have control over about one-fifth of the total budget. In Montevideo, a city of more than 1 million people, citizens decide more than half of all city funds. Residents of Mundo Novo, Brazil (population 16,000) meet in open town meetings to discuss every single item in the budget—including the mayor's salary.

There are immediate benefits of these deliberative processes. The first is an expansion of services to poor communities. For example, Montevideo found that Participatory Budgeting led to an "inversion of priorities" in which the poorest neighborhoods began to receive a larger portion of funds. Another benefit is increased civic participation by historically marginalized groups; women tend to play a larger role in community budgeting processes than they do in electoral politics. In Belem, Brazil, the budget council holds special meetings for Afro-Brazilians, children, and gays.

An important improvement that accompanies Participatory Budgets is an increase in city revenues. In Cuenca (Ecuador) and Campinas and Recife (Brazil) there was a significant growth in tax payments within a few years of instituting the process. This isn't surprising. If you are in charge of spending your own money, you are more likely to pay your full share of taxes.

But probably the most valuable benefit is something that isn't easily quantifiable: a feeling of individual empowerment. As citizens take control of their community resources, they feel a greater sense of ownership over their city. Civic participation leads to more civic participation, creating a kind of virtuous feedback loop.

"I was absolutely pleased and excited that our bid was successful, and that many other bids were successful in the whole process," Naweed Hussein, a resident of Bradford, England, told a local interviewer after a neighborhood budget assembly decided to fund a mosaic near his community garden. "I think it's been a very fair process. If we can continue using such practices in sharing the budget and looking at budgets together, I think we could accomplish many things."

Culture Shift in the
Land of the Giants

A California County
Redefines Corporate Rights

"Our Founding Fathers never intended for corporations to have this
kind of power."

— Anonymous citizen of Humboldt County

*When the largest recall effort in Humboldt County history was mounted
just weeks after the newly elected district attorney had taken office, residents were confused. When it came to light that a giant corporation was
behind the recall, residents were angry. Through a series of community
forums, a group of citizens who had studied the history of corporate rights
led the community not only to defeat the recall, but to a precedent-setting
campaign finance reform law that gets to the root of local control and real
democracy.*

In the spring of 2003, just a few weeks after Paul Gallegos took office as
the District Attorney of Humboldt County, California, a tough campaign
was already underway to recall him. True, he hadn't won by a landslide;
the margin of victory was 52-48 percent. But with hardly enough time to hang
law diplomas on the walls of his new office, how could Paul Gallegos have so
alienated himself from the voters who had put him there? The fact is, he didn't
have to. Alienating a Fortune 500 company was enough to spark a chain of
events that would change community politics in Humboldt and could help
redefine the way corporations do business across America. All this in a place
famous for its trees—*not* its politics.

One of the most serene landscapes in the United States, Humboldt County
is home to the majestic giant redwoods. Flanked by the rugged coast of the
Pacific Ocean, Humboldt is a land of foggy mountains, jeweled lakes and sage-
banked streams. With just 125,000 people lightly sprinkled over 4,000 square
miles, life is slower, cell phone reception is spotty, and neighbors can be hard to

glimpse outside of the county seat of Eureka and the nearby town of Arcata.

The population is overwhelmingly white, with a small mix of Latinos and Native Americans. It is also poor; four of every five children receive government lunches. But for those who live in Humboldt, it's hard to imagine any other place as home. "Folks here feel connected to this place, they care about what goes on here," said David Cobb, a transplant from Texas and a member of Democracy Unlimited of Humboldt County (DUHC), a collective that works to empower local citizens to take democratic control of their own community.

Throughout Humboldt, voter turnout is high. Support for local nonprofits serving the community is strong. While Arcata is politically progressive, the surrounding county is dominated by logging, ranching, and homesteading. As Cobb points out, "We've got a spectrum of types here, environmentalists, lots of Republicans, good ol' boy networks, and folks that don't trust the government at all." This makes politics in Humboldt County a tricky business.

It was in this climate that Humboldt DA Paul Gallegos made a move many called political suicide in his first few days of holding office. In March 2003, he sued the county's biggest employer, Pacific Lumber (PALCO), for $20 million, charging that the company submitted false information on an environmental impact study to expand logging rights into Humboldt's Headwaters Forest Preserve.

Just a scant few weeks later, a massive recall campaign had been mysteriously launched. PALCO and its parent company, the Texas-based giant Maxxam Corporation, initially denied instigating the effort. The recall committee, "SafetyFirst! The Committee to Recall Paul Gallegos," claimed no connection to Maxxam corporation and framed its efforts as a community safety issue, saying that Gallegos was "soft on crime." It would later be revealed that the corporation contributed over a quarter of a million dollars to the effort—a whopping 93 percent of the total recall coffer—and hired a team of media and political experts to mastermind it.

With a thin election mandate, the Maxxam effort could have marked the end of Gallegos' political career. Yet the citizenry rallied around their freshly elected DA, raising some $250,000 in mostly small donations for his defense—not because he was beloved, or even because they particularly challenged the notion that Gallegos wasn't safeguarding the community. Mostly, it wasn't even about Gallegos.

Something else was in play—a kind of community clarity. The people of Humboldt knew there was more at risk than Paul Gallegos' job. Democracy itself was in danger of being recalled. Residents were outraged that a corporation, particularly one that wasn't even local, could muscle its way into their electoral process.

Democracy Unlimited of Humboldt County (DUHC) had a lot to do with the county's political savvy. Traditional politics would have called for spending time and money battling the issue along the lines that the recall committee had set out—Gallegos' safety record. That is what the corporate-funded recall team expected. The locals wanted to have a different debate.

"We were involved as volunteers from the start of the recall, trying to keep the discussion around the *way* it happened instead," Kaitlin Sopoci Belknap, the director of DUHC, told us. "We published a series of op-eds and hosted workshops talking about the real issue, not whether Maxxam lied, or even whether Gallegos should be recalled, but rather who was in charge in this community. We can't allow a corporation to come in and buy an election. Why do they have a right to do this?"

It all sounds reasonable. But in the heat of the nasty mudslinging that comes with any big money recall, how could a handful of citizen-activists talking about corporate rights really have an impact? How could they pry open the debate, move beyond the name-calling, and get the community to talk about underlying issues of corporate rights and real democracy? Was it possible that people living together in a community—even one as politically diverse as Humboldt—still believe they are entitled to make decisions for themselves? That democracy "of, by, and for the people" is an ideal worth fighting for? Sopoci Belknap certainly thinks so.

"From local commercials, to the local media, to the DA himself, everyone really embraced the perspective that it was about *our* rights," she told us. "It was really exciting to see the actual shift in the discourse."

What the Maxxam team couldn't have known was that this community had long been prepared to talk about the role of corporations. All the money and media spin in the world wasn't going to convince residents that this was about their safety, or that Maxxam executives sitting in their plush offices in Texas cared about the well-being of the people in this remote corner of paradise. By making the wrong gamble, the Maxxam Corporation unwittingly revealed how strongly people feel about the basic democratic ideal that their votes should count. It makes for a strange irony, that this giant corporation helped pave the way for one of the strongest campaign finance reforms in the United States.

Democracy Unlimited's First Victory

How was it that the good citizens of Humboldt—in the heat of an election crisis—were prepared to sidestep traditional political mudslinging and instead make the recall about the role of corporations? "Preparing" the community to look at these deeper issues started much earlier. "Back in 1997, what would eventually become DUHC was more or less just an informal study group of about a dozen people who would just get together to learn the history of corporate rights," said Paul Cienfuegos, the co-founder of DUHC.

What that study group learned was shocking. The modern American corporation was originally chartered to perform limited tasks in service to the community, for short periods of time, and at the will of the people. Even banks held

Before Corporations Were King

When American colonists declared independence from England in 1776, they also freed themselves from control by English corporations that dominated trade and extracted wealth. After fighting a revolution to end this exploitation, our country's founders retained a healthy distrust of corporate power. They limited corporations to a strictly business role. Corporations were forbidden from influencing elections, public policy, and other areas of civil society. The privilege of incorporation was granted only for activities that benefited the public, such as construction of roads or canals. Enabling shareholders to profit was seen as a means to that end. The states imposed conditions (some of which remain on the books) like these:

- Corporate charters (licenses to exist) were granted for a limited time and could be promptly revoked for violating laws.

- Corporations could only engage in activities necessary to fulfill their chartered purpose.

- Corporations could not own stock in other corporations nor own property that was not essential to fulfilling their chartered purpose.

- Corporations were often terminated if they exceeded their authority or caused public harm.

- Owners and managers were responsible for criminal acts committed on the job.

- Corporations could not make any political or charitable contributions nor spend money to influence law making.

For 100 years after the American Revolution, legislators controlled the corporate chartering process. Because of widespread public opposition, early legislators granted very few corporate charters, and only after debate. Citizens governed corporations by detailing operating conditions not just in charters but also in state constitutions and state laws. Incorporated businesses were prohibited from taking any action that legislators did not specifically allow.

Unless a legislature renewed an expiring charter, the corporation was dissolved and its assets were divided among shareholders. Citizen authority clauses limited capitalization, debts, land holdings, and sometimes even profits. They required a company's accounting books to be turned over to a legislature upon request. The power of large shareholders was limited by scaled voting, so that large and small investors had equal voting rights. Interlocking directorates were outlawed. Shareholders had the right to remove directors at will.

Adapted from the Program on Corporations, Law and Democracy (www.poclad.org)

only six-month charters, and were required to demonstrate their community value and defend their record at public meetings before the charter could be renewed. Having uncovered this history, the group wondered, "So what happened?" They learned that despite the fact that the word "corporation" never appeared in the U.S. Constitution, over time the legal fiction known as the corporation has gained the same rights people have. These are often referred to as "Corporate Personhood" rights. Over the last 150 years, through heavy lobbying and massive funding, corporate directors have leveraged their access to the courts and legislatures to endow the corporate form with ever-expanding rights. Armed with these rights and lots of money, corporations now have free rein to wreak hazards and hardships on communities and nature while gaining broad access to decision making at the local, state, and national levels.

Addressing Root Causes

By examining the past, Cienfuegos, a longtime organizer, could suddenly see things in the present more clearly. "We had been fighting corporations that were clear-cutting the forests, but at the same time we were giving them the authority for it," he said. "You could take any issue and the core problem was that we had empowered the corporate form with rights to commit harm."

Corporations, legal fictions which were intended to be *property*, now had *personhood* rights—and with them, the ability to make key economic and political decisions. "Regular people can't compete with that, no way," Cienfuegos said. "After about a year of studying corporations' rights and how they got there, the study group decided to get active, to try to address an issue by the root causes, not in the usual, symptomatic way."

With this newfound understanding, Cienfuegos and the study group started Democracy Unlimited as a band of volunteers to change the rules locally, where the impacts of decisions touch the ground and affect people's lives. The first step was educating people about the proper roles for people and corporations.

"We needed to have a culture shift where people understood this relationship," Cienfuegos said. "Once people understood that they were being cheated, lied to, and virtually colonized by corporations, it was a short step to getting them to take action to change the rules."

Through a series of public education forums, DUHC began to shift the culture of the community. People in Humboldt began to look around and see just how much corporations were damaging their lives. Intensive extraction of natural resources resulted in such extensive over-fishing and clear-cutting that ecosystems were collapsing, and industry jobs were following suit. Abundant fish stocks had once supported more than 40,000 fishing jobs; by the 1990s, it was estimated that only 5,000 salmon—the primary fish population—remained. Under the Maxxam Corporation's heavy-handed approach, their employees' pension funds had been plundered, and rampant clear-cutting had sent vulnerable hillside soils plunging into the rivers during heavy rains.[1] The county's freshwater resources were under attack from a variety of corporations seeking to bottle and sell unsustainable quantities of the liquid gold. Chain retailers were forcing mom-and-pop stores out of business, virtually hollowing out the local economy. Enough was enough.

The Ballot Initiative

In the winter of 1997, about a dozen of those involved with Democracy Unlimited decided to test the political waters by running a ballot initiative addressing the political role of corporations.

"We didn't feel we were ready to change the law," said Cienfuegos, "but thought we'd try creating a government structure to reign in corporate rights, to make that task an official duty." They looked to other organizations for advice, such as the Program on Corporations, Law and Democracy (POCLAD), which helped them with the language of the ballot initiative and with suggestions for framing the issue. The team decided they were too small a group to take the initiative countywide, and limited the ballot initiative to the town of Arcata. The group organized a series of public meetings to discuss the proposal. Hundreds came, signaling that the issue resonated with the locals. The successful forum energized the DUHC volunteers, who started to believe that maybe there was something that could be done to create change.

The ballot initiative, Measure F, called for the creation of an official committee to "ensure democratic control over corporations conducting business within the city, in whatever ways are necessary to ensure the health and well-being of our community and its environment." The referendum passed overwhelmingly. Soon Arcata was hosting town hall meetings to establish the Committee for Democracy and Corporations (CDC) to review the role of corporations. An estimated 5 percent of the town's population attended the meetings.

"The CDC was the first and only standing government committee to address these issues, and all with real public participation," said Ryan Emenaker, a thoughtful and well-spoken twenty-something who currently serves as chair of the CDC and is also a member of the DUHC collective. "There have been many successes, including a formula restaurant cap and a prequalification contract, which makes it less likely that corporations with environmental or labor violations can win city contracts. We were also the second city in the U.S. to pass an anti-corporate personhood resolution."[2]

Despite its success, Measure F had taken its toll on the DUHC's volunteer team. "It took so much time; everybody was so exhausted, they just moved on," Paul Cienfuegos said, "Democracy Unlimited was more or less just a shell. We won, but had no long-term organization."

Enter Kaitlin Sopoci-Belknap, a young, vibrant southwesterner committed to environmental justice and determined to make a move to the Pacific Northwest. "I heard about the work they were doing in Arcata and I just decided to be part of it," she said. "I basically lived off of my savings for a while, and DUHC was more or less operating out of a corner of my flat. It was just Paul and me, and he was hoping to move on to do other projects."

After moving to Eureka, she met her partner and 2004 Green Party Presidential candidate, David Cobb, and convinced him to move to Humboldt. By 2004, Sopoci Belknap and others felt the group was ready to take on bigger things. They called a meeting of Democracy Unlimited to talk about the future. Sopoci-Belknap believed that it was "time to make a change, to formalize this group and make it a sustainable, viable organization." Now the director of Democracy Unlimited of Humboldt County, Sopoci Belknap said that meeting helped DUHC "rise from the ashes like a phoenix," transforming the group into what it is now: a county-wide education and action organization for local power, with an office, a staff, and a slew of volunteers. It was also at that meeting that the team decided DUHC should, as its first order of business, get involved in the campaign against the Maxxam Corporation's recall.

Stoking the Fires for Action

Inspired by a community equipped to talk about corporate power, fortified by the lessons learned during the Arcata CDC campaign, and invigorated with a newly organized crew of volunteers, the DUHC was well-prepared to battle the Gallegos recall. In the months leading to the March 2004 recall vote, citizens really *got* it. The campaign took on a life of its own as the anti-recall forces grew from the initial band of veteran activists to the community at large. County residents from all political persuasions joined the effort. You didn't have to be a long time radical to agree that an out-of-state corporation shouldn't decide who got to enforce the county's laws.

That community awareness was evident on Election Day. Not only was the recall defeated, but Gallegos actually *gained* support—winning 61 percent of the votes to keep him in office.

After the initial euphoria from winning the recall, a depression set in among those working on the campaign. "It was upsetting that we had to put aside what we were working on, all of us," Cobb said. "Our community shelled out $250,000 to fight it, and so much time was invested that could have been spent doing something else ... On the one hand, it was such a waste."

The citizens of Humboldt were angry. A fight that no one in the community had asked for had drained the community in many ways. And what was to stop another corporation from trampling their rights next time? "We knew we could take the next step because of the work that had been done already,"

Cobb told us with a grin. "We didn't get to strip corporate rights *that time,* but the community understood that you can't be for local control and community rights and also be for corporate rights." The citizens of Humboldt, unwilling to wait for the next corporate power-grab, were ready to take an offensive posture and ensure that nothing like that could ever happen again in their community.

The "Yes on T" Campaign

In the months following the recall, many folks turned to DUHC for leadership. The group hosted a series of meetings and conversations to discuss what could be done. They spoke with unions, elected officials, farmers, conservationists, business owners, teachers, students, and others. It was not an easy process, given the diversity of those involved. But everyone agreed on one key value: It was time to get big corporate dollars out of Humboldt politics forever. After much discussion and debate, a new citizen referendum, the "Ordinance to Protect Our Right to Fair Elections and Local Democracy," was born.

Better known as "Measure T," the referendum's central purpose was to bar out-of-town corporations from participating in local elections. But the measure's language also included a direct challenge to the legal doctrine that a corporation must be treated as a person with constitutional rights. The referendum text read: "Only natural persons possess civil and political rights. Corporations are creations of state law and possess no legitimate civil or political rights." By using such language to affirm the legality of restricting corporate political behavior, the measure reinforced the belief that corporations should be mechanisms to serve the people, not the other way around.

"It isn't about being anti-business," Cobb said. "There is a role for corporations, to serve the public good without exploiting people or the planet. It is about being pro-democracy; the current legal system is protecting property rights over people's rights."

In Humboldt, that radical idea (or commonsense one, depending upon your point of view) was gaining broader acceptance. From the start, volunteer energy drove the "Yes on T" campaign. A strikingly diverse coalition of organizations endorsed the measure, from the local Democratic Party and Green Party to a range of national environmental organizations and major labor unions. Dozens of local business owners also lent their name to the cause.

It was a clear example of how disparate groups can unite under a common agenda when the issue is about the rights of people to decide versus the rights of corporations to decide. "Put in this context," Cobb said, "it's a no-brainer."

The "Yes on T" campaign had a bit of luck in its naming. Ballot measures are labeled in alphabetical order, and the chance naming of the measure lent itself to making a historical connection with the Boston Tea Party. Although usually remembered as the opening salvo of the American Revolution, the Boston Tea Party was, for the partisans involved, also an act of defiance against the unchecked power of the largest corporation of the day—the British East India Company, a tea monopoly.

To help make that connection, the campaign had thousands of tea bags custom-made that worked as clever combination of hot beverage-makers and political fliers. Emblazoned with a "Vote Yes! Measure T" logo and the scales of justice, the tea bags were distributed at campaign rallies, outreach events, and local restaurants. Everyone wanted to take one. The tea bags were a fun—and effective—way of communicating with the counties' voters.

The measure was not without opposition; the county's business establishment, among others, was firmly against the idea. So as the campaign approached the June 2006 primary election, in which the measure would appear on the ballot, national political and campaign finance analysts were intently watching. As John Bonifaz of the National Voting Rights Institute put it, Measure T was "one of the most important local democracy efforts happening anywhere in the United States. If it passes, it will have profound ramifications for campaign finance reform efforts across the country."

Measure T passed with 55 percent of the vote. The cheers at the Democracy Unlimited office on election night were at a siren pitch.

Eliminating corporations' influence in the political system, the DUHC partisans say, is the future for corporations everywhere, not just in Humboldt

The "Yes on Measure T" campaign distributed thousands of tea bags stating, "It's time for a 'T' Party of our own. It's time for Measure T!"

County. The backers of the Humboldt measure encourage other cities and counties to join them changing the rules one city at a time.

"Democracy Unlimited is designed to work in solidarity with other communities," Sopoci Belknap said, with a twinkle in her eye. "We'd love to see a Democracy Unlimited in *every* community—just call us up."

CONVERSATION

Thomas Linzey, Esq.

Thomas Linzey thinks of himself as more than just a lawyer. A co-founder of the Community Environmental Legal Defense Fund (CELDF), Linzey is a practicing attorney, committed to the idea that change happens at the grassroots. Much of his activism occurs through CELDF's "Democracy Schools," an innovative curriculum that encourages people to go beyond the single issue they are working on to think of their struggle as part of a larger fight against corporate power. The schools prompt citizens to question basic assumptions behind our legal system. Linzey and his colleagues encourage communities to create local constitutions, or "home-rule charters," enumerating the rights of local citizens and backing up those rights with enforceable laws.

Q: Can you tell us about "democracy"? It's a word used by everyone and can mean so many things.

TL: Well, I don't think we have ever had a democracy in this country. I think it's a myth that majorities have ever been able to decide what happens to their communities and their lives. It goes back to the American Revolution when we jettisoned the king, but we didn't jettison the English structure of law. That structure of law developed at the same time England was developing into a global cultural empire. And the folks that wrote the U.S. Constitution, which serves as the DNA or hardwiring for this country, in essence worshiped English common law. We got rid of the King but we didn't get rid of an English structure of law that placed property and commerce over the rights of communities and nature.

Amazing as it might sound, a community that may want to stop toxic waste, or stop toxic sludge from coming in, or stop a big corporate hog factory farm from coming into the community, not only runs up against the corporations and the state regulatory agencies—it runs up against the Constitution.

Q: Some people might say you are anti-business. Is that the case?

TL: This work is not anti-business. In fact, it's not even anti-corporate, in many ways. We all need toilet paper and toothbrushes, stuff that needs to be made. But the question is: Who makes decisions about how those things are made? And, in addition, the question is whether those corporations should be governing entities, or should they merely be business entities? And over time, corporations and the few people that run them have become governing entities; they make governing decisions over us. When we try to make our own governing decisions, they slash us by using our own governmental institutions, legislation, and the courts. The work is not anti-business at all. It's simply a recognition that if you are a business entity, you should do the work of business, but you should not have constitutional rights. You should not have privately enforceable rights in the U.S. Constitution, and you should certainly not have the authority to nullify community authorities.

Q: Many people in this country don't understand that corporations have personhood rights. Why does this come as such a surprise to some people?

TL: That's a very good question. People only begin to peel back the layers of the legal opinions under which they are governed when they have something threaten them personally. One or our most able organizers—a woman named Jennifer England—is from southwestern Virginia. She has seven children. And she's an evangelical Christian. There were plans to dump sludge right next to her house. And it was that imminent threat to her kids, to her land, to her family, to her home, that drove Jennifer to start questioning how this entire structure of law is set up. She asked, "Why can't we just have a law that says 'no sludge can be spread in this community'?" So we had a conversation with her, and we told her that you can't do that, because it would be illegal. It's unconstitutional to ban something at the community level that the state has permitted, because it violates the corporation's constitutional rights. So the question is, as Jennifer asked, "Why?" When you explain to people like Jennifer that corporations are persons, it just doesn't make any sense to them.

The perplexed look on people's faces when they find out that corporations are deemed to be persons under the law generally leads to two things. Number one: asking questions about why corporations as persons do such damage to communities. The explanation is that when you pass a law at the local level and it somehow violates the corporation's constitutional rights, the corporation can use the federal or state courts to strike down the law. Number two: going on the offense, meaning that if you are going to pass a sludge ordinance or a factory farm ordinance, or some ordinance at the local level, it is absolutely foolish not to anticipate the challenge that will eventually come down the road, and to build into the ordinance a frontal challenge to the assertion of those rights of the corporation. And so the "Why?" being asked at the local level—why can't we control the destiny of our own communities?—is leading to an offense that's very sophisticated in terms of attempting to dismantle the structure of law.

Q: Speak about the regulatory system. It's supposed to keep corporations from doing harm, but everywhere you look—the water, the land, the air—everything is polluted.

TL: It's funny, because people come up to me and say that the regulatory system is broken. It's not protecting our health. It's not protecting our welfare. To which, increasingly, we look back at government and maybe we say the regulatory system is working perfectly because maybe its purpose was *not* to protect health and welfare. Maybe its purpose was to legalize corporate harms that would otherwise be illegal without a permitting system in place. In other words, we think of regulatory agencies as folks that attempt to save us from being harmed, but in reality the history of regulatory agencies is much different. In essence, it's about writing a script for our activism and channeling us down to a regulatory point where we can't win, and even if we do win, we don't win much of anything at all.

And of course when you regulate something, as opposed to when you ban or prohibit it, you are giving up your authority and, in this case, being stripped of your authority to decide what comes in and what doesn't. So I think if our activism is really going to evolve, we have to start seeing how the regulatory agencies really are enablers for the corporations to come in and do the damage that they do.

Q: Some believe that laws such as anti-corporate personhood ordinances are a waste of time because they will be challenged and shot down, so why bother? What is the logic behind civil disobedience to the law?

TL: Well, the law changes. The law changes when people stand up and say we can't take this any more, we are not going to do this any more. In fact, lawyers have never changed the law in this country. It's always been community organizers who are pressing up against existing structures of law that have changed anything in this country. Rosa Parks, she knew she was subject to a criminal conviction, but she did what she did anyway. The civil rights movement, those brave kids that sat down at the Woolworth's lunch counter, of course the police where going to arrest them, of course they were going to jail. How does that change anything? They change something when a spark happens. When people see other people doing democracy in a different way and it catches fire—then it has nothing to do with the individual law. It has to do with a movement that builds, with people no longer willing to live under a structure of law that continually screws them. Because there's nothing left to lose, and when there's nothing left to lose, people whose backs are against the wall tend to come out kicking.

What this work is about is knitting together those communities who are finally learning that they are always on the losing end of the stick, that the regulatory agencies are not a remedy, that they can't turn to their state legislature or their courts for a remedy because those courts are carrying out laws that are written by the corporations in the first place. And the legislatures are passing laws that were drafted and given to them by the corporations. And so the question is: Where do these folks turn for a remedy? They have to create their own remedy—just like the suffragists did, just like the abolitionists did, just like the great people's movements of this country did.

Q: Do you believe it's possible to change the role of corporations in our society?

TL: I think it's the beginning of the beginning of the beginning. And I think the people that are willing to change the structure of law are the ones that are directly affected by how law operates, are going to be the ones that push it forward. Which means it's not going to come from environmental organizations. It's not going to come from social justice organizations. It's not going to come from the top down, from existing organizations. It's going to be pushed upward by these groups of people who are courageous enough to come together around their kitchen table to say "we want this for our community" and are being told that they can't have it, and then they are pushing back and they are saying, "we are going to take it anyway."

The bulk of people who are going to be driving this stuff are the Jennifer Englands and other folks who are very different leaders than we perhaps expect to see. Leaders serve in that they are essentially facilitators and translators to explain to people how the system of law is operating, and why, when they try to stop sludge, they have to stop corporations as well. So I think when I say we are at the beginning of the beginning of the beginning, it's as if we are the abolitionists back in the 1830s, thirty-seven years before the 13th, 14th, and 15th amendments were written into the Constitution, and I think that's where we are now. It's an exciting time, because it allows us to lay the framework and the foundation in the right way so that the house doesn't fall over later. But it's also a fairly depressing time, because things are really bad and things are getting worse, and we want to see this thing accelerate.

Eventually, it means rewriting the state constitutions; eventually, it means rewriting the federal Constitution. And now in polite company, you can't even talk about those things yet. I think as the years roll on, more and more people will understand that we actually need to change the DNA of this country to have any chance. I think that as the ball starts rolling faster, more and more people will clearly see how the structure of law operates and the necessity of changing it.

Patriot Actions

Citizens Organize to Defend the Constitution

"The Constitution and the Bill of Rights don't belong to any political party."
    — Nancy Talanian, Bill of Rights Defense Committee

Six weeks after the September 11, 2001 attacks, Congress overwhelmingly approved the USA Patriot Act (Uniting and Strengthening America by Providing Appropriate Tools Required to Intercept and Obstruct Terrorism Act of 2001). This gave law enforcement officials sweeping new powers. But then civil liberties organizations on the left and libertarian groups on the right began voicing doubts about the wisdom of the law. Soon a national movement was underway to get local governments to overturn portions of the bill they said were unconstitutional. As they successfully lobbied hundreds of cities and towns to oppose the law, the patriots fighting the Patriot Act proved that Americans can set aside ideological divisions to defend common values.

When Chip Pitts sat down with 15 friends and colleagues at a Dallas Barnes & Noble café in June 2002 to plan a campaign for passing a local resolution opposing the Patriot Act, he wasn't especially optimistic. Dallas, after all, is a famously conservative town. As the number one source of donations for George W. Bush, and the hometown of many of his top political appointees, Dallas was very much the president's ideological base. So it seemed a long shot to think that the local city council would publicly oppose one of the pillars of the White House's post-9/11 national security strategy.

"It was a huge challenge," said Pitts, an attorney and long-time activist associated with Amnesty International and the American Civil Liberties Union. "This is the epicenter of the president's financial and political support. ...We actually had quite a few skeptics. Jan Sanders, for example, the wife of a federal judge here, said, 'Sorry, there is no way this will happen in Dallas.' A couple of members of the Green Party said, 'Sorry, this isn't worth our effort.'"

During the next year and a half, Pitts and his allies—a group that would eventually grow to more than 100 volunteers—would work tirelessly to prove the skeptics wrong. Through a wily combination of grassroots pressure, grass-tops lobbying, public education and hard-nosed political organizing, the Dallas chapter of the Bill of Rights Defense Committee succeeded in getting a majority of the city council to pass a resolution expressing their concerns about the Patriot Act's violation of key civil liberties. It was—in the game-day parlance often used to explain American politics—a stunning upset.

The political hurdles confronted by the Dallas activists may have been unique, but the group's accomplishment is not. As of this writing, more than 400 cities and counties across the country have passed anti-Patriot Act resolutions or more forceful ordinances that expressly forbid local law enforcement from cooperating with federal officials if their actions will violate the Bill of Rights. Eight states—from liberal ones, such as Hawaii and Vermont, to more conservative ones, such as Idaho and Montana—have also done so.

The locally organized—and nationally networked—opposition to the Patriot Act is yet another example of how citizens, working together, can make real change by focusing their efforts on those elected officials who are closest to them. What distinguishes the Patriot Act campaign from some of the other stories we tell is its self-consciously trans-partisan nature. The campaigns—which succeeded in small towns and big cities, in so-called blue states as well as staunchly red ones—did not just draw support from died-in-the-wool progressives. Rather, they deliberately enlisted the support of individuals from across the political spectrum. That type of broad-based political organizing was key to success in the Republican bastion of Dallas, among other locales.

"Some said this was the broadest coalition in the history of Dallas," Pitts recalled. "We had endorsements not only from the ACLU and the NAACP, but also from conservative groups like the Institute for Policy Innovation, the NRA, and the Republican Liberty Caucus. It showed this was a very mainstream, American-values effort."

"Values" is the key word here. The local campaigns defending the Bill of Rights prove that Americans are happy to drop the vitriol that often passes for political debate. Citizens will put aside the hot-button issues that mark the fault lines of U.S. politics (abortion, the Iraq War, religion's role in society) if they are enlisted in a collective effort to preserve shared beliefs. Consensus may be more common than popularly thought. If duplicated on other fronts—say, supporting local businesses struggling against Wal-Mart—this kind of non-ideological cooperation could usher in a re-alignment of American politics.

"The Constitution and the Bill of Rights don't belong to any political party," said Nancy Talanian, founding director of the national Bill of Rights Defense Committee (BORDC). "Conservatives, especially libertarians, are concerned about preserving rights. It makes for very obvious ways of bringing people together on common issues … You have to have a non-partisan approach when you're dealing with a city council. We have suggested to people that they reach out to everyone in the community and get as broad a base as possible."

Talanian knows that lesson from experience. As the director of the national BORDC, she has spent the last five years giving vital assistance to the local anti-Patriot Act initiatives, helping grassroots coordinators to plan and execute their community campaigns. In the process, she has refined a model of "netroots" activism that successfully shifted the debate over how to balance the needs for security with the demands of liberty.

21st-Century File-Sharing Activism

Passed six weeks after the September 11 attacks, the Patriot Act was designed to give law enforcement officials extra powers to track individuals planning terrorist strikes. Initially, the bill enjoyed extraordinary support from Democrats and Republicans alike. The legislation passed by sweeping margins in both houses of Congress during the emotional season following 9/11, a time when President Bush enjoyed broad public support. But as scrutiny focused on the legislation, a growing number of people began to express concerns about the wisdom of the new law.

Voices on the civil-liberties left and the libertarian right warned that the act had gone too far. For example, the new law gave law enforcement the power to monitor political or religious meetings even without suspicion of criminal activity, as well as the ability to listen in on conversations between attorneys and their clients in jail. Especially worrisome were so-called sneak-and-peak searches that would allow law enforcement to search suspects' homes without their knowledge, an apparent violation of the Fourth Amendment, and a provision to permit investigators to review individuals' library records and bookstore purchases. Critics said that these new law enforcement powers were a violation of key American freedoms.

"It was a flawed piece of legislation from the outset," Lisa Graves, deputy director of the Center for National Security Studies, told us. "The bill was a wish list, using September 11 to push through provisions that had nothing to do with preventing terrorism. … These programs are basically drift nets into the private lives of Americans who have done nothing wrong."

When she learned of the Patriot Act, Nancy Talanian was concerned—and she pledged to do something about it. A professional writer who prepared training manuals for corporations, Talanian had some past experience with grassroots organizing; she had been involved with the movement to end South African apartheid and with campaigns to promote human rights in Nigeria. Yet she had never been a full-time activist. This issue was different, however, and so Talanian decided to quit her corporate job and completely dedicate herself to beating back the Patriot Act.

"I felt that if we didn't do this now, we would have situations like the internment of the Japanese in World War II," Talanian said. "Who knew what would happen if we didn't put our foot down."

Talanian gathered together a group of friends and neighbors to form the Bill of Rights Defense Committee. They quickly set out to get their hometowns of Amherst and Northampton, Massachusetts, to pass ordinances opposed to the Patriot Act. The plan was modeled on the strategies of the anti-apartheid and nuclear-freeze movements, which had used city-council resolutions as a way to raise public awareness of their causes and build political support.

There was one key difference between past struggles and the BORDC's efforts. Whereas the anti-apartheid and nuclear-freeze resolutions had been largely symbolic—a local government can neither set foreign policy nor wage nuclear war—the civil-liberties campaign would have binding effect. The idea was to get the city council to pass an ordinance that would prohibit local police officers or local librarians from taking any action that would violate the Constitution. City officials would go on record refusing to participate in some aspects of the Patriot Act, and in the process, countermand federal policy.

"We needed something that a local city council could get into," Talanian said. "And that was that this law, though it's a national law, relies on local police to enforce it, and so it has an impact on local communities. We wanted cities to pass ordinances saying that their police would not engage in unconstitutional activities, even if allowed to do so by the Patriot Act."

As their proposed ordinance threaded its way through the local decision-making process, Talanian and her cohort documented each step of the way. They wrote detailed notes on how to introduce an ordinance, how to enlist allies on the city council, how to recruit supporters among the grassroots, how to work the media, and how to win. They knew that their campaign would only be successful if it could be duplicated in other cities, places that weren't as reliably liberal as western Massachusetts. And so they prepared a kind of road map for passing local legislation, a guide for other communities to follow their lead.

The plan worked. As soon as Amherst and Northampton passed their anti-Patriot Act resolutions in the spring of 2002, Talanian began receiving calls and emails from people across the nation who wanted to copy their success.

From the start, the Defense Committee's assistance to other groups was self-consciously hands-off. While the Massachusetts group was happy to share its name, the lessons from its own experience, and its template for victory, the national BORDC did not want to control the grassroots efforts. The BORDC staff in Massachusetts did not even select target cities; rather, they waited for people to come to them. Local autonomy was central to the coalition's strategy. The BORDC website provided groups with sample resolutions, downloadable public-information leaflets, and background information on the Patriot Act. But the rest of the work was up to the local organizers. Basically, the effort was a uniquely 21st century kind of file-sharing activism.

"I think that members of a city council are most moved by their own constituents," Talanian said. "They don't want to feel like they are being monkeyed with by outside agitators. So we felt it was really important that this came from people in the communities, and not from us. ... The local coordinators are people who are at least as creative as we are. All of the innovations, especially in the early days, came from other cities."

If the People Lead, the Leaders Will Follow

Glenn Devitt was a creative person who, after hearing about the growing Patriot Act opposition, decided to do something in his community—the burg of New York City. Like Chip Pitts in Dallas, Devitt faced some unique obstacles. While he enjoyed the advantage of living in a liberal city with a history of national leadership, he also had to grapple with New Yorkers' deep sensitivity to 9/11 related issues; New York City Hall is located just blocks from the crater where the World Trade Center once stood. Also, Devitt faced the daunting prospect of trying to make policy in a city of some 8 million people, a population bigger than that of many states. The campaign wouldn't be easy.

Like Pitts and Talanian, Devitt started with a small group of people—ten individuals in a Brooklyn living room plotting how to launch a campaign. The effort quickly snowballed. Soon, the New York Chapter of the BORDC had 99 organizations listed as co-sponsors, five subcommittees that met weekly, 80 core members, and another 300 volunteers—ranging in age from 17 to 84, who lived throughout the city. To keep volunteers engaged, Chip and the other coordinators focused people on tasks that dovetailed with their everyday interests—attorney volunteers worked on research, PR volunteers developed outreach materials, artists made signs and banners. Perhaps most important, given New York's sheer size, volunteers were split up by geography, with neighborhood teams assigned to target each one of the city council's 51 members.

"We went from all angles," said Devitt, who co-owns a multimedia website production firm. "We had quite a lobbying campaign. ... It was key for us to give council members the sense that they weren't leading the city—they were reflecting the city. Politicians are cautious. They don't want to do something unless they know they have popular support. They had to know there was a vocal sentiment behind what we were pushing."

Despite a supportive public, and many sympathetic politicians, there were still hurdles. As with any grassroots campaign, a key challenge was managing expectations and ensuring people didn't get dejected. Even at the local level, the legislative process moves at a tortoise pace. The institutional challenges were compounded by the ambivalence of the speaker of the city council, who kept postponing a vote on the Patriot Act measure. The repeated delays in the vote were starting to drag down morale.

Devitt and the other campaign coordinators maintained the volunteer activists' energy by setting medium-term goals to give people a sense of progress—say, doubling the number of volunteers from one month to the next, or getting another council member to commit to the resolution. At the same time, the coordinators tried to keep volunteers focused on the larger goal. As an organizer, Devitt's most valuable raw commodity was people's own hope; his task was to transform that feeling into empowerment.

"You do need to prepare for setbacks," Devitt said. "We were delayed from our vote for three or four months, and it was hard to keep people engaged because they were getting discouraged. ...But failure was not an option. It's not just that people could see they were making a difference, but that as we came together and did the lobbying training, people would walk away from that feeling much more empowered. They would call up their city council member on the phone, and get a meeting, and that was exciting to them, because they had never done that before."

In the end, of course, it worked. On February 4, 2004, New York City became the 256th jurisdiction to formally oppose the Patriot Act; Dallas followed less than three weeks later. The passage of the New York and Dallas resolutions in the same month gave fresh momentum to the national Bill of Rights Defense Committee campaign. They showed that one of the country's most conservative cities was not willing to sacrifice liberty for security, and neither was the epicenter of the September 11 attacks. The victories in those cities revealed to people just how much power they really have.

"It helped a lot of people overcome cynicism, the idea that they could actually influence their government, and that the elected officials would listen to them," Devitt said. "People learn that, at least at this local level, you can have an effect. This is, after all, a representative democracy."

What You Can Do

Take Over City Hall

The phrase "participatory democracy" is something of a redundancy. Without citizen involvement, democracy doesn't work; the concept is rendered meaningless.

Someone in your community is making the decisions that affect your life. If that someone isn't you, then who is it? And, more important, how do you influence them, and then start to make the decisions yourself?

The stories in this chapter show that there are a variety of ways to get involved in your community. Here are suggestions about participating in the decisions that affect your life.

Get Involved. Grassroots citizen campaigns depend on volunteer energy in order to succeed. Take a moment to think about the local issue that moves you the most—it could be the pollution of a nearby power plant, or the small budgets of your town's parks and schools. Then find a group that is working to address that concern. Offer whatever you can to help out, whether that means 10 hours a week, or one. Every minute you donate counts.

Sound the Alarm. Is there some injustice in your community that you can't bear to witness any longer? If so, help to uncover it. Write a letter to the editor of your local newspaper. Call the TV stations and radio shows and tell them what's going on. Hold a neighborhood meeting and start to spread the word.

Organize. If no one is working on the issue you care about, then you have to take charge. Leadership is easier than it looks. At its essence, it requires a vision of change, and the ability to communicate that vision to other people. Inspiration, it turns out, is a surplus commodity. Bring together your friends and neighbors to discuss the issue, agree on your goal for progress, map out a plan for how to get to that goal, and then get to work. The people in this chapter did it. So can you.

Campaign. If there is a candidate you believe in, get behind them—pick up the phone, knock on doors, hand out leaflets. Work to see that they get elected, and then, once they are in office, hold them accountable to the promises they made to get there.

Run for Office. We can't afford to leave politics to the career politicians. If you feel you have a vision for change, then enlist your friends in helping you create that vision. Start small: Run for a seat on the school board, or for the city council, or to be on the utilities commission. It's a gamble. But then, nothing was ever won by playing it safe. Only by risking going too far will you realize how far you can really go.

Section Four

Power to the People

Energy is so all-encompassing in our lives that being aware of it is like asking a fish to become aware of water. Energy powers our cars, heats our homes, illuminates our light bulbs, and keeps our laptops running. It is the lifeblood of our lifestyles.

The most basic energy we have is solar energy. Pre-industrial societies were very dependent on the sun for their survival. The sun grew the grass that fed the animals people used for extra muscle and for meat; it made the vegetation they used for food and fuel.

Then people figured out they could release the vast amounts of ancient solar energy embedded in oil, natural gas, and coal: the fossil fuels. Due to the voracious energy appetite of our industrial system we have managed in two hundred years to burn up solar energy that took two hundred *million* years to create. This is like taking apart the innards of your house and burning them in your fireplace to keep warm.

The relative accessibility of fossil fuel has allowed companies to extract these resources and sell them at a low financial price. But now society is becoming aware of the much greater, non-financial prices we pay when we burn fossil fuels.

Our "cheap" energy has encouraged us to make decisions that, upon inspection, appear quite stupid. For example, we have created sprawling suburbs that require millions of people to cram onto freeways inside oversized metal vehicles. We have recklessly polluted the air we breathe; we have poisoned our waters with oil spills; we have wrecked our pristine mountains through coal mining; and we have endangered our health by tolerating the smog that contributes to asthma, lung disease, and heart disease. Perhaps most insanely, we have invaded another country to maintain this lifestyle. If you doubt the Iraq invasion was in some way motivated by oil, ask yourself: Would we have tens of thousands of troops in Iraq if the Middle East's biggest export was broccoli?

And now, in what may become an act of collective suicide, our fossil fuel consumption is fundamentally changing the very weather of the planet, threatening the biological systems on which our civilization depends.

These combined crises have forced a growing number of people to realize that we must make a transition—as quickly as possible—toward conservation and renewable energy sources. There is no lack of smart alternatives; a combination of solar, wind, geothermal, mini-hydro, tidal, wave, and kinetic energies could meet our basic needs. As awareness of the potential of clean energy sinks in, policymakers and investors are starting to shift away from fossil fuels.

Some of the most exciting developments are at the grassroots, where ordinary people are driving the movement for sustainable energy. In this section you'll learn about how students are using friendly competition to spur developments on each others' campuses. You'll read about the more than 400 U.S. cities that—frustrated with inaction at the federal level—are reducing their carbon footprints. And you'll hear from members of the Sioux Nation, who are seeking to harness the incredible wind power that blows across their lands.

It's as if a collective light bulb is going off—a compact fluorescent one, of course. These stories will show you how to get plugged in.

Give Me an "E"

Rival Colleges Compete
for Sustainability

"It's so easy to focus on the challenges. You can lose sight of 'the right thing to do' ... but doing the right thing is extremely rewarding."
— Dayna Burtness, St. Olaf student who started a student-run organic farm on campus

Northfield, Minnesota's two colleges, Carleton and St. Olaf, compete on many levels: sports (their annual football game is among the oldest rivalries in college history); which institution is older (Carleton); and which boasts the largest student body (St. Olaf). In the last few years they have been competing for a new title—most sustainable campus. The two schools are in a race that involves erecting windmills, operating bicycle programs, growing school-lunch food on campus, and making biodiesel fuel from cafeteria grease. It is a competition that has implications far beyond campus life, and is emblematic of a wave of ecological activism at America's universities. Today's young people are, in many ways, sowing the seeds for a local, green economy.

Locals fondly liken Northfield, Minnesota to Garrison Keillor's Lake Wobegon. A sign on the road into town boasts, "Cows, Colleges and Contentment." Although the character of the town is slowly changing due to the impact of the Mall of America and the steady creep of the Minneapolis suburbs, Northfield is still a quaint hamlet. It is the home of the Malt-O-Meal factory and a 125-year-old rivalry between the town's two colleges—Carleton and St. Olaf, whose combined enrollment comprise 5,000 students, about one-fourth of the local population.

The annual "Cereal Bowl" football match between the schools is a highly anticipated community event. The winning team holds the coveted "Goat Trophy," which, St. Olaf alums and fans are happy to tell visitors, the "Oles" have retained every year for the last decade. In the century-long history of these schools, friendly rivalries have developed over many things. In recent years, it's bragging rights to campus sustainability and energy efficiency.

Pondering the origins of the rivalry, Katie Godfrey, a member of the St. Olaf student environmental coalition, said, "Carleton and St. Olaf are really pretty different, even though they're just a couple of miles apart." Carleton is the more liberal of the two. "St. Olaf is a Lutheran college," Godfrey said. "It's more conservative and attracts more Minnesotans."

Despite these differences, students, faculty, and administrators from both colleges see that transitioning the campus ecology toward a self-reliant model is an important strategy for financial survival and an increasingly significant status symbol of collegiate leadership.

Green Campus, Green Coffers

The Carleton and St. Olaf experiences are not unique. Campus "greening" is a trend that is sprouting on campuses nationwide. In recent years, students at Oberlin College in Ohio have reduced by one-half the electricity they use in dorm rooms. New York University has committed to buying most of its power from renewable wind sources. University of California students are pushing the giant UC system to adopt a sustainable food policy and have already convinced the administration to reduce fuel use of campus transportation fleets.

"College students really get the big ideas of our time—climate change and the critical balance between nature and people—and they have been pushing the schools on ecology for years," DeVere Pentony, a retired professor and administrator at San Francisco State University, told us.

Young environmental activists are growing in numbers at a rate almost too fast to track, and as their numbers increase, so does their power to win sustainability campaigns. The demand for campus sustainability is driven in large part by the threat of climate change. Young people understand that unchecked carbon dioxide emissions—the main cause of global climate change—pose a real danger to their future, and they are determined to do something about it. In taking on this challenge, the campus activists are further proof of the power of human creativity. The college climate efforts have produced a slew of solutions for reducing our ecological footprint. Many are not only ecologically smart, but also economically savvy.

The "bottom line" is being redefined, and it's no longer just about immediate costs. Colleges are seeing that investing in green technologies, such as renewable electricity or energy efficiency, saves them money over the long run.

"As more students remind administrators of the 'triple bottom line'—the need to weigh environmental and social factors along with cost factors—the better the odds that environmentally- and socially-minded decisions will get made," said Judy Walton, Executive Director of the Association for the Advancement of Sustainability in Higher Education (AASHE). "More and more campuses are realizing that part of their mission is to responsibly lead society toward a better future for all."

According to Walton, there are more than 600 schools undertaking sustainability projects in the United States, including over 30 campuses with functioning wind turbines. More and more, she says, they are working together and using friendly competition as a way to collectively boost results. Recycle-Mania, for example, is an annual college and university recycling competition. In 2006, over 100 campuses from 33 states participated, with California State University San Marcos winning the grand championship.

Often, students are simply asking administrators to satisfy campus mission statements and the mottoes emblazoned on school seals—where words like stewardship, leadership, and innovation can be found. That's what the Carleton students did when they lobbied their school president and administration for a plan to make the college carbon-neutral. Their successful campaign has distinguished the small liberal arts college as having the strongest climate commitment of any school in the nation. But that title may not hold for long, as more and more campuses join the competition to fight global warming.

It's Getting Hot in Here

The debate is over. The warning signs of a planetary meltdown are everywhere: chaotic weather, harsher and more frequent hurricanes, entire islands sinking beneath the sea, drowning polar bears unable to find ice in their Arctic hunting grounds. And it's going to get worse. This is the planet our youth are inheriting from their parents and grandparents. Students see that decades of environmentally- and socially-bankrupt industrial practices and government inaction have put short-term profits before their long-term well-being.

Unwilling to simply blame adults—or to wait for a techno-fix, or for governments or industry to change course—students are demanding action to halt carbon emissions. They are building a movement to stabilize the climate and secure their future.

The impact and influence of student actions stretch beyond the ivory tower. Students have taken resolutions they passed on campus—for wind energy and green transportation fleets—and leveraged those policies to get their cities to make similar commitments. By showing the benefits their campuses have reaped, the students have contributed to city, state, and regional action.

A example of student power occurred in the fall of 2005, when youth from around the world converged on Montreal for an international climate summit. They participated in official and unofficial capacities, doing anything they could to pressure the delegates to curb greenhouse gasses. As Mike Hudema of Global Exchange's Freedom from Oil Campaign said, "They were there to tell the world what they want, what governments need to do." The youth demands were then taken to the International Conference of Mayors, which adopted the students' recommendations and is now using the climate targets fashioned by youth. The Campus Climate Challenge (CCC), begun after the Montreal actions, is a project of more than 30 leading youth and environmental organizations throughout the United States and Canada. The CCC leverages the power of thousands of young people to win 100 percent clean-energy policies at their schools.

In 2001, Julian Dautremont-Smith was a student at Lewis and Clark College, and helped lead the campus to become the first Kyoto-compliant campus in the country. Now he leads AASHE's involvement in the CCC.

"The overall goal of the CCC is to build a generation-wide movement to stop global warming," Dautremont Smith said. "The CCC aims to do this by mobilizing students at North American colleges and universities to work for solutions to global warming on their campuses and in their communities."

By eliminating pollution from high schools and colleges, Climate Challenge is leading the broader society to a clean-energy future.

Windmills and Garden Beds

Score one for Carleton: In 2004, Carleton erected a 1.65 megawatt wind turbine to offset the rising costs of electricity. Carleton's turbine has the capacity to produce about 40 percent of the school's electricity. It sells the energy to the local utility company and buys back what it needs.

Bristling with a tinge of friendly competition, student Katie Godfrey is quick to brag about what her own school is doing. "At St. Olaf, we got our windmill this year," she said, "and in fact we ordered ours first, before Carleton got theirs." St. Olaf's turbine will provide energy directly to the school, meeting about one-third of the campus's total energy needs. According to the school's calculations, the turbine will save the college as much as $300,000 per year, and once the initial investment is recouped (in about seven years), it will become a source of profit.

Carleton philosophy professor Jennifer Everett, who teaches Environmental Ethics, has enjoyed the surge of positive competition between the two schools. "It's true," she told us, "the wind turbine was a high-visibility item for Carleton. But after it was dedicated, we began to hear how many impressive and pervasive things Olaf was doing—especially to connect to the curriculum—that some thought put Carleton to shame." She added with a laugh, "Of course, we're insecure over-achievers at Carleton, so it's easy to trigger perceptions and worries about being bested."

True enough. Over at St. Olaf, sustainability is measured not only in wind, but in energy-efficient lighting, composting cafeteria garbage, and campus-wide conservation efforts. First-year students get to buddy-up with older students and learn about on-campus greening and how to participate. One program they learn about is the Green Machine Bicycle Program, which recycles used and discarded bikes for students living on campus. They also learn how fry grease from the cafeteria is being used to replace gasoline for all campus vehicles. They are also encouraged to help out with a student-run organic farm on campus that sells fresh veggies to the cafeteria and teaches students about the importance of knowing where food comes from.

But students are not just sitting around waiting for administrators to "get it." They are taking the future of the planet—their future—into their own hands. The way students see it, there isn't any time to waste, and waiting around for the system to fix itself just isn't enough.

Oles student Dayna Burtness is one such campus activist. She started the Olaf farming project without permission from the school, and was determined to overcome any resistance she might meet. "I'm stubborn; I wouldn't take no for an answer," Burtness said. "I think they had a bad experience with a student-run project before, and were a little skeptical that I could really make it happen." But she did. She recruited other students to help out, located some land, found a market, and then got to work.

"There are 400 acres of farmland on campus, and we found a small backyard field run by the Cannon River Watershed Partnership, a environmental non-profit, that rents an old farmhouse on the outskirts of campus for their headquarters," Burtness said. "We asked them if we could farm on their yard, since it was currently unused. It used to be a horse corral; the manure made great fertilizer."

Acquiring some land was only part of the problem. Burtness and her student farm crew needed a market to sell their vegetables, and they needed an infusion of capital for seeds and equipment. "We approached the food service management company, Bon Appétit, which runs the school cafeteria," Burtness said. "We had no way to project yields or anything, but they shocked us, telling us that they would buy all the produce we could grow, giving us a guaranteed market." With land and market in hand, the campus farmers petitioned the school government association for a grant of $6,400. The student government loved the idea of a student-run farm, and the funds were used to purchase a greenhouse, a tiller, and other equipment. The school entrepreneur program gave the farm an additional grant of $2,000 to support a farm staffer for the summer.

Having proven they were serious and viable, the farmers got permission from the college to operate officially. Despite some rookie mistakes in planting, the first season was phenomenal, selling over $10,000 worth of produce to the school cafeteria. Profits were reinvested in the farm, used to hire four more student staff and expand the farm by 70 percent. One of the farm's most impressive successes was the degree of student enthusiasm the project attracted.

"We had volunteer days, threw a fall harvest party," Burtness told us. "We've done garden and organics education, and people really enjoy eating food their friends have grown. All the food in the cafeteria is now source-labeled, so everyone knows where the food comes from that they are putting in their mouths."

Dayna Burtness didn't grow up anywhere near a farm. Raised in a suburb of Minneapolis, Burtness had very little connection to agriculture until she spent a summer working on an organic farm with a community supported agriculture (CSA) program. The experience gave her a fresh appreciation for the craft of farming, and cultivated in her a commitment to share her passion with her peers. For Burtness, the on-campus farm is a way to encourage people to understand how profoundly we rely on biological systems. It's important, she believes, that people recognize that food is more than industrial supermarket magic.

"Coming from the 'burbs, I thought farming would be dull, isolating, backwards—and it is just not the case," Burtness said. "It is intellectually stimulating. There are a ton of variables, lots of problem solving, and I love the culture. It's extremely community-oriented. ... In general, folks don't care where their food comes from or know how to grow it. I had to start a farm to give people this experience."

But students at St. Olaf are not just interested in where the food comes from—they also want to know where it goes when they're finished with it. About 1,000 pounds of food waste are generated on campus each day, waste that used to go straight to the landfill, where it does not get enough oxygen to decompose, but just piles up like the rest of the trash. This year the school invested in a high-powered composter for the cafeteria. The students separate the food from the garbage and recyclable materials, and then squeeze the liquid out of the food. The result is a high-quality liquid fertilizer for the school flower beds. "We're also testing the compost now, to see if we can use it on the farm," Burtness said.

Grease Into Gas

Back at Carleton, senior Daniel Pulver has been working on a cafeteria recycling project of his own, converting used vegetable oil into biodiesel fuel that can run the campus vehicles, a project he started by experimenting in his kitchen. The school kitchen at Carleton dumps over 1,000 gallons of vegetable oil each year, which could be converted into savings of energy and money.

At St. Olaf, Dan Borek, Burtness' farm partner, is also working on a biodiesel project. St. Olaf's facilities team converted the school fleet of lawn mowers, snowplows, tractors, and other vehicles to a 20 percent biodiesel mix.

Students in St. Olaf's Campus Ecology class calculated the rough automotive mileage for the faculty, students, delivery trucks, and visitors to and from school each day, estimating that the campus community collectively drives nearly 20,000 miles—almost enough driving to circumnavigate the globe—each day. The result of this study has spawned public awareness campaigns and bicycle programs at both schools. Subsequent years' Campus Ecology students will chart the school's progress, examining the campus as a system of resource flows, a microcosm of American consumption patterns.

The students say a few enlightened professors and the attention of some administrators have empowered students to demand changes—and there may be a bit of competitiveness there, too. Daniel Pulver gives credit for his biodiesel experiment to his Carleton Environmental Ethics professor, Jennifer Everett, who firmly believes that sustainability must be the centerpiece of education. The keys to success, Everett said, are "enthusiastic students who know they face a frightening future; a few committed people to get the ball rolling; and around here, a regional identity built in part around affection for the prairie."

Jim Farrell, who teaches Campus Ecology at St. Olaf, is equally praised by his students for inspiring them not only to think outside the box, but to take action. "I will say that our farming project came along at a good time," campus grower Burtness said in discussing Farrell's contributions. "There were already energy-related sustainability projects on campus, thanks to teachers like Jim Farrell and our Vice President of Facilities, Pete Sandberg. Pete takes lot of his own time to work on green projects, and put together a sustainability task force, which is a cross-section of the whole campus. So there were already folks thinking about this stuff."

Burtness and others would like to see more collaboration between the schools. "It's been kind of funny, this rivalry thing," she said with a smile. "Carleton got their wind turbine first, but now they are setting up a student farm over there. ... It would be fun to swap farms, work on ideas together, even put our resources together."

And thanks to more student pushing, that is exactly what is beginning to happen, starting with a summer conference in 2006 aimed at how environmental learning can be further incorporated into the classrooms of both schools. "And not just the ecology classes," Katie Godfrey of the St. Olaf environmental group said, "but all classes, across the entire curriculum, from art to economics."

February 2007 marks the schools' annual Energy Month competition. But this year the rivals are not just challenging each other; the competition has grown into a Minnesota-wide effort to see who can reduce energy consumption the most.

Taking a brief break from her tireless activism, Dayna Burtness wonders if the trend toward working together on environmental stewardship can't also address a perennial problem: the dating imbalance at St. Olaf, where female students far outnumber their male counterparts. "The latest idea is to bring Carleton and the Oles together to boost the dating scene. We're planning a square dance in the middle of town, where we will bring together the environmental communities from both schools, along with the larger community of Northfield." She added teasingly, "I mean, anybody can square dance, right?"

CONVERSATION

David Morris

David Morris is a Co-Founder and Vice President of the Institute for Local Self Reliance (ilsr.org) in Minneapolis. He is the director of their New Rules Project (newrules.org), an excellent resource on the best practices for getting local control over energy, agriculture, retail development, finance, and other key areas. He is the author of many books and reports, which are available from the New Rules website. His regular articles are featured on AlterNet.org.

Q: Why does local control of energy make sense?

DM: Local control of *everything* makes sense. But local control of energy makes sense for two reasons: one is that ten cents on the local dollar of the community goes directly to pay for fuel, and all of it is imported. Only between ten and fifteen cents on the dollar spent on that fuel stays in the local community. So from an economic development standpoint, it is probably the worst expenditure that you can make in a community. The other reason is that you don't have to. Cities, unless they are high-density cities, can in fact generate much, if not all, of their own energy, either internal to themselves or within 50 to 100 miles.

Q: What has been the federal government's role on these issues? Is it getting better or worse?

DM: The federal government has not been wise on these things, ever. On the issue of decentralization and energy being produced from the bottom up, the federal government's policies undermine it at almost every level. And it doesn't matter whether it's been Democrats or Republicans; there has been no change in that whatsoever. The federal government wants more energy, but they are either indifferent to where the generation occurs, or they encourage large absentee-owned facilities in most of their incentives and regulatory policies.

Q: Could you give us some specifics on how federal government policies undermine local energy production?

DM: Sure, one is that the federal government has preempted a significant amount of state authority on the siting of high-voltage transmission lines. The federal government is doing everything in its power to build these transmission lines like a national highway. They argue that this is "efficient," and I disagree, but that is their argument. What it does is encourage the generation of energy far away from where people tend to use it. The federal government has also encouraged absentee ownership of energy facilities. For example, in wind, if you have a wind turbine and you only meet your own internal needs, you actually don't qualify for federal incentives. The only time you qualify for them is if you sell the energy into the grid system—then you can qualify for a tax incentive. There are many examples like this, and the federal government would probably admit it. Their feeling is that large is better than small, absentee is better than locally owned, and it's much better to attract the capital of Wall Street and global investment firms than it is to attract local finance.

Q: How does the issue of net metering factor into this?

DM: Net metering was a revolution, a very quiet revolution. It said that the utility companies had to allow you to turn your meter backwards. Since 1979, by federal law, the utility companies had to agree to buy your electricity if you had solar panels, but they could put any conditions they wanted on it, and they put on conditions that made it uneconomical for you to do that. So what net metering says is that the utility can't charge you for a second meter; it has to allow the meter to run backwards, which means you get the retail price for your electricity. So that redefines the electric system as a two-way system, by law.

Q: Is there any state with full net metering, where if I put more into the grid than I take out, they have to pay me for the electricity I put back into the grid?

DM: Yes, there are many states that allow that, but every one is different. There are some that have a carry-over from month to month and at the end of the year you settle up. There are some that have a carry-over from month to month and at the end of the year you lose any surplus you might have. There are some that require them to pay you, but they would pay you for the voided costs, they're not going to pay you the retail price. You could turn your meter backwards, in effect getting the retail price, but when you get a surplus you're getting a voided cost (between a penny-and-a-half to two cents a kilowatt hour) instead of getting the displaced retail price of anywhere from 7 to 15 cents a kilowatt hour.

Q. Can you discuss the biofuels debate?

DM: The key issue is ownership. In 2002 almost 50 percent of all ethanol facilities in this country were majority farmer-owned, and about 80 percent of all the new ones coming on line were majority farmer-owned. By 2007, about 95 percent of all the new ones are absentee-owned. So we've had a big change in the ownership structure of ethanol.

Q: What caused such a big shift?

DM: Wall Street came in. We had oil going for 60 to 70 dollars a barrel, and we had a mandate for ethanol at a national level. Wall Street found out it could earn 30 to 40 percent turnaround on its investments, and they flooded in and began building 100 million gallon-a-year plants rather than 30 or 40 million gallon-a-year plants. If that becomes your basic size template, that's too large for any local equity to get control of. So that's a serious problem.

Q: What about the issue of taking land away from food production by growing corn for ethanol instead of for human consumption? Or the issue of horrible working conditions for sugarcane workers in Brazil?

DM: Previously, the majority of sugarcane in Brazil was family owned. Now, with the ethanol market taking off, they're getting Japanese capital, Chinese capital, American capital pouring in there, and they have to deal with the absentee ownership in terms of bad working conditions. In terms of the food vs. fuel issue, the point is that if you want to go to a renewable sustainable future, then the question is: "What materials do you rely on?" And when it comes to energy, you can say, "Well, let's rely on direct sunlight," and "Let's rely on wind." And that's fine, as long as you don't need storage. But if you need storage, you need matter, you need molecules—and where is the material for that going to come from? Furthermore, where are the molecules going to come from for everything else? For desks and for cars and so forth, where's that going to come from? You have two alternatives: vegetables or minerals. So if you want minerals, with recycling you can do a lot, but in the longer term you want to shift to vegetables. I wrote a book in 1992 called *The Carbohydrate Economy* and I will stand by the fact that it has to be a piece of the renewable materials puzzle. Then the question becomes, what do you use that biomatter for, aside from food and feed—it's an interesting question. It's a challenge to design public policy correctly because obviously, nutrition should be the highest priority. But when you get below food and medicine, what should it be: should it be liquid fuels, electricity, heat, biochemicals, construction materials, what should it be? That's the real challenge in designing these policies.

Right now, corn farmers without government subsidies are earning more than the cost of production of corn for the first time since the drought year in 1996. Since the 1930s we've had a federal policy whereby the taxpayer pays 20 to 35 percent of the cost of production and in return the grain is artificially low-priced. We find now that the corn is priced slightly higher than it probably should be, and people are screaming that everyone's going to starve to death should they have to pay the real costs of growing these things. It would be laughable if it weren't so sad. Farmers in other parts of the world have been complaining for many years about the U.S. dumping our cheap, subsidized grain on the world market and driving them out of business.

Q: You've written about energizing rural America through the farm bill and trade policy. Can you talk about the link between increased rural prosperity and energy security?

DM: Rural areas have a competitive advantage in only a few things. The primary one is that they're got a lot of land and relatively few people. It also turns out that the wind blows better and more consistently in rural areas. So that's their competitive advantage: plant matter and wind. Right now those are national priorities, and I'm saying, let's do it right this time. The federal government favors quantitative goals. They want more and I want better.

We did it wrong last time. We should have learned from that experience, and the best way to do it right this time is to let the farmers and local owners control the process so they're not 100 percent dependent on a commodity price they don't control.

Q: Can you talk about green-energy pricing programs?

DM: We're opposed to green pricing programs and I've always been opposed to them. There is a difference between green pricing and green citizenship. Green citizenship says that if the majority supports renewable energy, then the majority should pay for it through the utility bills that go to everyone. Standards are mandates that the majority imposes on themselves, and if there are any increased costs, they are spread out over all the ratepayers. Green pricing, on the other hand, says that I, in return for taking a moral stand, I will pay a significantly higher price for my electricity because I want renewable sources. This punishes ratepayers who want renewable energy—making them pay 10-25 percent more for their electricity—while those who don't choose renewable sources pay less. If we want green electricity then we should demand it and everyone should pay for it.

Beyond Hot Air

Cities Lead the U.S. on Tackling Climate Change

"There were lots of people who were relieved that we would be solving a big problem in our little corner of the world"
—Chris Hayday, organizer, Columbia, Missouri

The science is unequivocal: The earth is getting hotter, and humans are to blame. The U.S. political leadership, however, has been in a state of denial when it comes to the threat of climate change. But while Washington dawdles, local leaders are taking action. More than 400 mayors have signed a pledge committing their towns and cities to reduce their greenhouse gas emissions. The activity at the municipal level shows that there is a range of actions communities can take to address a pressing global challenge. It's also a hopeful sign that if local communities lead, the "leaders" in the nation's capital will follow.

The Roanoke Valley of southern Virginia is not known as a hotbed of activism. Nestled at the base of the Appalachian Mountains, Roanoke is a quiet region of soft green hills and scattered farms. Home to some quarter of a million people, the Valley boasts a modest economy anchored by auto parts manufacturers, health care companies, and small businesses. In the 2004 presidential election, George W. Bush won Roanoke County by a nearly two-to-one margin.

Roanoke may seem an unlikely place to wage a campaign to address the threat of global climate change, which until quite recently was thought of as a "liberal conspiracy." But that is exactly what's happening there. A coalition called the Roanoke Valley Cool Cities Campaign is spearheading an effort to get the region's governments to slash their greenhouse gas emissions. By bringing together businesses, non-profit groups, and elected officials, the Roanoke Cool Cities Campaign is tapping into political conservatives' instincts for local governance, and in the process is convincing people to see how tackling global warming can lead to real community benefits.

173

"We said we wanted a base of operations that wasn't just the Sierra Club treehuggers, but was really a cross section of the community," Mark McClain, chair of the Roanoke Sierra Club and a co-coordinator of the Cool Cities Campaign, told us. "We now have 41 affiliates, and they range from Hollins University to a dozen or so community leaders—including a former city council member of Roanoke—to a lot of companies. ... We still have a few skeptics. But when we sit down and explain things to people, they acknowledge that [climate change] is a big problem."

The Roanoke organizing is just one piece of a larger national campaign to get local governments to do whatever they can to reduce their CO_2 emissions. Across the United States, communities are working to stop climate change. Lincoln, Nebraska, for example, is running its city buses on biodiesel. Waverly, Iowa has built its own windmills to generate electricity. Houston, the fourth largest city in the country, is converting its fleet of municipal cars and trucks to hybrid models. Chicago is encouraging the construction of energy-saving green roofs. And in November 2006, voters in Boulder, Colorado, passed the country's first carbon tax to discourage homes and businesses from using too much electricity.

As of this writing, more than 400 local leaders representing nearly 60 million Americans have signed the Mayors Climate Protection Agreement, which calls for cities and towns to cut their carbon emissions to seven percent below 1990 levels by 2012—in effect implementing the Kyoto Protocol on Climate Change.

Localities' energetic response to the threat of global warming is due in large part to inaction at the federal level. Under both Democratic and Republican control, the U.S. Senate has refused to ratify the Kyoto Protocol, which has been adopted by every advanced industrial nation except Australia. The Bush Administration has been particularly hostile to international efforts to halt climate change; one of Bush's first acts after taking office in 2001 was to express White House opposition to the Kyoto plan, which the president called an "unrealistic and ever-tightening straightjacket."

Leadership, however, abhors a vacuum. In the space left by federal officials, local leaders have stepped up to craft their own solutions. Mayors have shown that there is a range of actions that governments at any level can take to cut greenhouse gases.

In doing so, the mayors and the grassroots groups supporting them are showing how leadership often percolates up from the bottom. There's a saying that community organizers like to quote: "If the people lead, the leaders will follow." By making meaningful reductions in greenhouse gases, the country's mayors are hoping to show that if the cities lead, the federal government will follow.

"We have been stuck in a stalemate in global warming at the federal level forever," said Glen Brand, a national Sierra Club staffer who coordinates the various Cool Cities campaigns. "The way to break that is to build public pressure on a number of levels ... I think it's important that the entire Cool Cities movement is a positive, solutions-based message, which is desperately what we need and is why the public is responding to it. That kind of can-do attitude has been infectious."

Strength in Numbers

Our gasoline-powered cars, coal-burning power plants, and natural-gas stoves and heaters release tons of carbon dioxide into the air every year, gases that trap heat, much like a greenhouse. The effects of a warming climate can already be seen. Polar ice is melting faster than previously predicted. The weather is becoming increasingly bizarre, as storms strengthen and flower bulbs blossom in winter. Some forecast models predict a rise in sea levels that will swamp many major cities and all but drown low-lying countries such as Bangladesh.

Despite the broad scientific consensus on global warming, the U.S. political class has been in a deep state of denial. For years, many conservatives have not even wanted to admit there is a problem. And liberals have been hesitant to back changes that would make a real difference—like government-mandated improvements in automobile efficiency—since such reforms would roil the politically powerful carbon barons.

While U.S. leaders have squabbled, the rest of the world is taking action. The centerpiece of international efforts to address climate change is the Kyoto Protocol. Ratified by 169 countries, the agreement calls for nations to cut their greenhouse gas emissions to below 1990 levels by 2012. Many environmentalists have complained that the Kyoto agreement does not go far enough in slashing carbon emissions, given the precarious state of the earth's atmosphere. True. But the agreement at least represents a collective plan to address a common problem, and in that, the protocol is a step forward and an important example of international partnership. As noted, the United States is conspicuous by its absence.

Planetary climate change is among the most international of problems. It will require consistent and committed collaboration among nations to slow down greenhouse gas accumulations. But remember the old bumper sticker: "Think Global, Act Local." Yes, international actions are required; at the same time, there are steps local governments can take to do their part in stopping climate change. Those local actions are especially important given that the

United States is responsible for nearly one-quarter of all greenhouse gases.

In 2005, a group of progressive minded mayors, frustrated with U.S. inaction, decided to use their influence to confront the climate crisis. On the day Kyoto formally went into effect—February 16, 2005—Mayor Greg Nickels of Seattle called on his fellow mayors to join Seattle in sharply reducing CO_2. Nickels' "Mayors Climate Protection Agreement" set out a 12-point plan for cities to cut their greenhouse gases, called on the federal and state governments to meet or beat the Kyoto requirements, and urged national lawmakers to "reduce the United States' dependence on fossil fuels and accelerate the development of clean, economical energy." Nickels said that confronting climate change was a "national debate we can't really sidestep."

Longtime climate activists say that the arrival of leadership at the municipal level gave a major boost to grassroots campaigns that had been trying to get traction on the issue for years. "It's really been in the last two years that the engagement by local governments has been incredible," said Michelle Wyman, director of the U.S. arm of the International Council for Local Environmental Initiatives (ICLEI).

Since 1993, ICLEI had been promoting a Cities for Climate Protection Campaign. But the effort had failed to take off, partly due to ignorance and confusion about climate change science, as well as the lack of a leader willing to champion the issue. When Nickels became that champion, the campaign received a shot of momentum.

The Seattle mayor was soon joined by the mayors of Minneapolis, Salt Lake City, San Francisco, and seven other cities, who together released an appeal to their fellow mayors to sign the climate agreement. From there, the effort snowballed. In June 2005, the U.S. Conference of Mayors unanimously endorsed the protection plan. Then one by one, month after month, mayors added their cities' names to the agreement, pledging to inventory their current greenhouse gas emissions and then take immediate steps to reverse them.

The steady buildup of mayoral involvement on global warming reveals an important dynamic of leadership: courage breeds courage. When a critical mass of cities publicly committed to tackle climate change, it was like a green light—visible only to elected leaders—went off, giving mayors the go-ahead to address the issue. As the number of cities involved with the Climate Protection Agreement grew, mayors received confidence from each other to go further with their commitments. City officials started to swap stories of their efforts, trading lessons and experiences.

"When the mayors get together, there is strength in numbers," Wyman told us. "They get empowered by each other. The strength is in the network itself. We've seen how networks learn from each other."

A good example of this leadership dynamic, Wyman said, is Anchorage mayor Mark Begich. The Alaska native had been a skeptic of climate change, Wyman said, until he attended one of ICLEI's annual "Sundance Summits." He left the summit convinced that CO_2 emissions were a problem, and immediately set to work to get Anchorage to limit its carbon footprint. Begich has since become a prominent climate activist, encouraging mayors of similarly conservative communities to get involved. He has used his unique position as the mayor of a famously oil-rich region to spur other mayors to action.

"The idea behind the Sundance Summit is to bring together mayors who have done nothing at all, or who are naysayers—and thank God there are fewer of them—and get them to leave as leaders," Wyman said. "Mayors who have never done anything before now want to do something. The network makes the new guys more confident to step out."

That confidence has been easier to cultivate as the public's perception of climate change has shifted. The Hurricane Katrina catastrophe, weirder and weirder weather, and the success of the climate documentary *An Inconvenient Truth* have made it difficult for most people to ignore the harsh reality of what is happening to the planet.

The political moment for creating a broad-based climate justice movement has finally arrived.

Let's Talk About Clean Air

The political opportunities for addressing climate change can be witnessed in the experience of Columbia, Missouri. In 2004—even before the watershed events that shifted public opinion—residents of Columbia voted to require the city's municipal utility to purchase electricity from renewable energy sources. To be sure, Columbia is a stereotypically open-minded college town, home to the state's largest university. Yet the community of 90,000 is set in the middle of Missouri, a state well known for its hard-headed practicality; Missouri's motto is "The Show Me State."

The organizers behind the renewable-energy proposition said that tapping into the Missouri spirit of pragmatism was key to the campaign's success. For city residents who agreed that climate change poses a threat, the measure's backers offered the proposal as a sensible way to make a difference—steady increases in the city's renewable energy portfolio, from 2 percent of all electricity in 2007 to 15 percent by 2022. For those who still doubted the science on global warming, the organizers promoted the initiative as a way to improve local air quality and reduce imported energy—commonsense concerns.

"People were waiting for someone to be doing this; they were excited to have someone grab the bull by the horns," Chris Hayday, a coordinator of the Co-lumbia effort, told us. "The people who were going to be suspicious or critical, what got them on board was the idea of being energy independent, and not wanting to be reliant on politically sensitive and unstable regions. They were able to make that connection. There were lots of people who were relieved that they could vote for this and that we would be solving a big problem in our little corner of the world."

The approach worked. With a $5,000 budget and a crew of 40 volunteers, the campaign easily collected the 3,500 signatures needed to get the renew-able energy proposition on the ballot. On election day in November 2004, the measure passed by a wide margin, 78 to 22 percent.

A non-ideological style has been key to the success of the local climate cam-paigns. Viewed from a national perspective, the various global warming cam-paigns are best-practices examples of how to combine grassroots muscle with grasstops expertise. Groups like the Sierra Club and Kyoto USA supply the foot soldiers who do the public education work and community organizing that builds consensus for taking action. Then ICLEI comes in and helps may-ors and city employees translate that consensus into concrete improvement. Together, it makes for a powerful mix of thematic organizing and technocratic capacity-building, a kind of political vanilla and chocolate swirl. The combi-nation gives meaning to the classic tactician's mantra, "Inside, outside—we're all on the same side."

At the heart of this strategy is an attentiveness to local conditions. The ICLEI staffers are very deliberate about offering municipalities a smorgasbord of op-tions. First ICLEI helps the city conduct an inventory of current emissions. Then it suggests a variety of ways to reduce those emissions. Some communi-ties, like Charlotte, North Carolina, and Marion County, Florida, decided to focus on greening their municipal auto fleets by switching to hybrid and biodiesel vehicles. Other places—for example, Twin Falls, Idaho, and St. Paul, Minnesota—have concentrated on energy efficiency by installing compact fluorescent bulbs and updating heating systems. A third avenue for change is to commit to buying more renewable energy, which is what Ft. Collins, Colo-rado, did when it set a policy aiming to get 15 percent of the town's electricity from renewable sources by 2017.

"We don't take a punitive or apocalyptic approach," Michelle Wyman of ICLEI said. "The idea is to be hopeful, and give the mayors real tools. You have to offer a variety of tools, because every city is of a different size and has a different budget."

The ICLEI staffers are also flexible in how they discuss climate change. In some more reactionary communities, taking on global warming is not a vote-getter. And so the ICLEI staffers help local leaders frame the reforms as efforts to reduce air pollution, increase quality of life, or cut traffic congestion—bread-and-butter issues. The ICLEI team is also careful to promote the cost benefits of reforms by showing how an investment in energy efficiency today will lead to lower costs in the future.

"We don't talk about the politics of climate change, but say this is about improving air quality and city livability and shoring up your transportation infrastructure and, guess what, this also leads to climate protection," Wyman said. "That's what we ran into when we worked with Texas mayors. The first thing they said is, 'We don't want to talk about global warming down here. Can we talk about something else?' And I said, 'Sure. Let's talk about cleaner air.'"

That kind of emphasis on standard quality-of-life issues is especially helpful toward encouraging reforms in historically conservative places such as Roanoke.

"The mayor of Roanoke has been reluctant to sign on to something that says 'Kyoto,'" Mark McClain of the Roanoke Valley Cool Cities Campaign told us. "But Roanoke has already done a lot with [improving the efficiency of] their lighting, and they have already purchased some hybrids for their fleet. ... Even if they don't agree with us on global warming, they say 'I agree with what you're doing, because you're reducing oil dependence, and cutting air pollution, and reducing utility costs, and cutting back on coal mining in West Virginia.' ... The hardest thing is to change people's momentum. There's no silver bullet. There's no quick fix."

Pragmatism, Not Politics

The local climate campaigns' emphasis on results reveals an important characteristic about the movement for a local, green economy. The movement is, above all, a pragmatic one, more interested in real progress than in spiffy political theories.

"Our angle, the mayor's angle, is that this is very, very local," Sadhu Johnston, Commissioner of Chicago's Department of the Environment, told us, referring to the city's environmental agenda. Under the leadership of Mayor Richard Daley, Chicago has become one of the greenest cities in the country. The city is buying $5 million of solar panels; has distributed half a million compact fluorescent light bulbs to residents; and is encouraging sustainable building practices, among other initiatives. The city is cutting its carbon emission by one percent a year. "Sure, there are global benefits, but this is about increasing the quality of life for the people of Chicago. Ultimately, we emphasize that green technology and sustainability is about improving quality of life."

The desire for tangible change shows how hungry people are for solutions, and how eager they are to do something—anything—that will make a positive difference. If you give people a toolbox of reforms, they will gladly get right to work.

"It's that idea of the Show Me State," Missouri organizer Chris Hayday said. "It becomes, 'We can do this ourselves.' We don't have to rely on anyone else. We are self-sufficient. 'Think Globally, Act Locally' also works for conservatives."

That commitment to self-sufficiency is a vital part of the emerging green economy. It's proof of the potential that exists to create local and regional economies. The climate initiatives show that there is a wealth of knowledge and vision within communities to form a more sustainable and equitable economy.

By leading U.S. efforts to combat global warming, cities are showing that they don't need the federal government to set the course. Yes, federal and state participation is going to be key to making the big changes that have to occur in order to deal with global climate change. But until that participation happens, cities are relying on themselves. In the process, they are setting an inspiring example of grassroots progressive reform.

"This is just the power of people realizing that the world is changing very fast, and that we have to do something about it," said Tom Kelly, co-founder of Kyoto USA, an organization that has worked with ICLEI and the Sierra Club to promote local climate initiatives. "People are willing to do more, so you have to give them things to do. We want something practical that will have a multiplier effect. ... What we're doing is re-democratizing America. Let's roll up our sleeves and get to it."

CONVERSATION

Ben Namakin

The international movement to halt carbon emissions is being led in large part by young people, whose futures are jeopardized by the risk of climate chaos. Twenty-six-year-old Ben Namakin is one of those youth leaders. A resident of the Pacific island of Kiribati in Micronesia, Namakin has already witnessed some of the effects of climate change, as the aquifers on his island home suffer salt-water intrusion. In an effort to highlight the human costs of climate change, Namakin has traveled the world to talk about the environmental challenges his community faces. We sat down with him on his way to New York to participate in a climate justice summit coinciding with the United Nations General Assembly meeting in 2006.

Q: Tell us what life is like in Micronesia.

BN: Micronesia, or the Pacific region, is among the most peaceful places on earth. We are a very loving people, and we welcome every single non-Micronesian/Pacific Islander who makes the effort to come out and visit our small island nations. We may not have enough to offer, but we offer what we think is best to strangers who come to our islands. This is something unique about us—our love for others, our intact culture. Therefore we are proud to be Micronesians/Pacific Islanders.

Q: Why is climate change an important issue to you?

BN: From what I see in the Pacific Islands, we don't cause it, but we are among those who are at greatest risk from its negative impact. Fishing, tourism, and agriculture, which are the main economies in the Pacific, are severely affected by climate change.

This issue is very important to me because it does not affect only Micronesia and the Pacific Island nations; it's affecting the entire world. I feel very sad for every single child on this planet, for their future has begun to be destroyed.

I am pleasantly surprised that, these days, among the top news stories—aside from the crisis in the Middle East—are reports about storms, typhoons and flooding around the world. It is obvious to the international community that natural disasters are happening more frequently and intensely in most parts of the world. We in the small island nations suffer from it because we are the most vulnerable to it.

Q: What is climate change doing to small island nations like Micronesia?

BN: Climate change's effect on small island nations is the saddest part of the story of climate change. I can talk easily about this, because I can see it and feel it. We can start to see the problem with the rise in sea levels. All atoll islands, like Marshall Island, Kiribati, Tuvalu, outer islands in the FSM (Federated States of Micronesia), Cook Island, and others, will be the first to suffer this.

How sad to see your island sinking! Kiribati, where I grew up, is only two to three meters high. You can imagine what will happen in the next 25 years or so if no action is taken. My home, my history, will be gone.

Also, saltwater intrusion is a big problem for our small gardens and taro patches. During high tides, seawater slowly seeps into the thin wedge of the ground and affects the quality of the water in the taro patches and in our drinking-well water.

Though volcanic islands in Micronesia and the Pacific won't be underwater soon, still they will suffer coral bleaching that has occurred in some parts of the Pacific, which causes a drop in tourism. It also makes it more difficult for us to find the fish and marine organisms we need to survive. We are experiencing coastal erosion, and landslides that killed people in Micronesia. We just never thought of experiencing all these. We are the canaries in the coal mine.

Q: Some people say it's too late to do anything about climate change. What would you say to these people?

BN: No! It's not too late at all. We have different types of technology available that can shift us back from oil to the use of biofuel and other renewable energy sources. It's just a matter of our government leaders adopting the idea.

To my fellow youth in Micronesia and around the world—now that we understand that deforestation is also contributing to global warming—we have the knowledge and skills that we can use to build awareness within those who are not aware. It's not too late.

Also, each individual can make a difference. If our government leaders are not worrying, we don't have to wait. We can go ahead and do such things. For example, we can make sure that our air conditioner, car, refrigerator, lights, etc., are turned off when not in use; implement conservation projects; create public awareness; and much more. From doing just this, little by little of that percentage of the greenhouse gas emissions will slowly go down.

Each individual can make a difference. This is a long-term solution, but I want to remind us all that this will mean a lot for the next generation on this planet. We owe it to our children.

Crude Awakening

The Peak Oil Challenge

One of the most powerful ideas motivating people to advocate for a local, green economy is the concept of peak oil: the argument that at some point in the not-to-distant future, we are going to face acute petroleum scarcities that will demand a complete overhaul of our society and economy.

Defenders of the peak oil theory say you don't have to be a shrieking Cassandra to believe that the oil-and-gas age is coming to a close. You simply have to recognize the basic laws of science. As we all learned in elementary school, fossil fuels are not a renewable commodity. To wonder when the petroleum we depend on will start running out misses the point: We've been running out ever since the first commercial oil well was drilled in Pennsylvania in 1859.

The rules of geology mean that at some time, oil production will decline. Already, the petroleum firms are going to extreme lengths—pursuing deep-sea drilling, exploring for oil in tar sands and shale deposits, trying to wring the last drops from existing wells using high-powered steam—to eke out the globe's remaining oil. A common misconception is that society will face an energy crisis when we reach the last drop of oil. But the trouble will start long before that, as soon as we have used up more than half of all the oil that exists. Because after that point—the peak of global petroleum production—the laws of supply and demand will kick in, making oil increasingly expensive, so that it is no longer financially feasible for society to rely on it as we currently do.

When will we hit that peak? No one knows for sure. Many geologists and observers believe that we will hit the peak sometime in the next 10 years. Others say it's farther in the future. In any case, it's clear that anyone born in the last quarter of the 20th century will live to see a post-oil age.

For a time, natural gas may be able to fill the gap. But gas, like oil, is also held hostage to the rules of science. Geologists expect natural gas production to climax within a few decades of the petroleum peak. Clean energy sources such as wind, solar, and mini-hydro will be able to make up some of the difference. New research and development may uncover energy sources never even imagined. Yet the contribution of all these sources is limited. There is simply nothing as energy dense and as easily transportable as petroleum, no quick-fix alternative.

So what will Peak Oil mean for our lives? For one thing, cheap travel will become a thing of the past—goodbye, backpacking trips to Bali and cross-country road trips. Our transportation infrastructure is utterly dependent on oil. Forty percent of all the petroleum we consume goes into our personal cars and trucks, and another 20 percent is burned by our trains, semi trucks, and airplanes. As fuel costs rise, our freeways could crawl to a stop, our airports could be shuttered. The process of economic globalization, which is so dependent on inexpensive transport, will hit a brick wall.

Then things could get really ugly. Modern agriculture has become completely reliant on carbon energy inputs. The synthetic nitrogen fertilizers that are essential for high crop yields are a by-product of natural gas. Gasoline and diesel fuels power the combines that rumble through the grain fields. Countless kilowatts of electricity are burned up in the factories that process all the packaged goods that line the supermarket shelves. And then there's the gasoline required simply to get food to market. Without the help of fossil fuels, farming as we know it would collapse.

Authors such as Richard Heinberg (*The Party's Over*) and James Howard Kunstler (*The Long Emergency*) have sold thousands of books detailing the nightmare scenarios of a post-oil age. But, as these writes show, the future doesn't have to be gloom-and-doom; our fate remains in our own hands. If we can find a way to re-localize our economies—to make them more reliant on regionally available resources—then we may be able to avoid the apocalypse some fear.

If not? Then, as David Goodstein, another Peak Oil author, warns, we are in big trouble. Goodstein is no greenie; a former provost of California Polytechnic State University, he is firmly in the scientific mainstream. Goodstein worries that society is ill-prepared to manage the transition. In his book *Out of Gas*, he writes: "Civilization as we know it will not survive unless we can find a way to live without fossil fuels."

Sweden Declares
Independence
from Oil

To cope with the inevitable post-petroleum age—whether forced by the onset of peak oil or pushed by the increasingly fearful impacts of global climate change—some communities are already hard at work laying detailed plans for how to live without oil. The city council in Portland, Oregon, for example, has established a citizen-directed Peak Oil Task Force to examine how to reduce the city's fossil fuel use 50 percent by 2032. In the town of Willits, California, residents came together in 2004 to form Willits Economic LocaLization (or WELL) to survey the area's existing resources, and to determine how to make those resources meet the community's needs. The group has nine teams working on plans to build local, sustainable systems for the town's businesses, food, energy, water, healthcare, and culture, among other items. WELL's founding statement, which has been endorsed by the local Chamber of Commerce, calls on the town's residents "to learn about why and how we can reorganize our economy, and then add your ideas toward creating a place that is even more beautiful."

It's one thing for a small town like Willits (population 5,000) to chart a course for energy independence. But it's quite another task for an entire nation to do so. That's what's happening in Sweden, a large, sparsely populated country of some 9 million people. Sweden is already famous for its progressive public policies, including a strong social safety net, generous parental leave (for fathers as well as mothers), foreign aid largesse, and staunch geopolitical neutrality. Sweden is also a pioneer when it comes to environmental policy, ranking second (behind New Zealand) in Yale University's Global Environmental Performance Index. With its commitment to slash petroleum use, it appears that the country is bucking for first.

In December 2005, the Swedish government announced a pledge to be independent from oil by 2020. Environmentalists around the world greeted the announcement with excitement and astonishment, in part generated by the misunderstanding that the country's leaders were determined to be "oil-free" by that date. More accurately, the Swedes have committed to being "free from oil." That is, to still use oil, but to no longer be so reliant on petroleum that it handicaps the economy. The Swedish plan stands out as one of the most ambitious on the planet, especially when compared to countries such as the United States, where oil imports have increased steadily for more than 20 years.

"The most important thing about having ambitious and long-term goals is that you get clarity about the direction," Martina Krüger, an energy campaigner with Greenpeace Nordic, explained to us. "It is also giving the industry the right information about which investment makes sense. If you think that you need to reduce emissions by 10 percent and not more, you will choose different options than if you know that in the long term you have to reduce by 50 or 80 percent. The cost-benefit analyses make more sense."

The Swedish government's pledge was not the consequence of any focused campaign by grassroots green groups to demand such a pledge. Rather, according to Krüger, the move came about as the organic result of years of environmental organizing and consciousness-raising. Because environmental awareness in Sweden is widespread, there was no political risk for the government to make the pledge; it was right in line with public opinion. "Climate change is high on the agenda in Sweden," Krüger wrote to us in an email. "Greenpeace and other environmental groups have been educating the public and the media, and pushed the climate threat since the late 80s. So this is now leading to the public and media and government agreeing that climate change is a problem that we cannot ignore ... There is not a day going by without a major climate story in the news, be it print or TV."

As far back as 1980, Swedish citizens demonstrated their energy awareness by voting in favor of a national referendum that called for phasing out nuclear power and switching to renewable energy. The government announced a plan in 1997 to phase out all Sweden's nuclear reactors. But the reason half of Sweden's nuclear power plants are currently idle is a bit more sinister: A near-meltdown at the Forsmark Nuclear Power Plant in 2006 revealed a technical flaw that could be common to many other nuclear plants. The resulting publicity and plant closures fortified public sentiment that it was time for a major change in energy policy.

The Swedish example proves again that if the people lead, the leaders will follow. Public policy is an expression of the broader culture, and so the movement for a local green economy is in large part a cultural struggle, an effort to redefine social priorities. In Sweden, the culture's priorities have moved significantly in the direction of ecological sustainability.

The Swedish plan for reducing oil use is straightforward. The country hopes to make the biggest cuts by eliminating home heating oil, currently the number-one petroleum use. Government officials figure they can keep the country warm by burning pellet-size wood chips and other biomass that are the leftovers of Sweden's sizeable forestry industry. At the same time, they want to cut gasoline and diesel consumption by 40 to 50 percent, partially by increasing production of biofuels (again from Sweden's forests) and also through improving and modernizing the mass transit system. To help the industrial sector cut back on oil usage, the country believes it could get up to 30 percent of all its electricity from wind power.

To be sure, Sweden's crusade for oil independence enjoys special advantages, among them huge forest resources, impressive hydro power, and a low baseline—compared with some other industrial nations, Sweden doesn't use that much oil to begin with. Still, the commitment will demand significant changes in the lives of ordinary Swedes; some sacrifice will be involved. "There is no silver bullet," acknowledges Krüger.

The Swedish experience proves that the barriers to creating a sustainable economy are political and ideological—not technological. The tools exist for becoming independent from oil. The question, at least for those of us living in the United States, is whether we really want to get there. Because if Sweden can become free from oil, why can't we?

Harnessing the Saudi Arabia of Wind

The Rosebud Sioux Bring Renewable Energy to the Dakotas

"The wind is a blessing. Harnessing this gift can benefit our people, help reduce the impact of global warming, and provide economic restoration. I've never seen a situation quite like it. It's win-win-win."
— Patrick Spears, President, Intertribal COUP

As signs of global warming become increasingly dramatic, concerns are growing about how to arrive at the clean energy future. While governments and industry drag their feet on big picture solutions, some communities are taking action at the local level to develop their own response. In the Great Plains alone, wind energy potential could provide as much as 75 percent of the electricity needs of the continental United States. The Rosebud Sioux tribe of south-central South Dakota has taken a huge leap in harnessing this potential, constructing the first Native-owned wind turbine on reservation land. In so doing, the tribe has carved a path to self-sufficiency for the Lakota people and a route for others to follow.

So the story goes, an elder from a southwest Pueblo visiting the Rosebud Sioux tribe asked, "Say, all your animals up here kind of lean over to one side. Do they fall over when the wind stops?" The Sioux answered, "We don't know. It never stops blowing."

The constant wind through the Rosebud reservation carries ancestral voices of warriors like Sitting Bull and Crazy Horse, and the ancient traditions of a way of life that lived in harmony with nature. Roaming buffalo, big sky, and open prairies are still there, but they are only part of the picture. Casinos, ruthless winters with temperatures dipping 30 degrees below zero, wrenching poverty, a multitude of health concerns, and an average wind of 18 miles per hour are another part of the story.

For Native Americans living on the reservation, life is a daily challenge. Work is in short supply. Casinos, ranching, and the reservation school system provide the bulk of the available jobs, but most of them are low paying. The farming season is brief, which means healthful food is hard to come by or must be trucked in—an expensive luxury in a community where families often share cramped houses, as many as seven to a bedroom.

While South Dakota, the state that surrounds the Rosebud reservation, boasts the lowest unemployment rate in the United States at 3.6 percent (the U.S. average is 6 percent), on the reservation unemployment is a staggering 34 percent, according to official U.S. figures.[1] Tribal officials say the figure is closer to 80 percent. Tony Rogers, director of the Rosebud Sioux Tribal Utilities Commission (RSTUC), says mistrust and fear are at the heart of this discrepancy between U.S. and tribal unemployment figures. "Unemployment on the reservation is high, it's close to 90 percent, but the U.S. figures come from the census," Rogers said. "Our people don't always answer the door. Many are afraid of talking to U.S. government folks."

Sioux leaders say the pervasive poverty, fear and mistrust on the reservation goes back at least to 1944, when the U.S. government decided to dam the Missouri River, forcing most Plains Indians to relocate away from the river basin. The Flood Control Act authorized six dams to be built along the once-mighty Missouri River. The last dam was built in 1963. For the Great Plains tribes, the river was the source of life. They depended on it for fishing, hunting, and farming; all their subsistence needs centered on the river. When the dams went up, the Sioux members were relocated to less-hospitable lands with poor soil, poor water delivery, and harsher weather.

As Patrick Spears, president of Intertribal Council on Utility Policy (Intertribal COUP), a consortium of 12 Plains tribes working to bring lucrative, green power to reservations, told us: "The flooding of the Missouri River was the second most destructive blow to our basin people since the killing of the buffalo." He should know. Spears was 13 years old when the river where his grandfather took him hunting and fishing was flooded. In a curiously matter-of-fact tone, Spears said, "It's a serious emotional issue for us. We've been flooded, and moved. The animals had to move and we lost our best timberlands. … That was our land, our way of life … We were giving up our land for the public good, for the rest of America."

Most of the people moved to new, poorly planned communities on the reservation, but many moved away to find work. During the relocation process, the U.S. government tried to move Native peoples to more urban areas. The adjustment was tough: the Sioux struggled with challenges of racism and bigotry. Many languished in ghettos, unable to transition to the urban setting.

Unhappy in the cities, the Sioux returned to the reservation, despite the poverty and harsh conditions. According to Spears, "Over 90 percent live in a different community now: clustered housing, no jobs, no food, little garden space, no topsoil like we had on the river. It wasn't our choice to move, but we're doing the best with what remains. ... They come back, despite the poverty, because these are our homelands."

Another challenge facing the Sioux was the difficulty of providing its people with one of the basics of modern living: electricity. Some 5 percent of reservation inhabitants live without electricity, nearly quadruple the U.S. national percentage.[2]

In the 1990s, the federal housing officials introduced a well-intentioned energy-saving measure, retrofitting reservation homes with vapor-barriers that retained heat. But the barriers also trapped moisture inside, exacerbating a persistent mold problem that now affects 75 percent of reservation houses. Mushrooms have sprouted in the dark corners of some homes.

Throughout these travails, the wind kept blowing as always. Then one day something new could be heard on the breeze—the promise of a clean energy future, and a fresh hope for tribal prosperity and self-reliance. In the late 1980s, while searching for a low-cost energy source, the Rosebud Sioux learned that the wind on their reservation alone could potentially meet one-twelfth of U.S. energy needs. "Our jaws dropped," Robert Gough, secretary of Intertribal COUP told *Fortune Small Business*.[3]

Despite a lack of experience of any kind in wind technology or energy policy, the tribe determined to harness what people were calling "the Saudi Arabia of wind"—the tri-state area of North and South Dakota and Nebraska.

Without funding or experience with wind-energy technology, the tribe succeeded in erecting the first Native-owned and operated wind turbine on reservation land. Through hard work and tribal unity, the Rosebud Sioux have distinguished themselves as enterprising leaders on the razor edge of eco-energy technology. They have shown how communities can take advantage of their unique local resources to bolster their economic self-sufficiency.

By choosing a green solution that honors their spiritual beliefs of living in balance with nature, the Rosebud Sioux have also contributed to addressing the U.S. energy challenge and the threat of global warming. Their success has inspired tribes throughout the wind belt to take power into their own hands. Perhaps most importantly, the success of the turbine has restored some of the trust that the community lost during generations of abuse and oppression.

Dinosaurs and Windmills

It is difficult to overestimate the potential for wind energy. Wind power is the cleanest of all the energy resources, and like solar power, it will never disappear. It does not pollute or require painful extraction methods such as mountaintop removal for coal or superheating the earth for oil. Wind power does not even require dedicated land—cattle and buffalo can graze and farmers can till around relatively unobtrusive wind towers.

Wind energy is a multi-billion dollar industry in the United States, and is the fastest growing energy technology in the country. According to the American Wind Energy Association, worldwide wind-generating capacity increased by 27 percent in 2006, continuing a trend of speedy growth in recent years. More than 90 percent of that capacity was installed in the United States and Europe. In 2004 alone, installed capacity of windmills increased 36 percent—enough to light the city of Detroit. Yet despite the ready availability of wind and the industry's technological advances, less than 1 percent of total electricity in this country is currently generated from wind.

U.S. reliance on dirty electricity-generation methods—such as the burning of oil, gas, and coal—is often defended by industry proponents as a matter of cost savings. They point out that a switch would require a burdensome infrastructure investment in higher-priced, clean energy sources, such as wind and solar. But costs for wind energy are dropping with each investment. The definition of "cheaper" is called into question by about $6 billion a year of federal subsidies for dirty energy.[4]

The fossil fuel companies are quite satisfied with the *status quo*. According to the 2006 Fortune 500 ranking of America's Largest Corporations, six of the top ten earners were oil and energy corporations or auto makers, including ExxonMobil, General Motors, Chevron, Ford Motor Company, ConocoPhillips, and General Electric. Only the world's largest retailer, Wal-Mart (which came in at number two) broke the fossil-fuel industry's sweep of all top seven spots.

Yet as corporate profits have soared, so too have consumer energy costs. Between late January and early March 2007 alone, the price of gas at the pump increased 60 cents per gallon. Home heating costs surged an estimated 62 percent between 2003 and 2006, with more increases predicted.

While corporate executives blame war abroad and a lack of refinery capacity at home for increased oil costs, clearly those factors are not hampering shareholder's profits. Our government, rather than investing in a renewable infrastructure, is subsidizing major "external" costs of the fossil fuel model. For example, the expensive war in Iraq and major U.S. military bases throughout the Middle East are not reflected in the prices we pay at the gas pump. Not included in the cost of our home-heating oil or electricity is the price we pay for air pollution and its attendant health problems. Were such externalities factored into the true cost of our addiction to fossil fuels, the price of developing wind technology—already competitive—would be far lower than traditional sources of energy. And of course, wind and solar are clean, and do not contribute to global warming, which, as Hurricane Katrina proved, has huge costs. As Native American leader and environmental activist Winona LaDuke has written, the wind potential on Native American lands is "enough to reduce output from coal plants by 30 percent and reduce our electricity-based global warming pollution by 25 percent."[5]

The Power of Four Winds and a Little Soldier

For the Rosebud Sioux, wind power offered the possibility of creating self-sustaining economic assets, and also fit with the environmental values and cultural spirit of the tribe. Spears told us, "The four winds have great significance for Native peoples. For Lakota people, they are prominent in our ceremonies, and in recognition of the powers of the great spirit."

As Tony Rogers—and everyone involved with the wind turbine—will tell you, the inspiration for the turbine came from the late Alex "Little Soldier" Lunderman. Trained as a public defender, Lunderman was vice president of the Rosebud tribe, and twice served as president of the Rosebud Utilities Council, including between 1991-1993, when the utilities code was passed, green-lighting the turbine. "It was his vision. He believed that we could use modern technology and nature's resources in a way that was compatible with our values," Rogers said. "It was his vision that we could break down barriers. We ran into many, including from our own people."

Strange, perhaps, to those unfamiliar with the shared experiences of Native peoples, but the biggest barrier was internal. Despite a range of technological and financial obstacles, the highest hurdle was the pervasive fear and mistrust among the Sioux. Rogers told us, "When you lose a war, like the Indian wars, and the people are put on reservations—they were like prison camps, initially—well, it has taken generations for people to trust. Some thought maybe by creating our own energy we would be making trouble with the local electric cooperative, that maybe they would disconnect their service."

It required countless meetings and conversations to overcome tribal apprehensions. Even then, there was a long way to go. The tribe had no background in the field of wind energy. They had no energy economists, nor did they have the capital needed for the building of a wind turbine.

Despite never having worked in the industry, and not having a specialized degree, Tony Rogers was tasked with heading up the Rosebud Sioux Tribal Utilities Commission. To many non-Native peoples, it would seem natural for the tribe to look outside the reservation for leadership on the project. But the Rosebud had a commitment to investing in their own people. The decision to put someone with no expert knowledge in charge of such a project would be unthinkable to many, but it was part of a larger vision of tribal self-sufficiency.

Tribal attorney Bob Gough assisted in the development of the Rosebud Tribal Utility Commission, serving as the first acting director, a temporary position because he was not a tribal member. After seating the initial commission and raising funds, he stayed on as a consultant. Spears was also hired by the RSTUC to assist with the wind turbine project. Gough and Spears contracted with the NREL Wind Technology Center to provide assistance.

"If you had asked me in 1996 how to do this, I'd say, 'I'll get back to you,'" Rogers said with a laugh. "We had to teach ourselves. The elders told us to be patient, to bring back the knowledge and teach us. I had some good teachers. There was one good, good gentleman, Dale Osborne out of Denver; he just wanted to help us. That is how we learned."

Dale Osborne was indeed a well-qualified teacher. He is widely credited with leading the U.S. wind industry from its infancy in the 1980s, when it was just a handful of small firms, to its more robust and technologically advanced state today. After years as an industry executive, he now runs a small wind firm, DISGEN, which enabled him to work with the tribe and help them achieve their goals. As Osborne told an interviewer with the Department of Energy (DOE):

> Many Native Americans residing on reservations live in conditions that would not be tolerated anywhere else in the United States. My belief is that developing wind energy represents the greatest economic development opportunity ... for rural America in my lifetime. Indian reservations are as rural as it gets. So, if we can determine how to develop wind projects on tribal lands and create the maximum economic benefits for tribes and their members, then new jobs and revenues from sales of power will help tribes to manage other, almost overwhelming, issues in their lives.[6]

The tribe spent the next two years researching what was needed, and consulting among themselves how they would organize the momentous tasks before them. By 1995 they had installed an anemometer to collect wind data. Many couldn't even pronounce it then, much less understand its readings. Testing determined the most beneficial places on the reservation and the exact height that would capture the most continuous wind. As Rogers recalled, the anemometer was up for two years collecting data. "Eighteen miles per hour," he told us was the average. "That's a class five resource. Excellent!"

Financing would prove the most difficult task. The cost of erecting the turbine was more than $1 million and the tribe was insistent that control remain in their hands. "We had to find our own funding, which came from a few places. We got a cooperative grant, a 50-50 grant, we had to match it," Rogers said. "We had to show the Rural Utility Services that it was feasible overall. It was understood that this was a private project; they were used to working with electrical cooperatives. We had a lot of people to convince."

To gain the trust of possible investors, Rogers and his tribal colleagues were engaged in constant discussions. There were a dozen agencies to contend with, hundreds of bureaucratic hurdles and countless meetings.

In the end, the funding came from a variety of sources, including a grant from the DOE in 1998 and a loan from the U.S. Rural Utility Service. The tribe's first customer, Ellsworth Air Force Base, bought five years' worth of the turbine's capacity up front. This was enough to break ground on the project in 2001. But perhaps the most critical support came from a partnership with a one-year-old alternative energy company, NativeEnergy.

What NativeEnergy brought to the table was a bold marketing plan that would ensure tribal autonomy over the commercial turbine by raising $250,000 of the capital needed through the sale of "Green Tags," otherwise known as renewable energy credits. Intertribal COUP was also involved in the hunt for resources for the turbine. As Spears recalled, "We were looking at other Green Tags out there, and found NativeEnergy. We asked them, 'Are you Native?' They said, 'No, we meant "native" as in "homegrown".' We said, 'Good. We like that. How do you do that?'"

NativeEnergy markets Green Tags to the general public through its website, usually selling the carbon offsets in relatively small numbers. Financing the Rosebud project would require a larger effort. So NativeEnergy bought the remaining Green Tags up front, and then sold them to green-friendly companies, including Ben & Jerry's, Stonyfield Farms, and the Dave Matthews Band. What was in it for businesses such as Ben & Jerry's? As the company's natural resources manager Andrea Asch told *Fortune Small Business*, "It solidified what our brand stands for and why people buy our product. The investment comes back fourfold in recognition."[7]

It wasn't just the green enterprisers that stepped forward. Turner Network Television—which was filming a movie on Lakota lands called *Into the West*— also wanted to green its practices. TNT bought enough Green Tags to offset the CO_2 emissions for the movie's premiere, offsetting more than 175 tons of greenhouse gasses and highlighting the turbine project and the Green Tags while touting its own green practices. More than 1,000 individuals also purchased Green Tags that would ultimately finance the Rosebud turbine.

The plan was a win-win for all involved, as the funding enabled the project to make it to the finish line. In February 2005—after an eight-year process—a 190-foot, 750-kilowatt, commercial turbine was installed, enough to power 220 homes. It is named "Little Soldier" in honor of Alex Lunderman, who passed away in 1999, but whose vision of the tribe blending technology with ecological balance inspired the process.

The turbine supplies power to the Rosebud casino, but the windmill's output is more than the casino can use, so it is also connected to the local grid, run by Basin Electric Power Cooperative. Basin Electric, which services the Rosebud reservation and surrounding communities, was the country's most polluting utility, according to a recent report by a national coalition of environmental groups. Now, some of that dirty energy has been replaced with Rosebud's clean wind energy. Looking toward the future, over the next 25 years this single windmill will eliminate 50,000 tons of carbon dioxide, comparable to the emissions from 8,300 cars during that same time.[8]

What Are Green Tags?

Feeling bad about climate change, greenhouse gases, and your own ecological footprint? A single round-trip, cross-country flight emits 8,160 pounds of greenhouse gases into the atmosphere. The average U.S. household creates 35,000 pounds of CO_2 and other pollutants each year. Unlike power generated from fossil fuels, renewable energy sources such as wind or solar do not contribute to global warming. So every time conventional power is replaced with renewable resources anywhere in the world, the overall effect is to reduce global greenhouse gas emissions. But renewable energy is not yet available in every electricity market, leaving some consumers with no option other than traditional dirty energy to meet their needs. Green Tags offer a solution.

Green Tags are a way for purchasers with no access to clean energy to offset the climate change caused by their daily energy consumption. This is done by paying a little more—through a Green Tag purchase—for someone else to switch to clean energy where it is available. For every Green Tag purchased, a set amount of energy that would have come from a polluting source is instead generated from a renewable "green" source. Or the Green Tag can be used to erect new wind turbines, as Native Energy promotes, thus creating new sources of green energy for the future. It does not matter to the atmosphere where the Green Tags are purchased or where emissions are generated—therefore a Green Tag purchased in Oregon results in an overall reduction in emissions, even if the Green Tag is applied in South Dakota.

A Thousand Little Soldiers

If the Rosebud turbine story ended here, it would be a great victory. But the story continues, and the success grows. "What it has done—we've been able to show other tribes how we did this. We ended up owning this 100 percent," Rogers said.

In 2007, construction began on a 30-megawatt wind farm on the Rosebud reservation with as many as 18 "Little Soldiers." Two other nearby sites are being examined for similar wind farms. Rogers said, "We are talking to other wind developers, and we're hoping to produce 50 megawatts by 2010, right here on the Rosebud." As Spears explained, a single megawatt is enough to power 250 homes, or one average energy-intensive Wal-Mart.

The project has created several spin-offs for the Rosebud that will increase tribal income and job opportunities in the field of energy conservation. In cooperation with the local housing authority, Intertribal COUP, the Lakota Solar Enterprise, and other agencies and partners, a special single-family solar home has been built on the reservation. "Little Thunder," as it is called, is a model energy-efficiency project, with a real family living inside. Through a series of innovations—including solar heat panels, a wood burning stove, a family-sized windmill and 13 trees for windbreaks and shade—the goal, according to Rogers, is to "see if we can get the cost of energy to zero." If successful, this will be a new area of green enterprise for the tribe that will also improve conditions on the reservation. Yet the real excitement remains in the wind sector. As Spears told us: "We're well-positioned to develop this resource and provide power to the rest of the region. With help from our treaty partners, we can move it to urban areas where growth is anticipated. We can reduce the number of coal plants that are being planned. If we can do this, grandmother Earth gets the benefits, and all the ecosystems and humans too."

The damming of the Missouri river that forced tens of thousands of Native Americans to move was supposed to provide a lifetime of hydropower for the region, but that promise is evaporating. Persistent droughts and low water flows—perhaps related to climate change—have reduced electricity generation, requiring more electricity generated from fossil fuels. When the river is so low it can't produce energy, the regional power authority has a contract to buy fossil fuel energy from other utilities, usually at peak rates.

"We've been witnessing reduced water levels on the Missouri River for the last 15 years," Spears said. "Reduced water, global warming, and a seven-year drought. Some say it's a cycle. Yes, it's the beginning of a new cycle, but one like you've never seen before. Everything is happening at the wrong times. It's confusing to the animals when creation is out of balance."

The irony that climate change begets more climate change is not lost on Spears. "It's definitely a negative-feedback cycle," he said. "We've got to do something." And Intertribal COUP is positioning itself to do just that. They think the government should be buying wind power to replace (and to conserve) the diminishing water source, which they point out would also save money. The existing utility contracts, however, are set in place. But the Sioux believe that after all they have accomplished so far, there are ways to work around that obstacle too. "It is a cultural and spiritual issue for us, that is what drives us to pursue this despite the barriers," Spears said.

As the centerpiece of its tribal empowerment strategy, Intertribal COUP purchased a controlling interest in NativeEnergy in 2005, making it truly Native—as in Native-owned. The Green Tags will help support new reservation energy development, and it means the Native nations will not have to rely on federal government grants or loans in the future.

According to both Spears and Rogers, tribes throughout the United States are now examining wind energy. Tribes located in regions where wind generation is not a promising option are looking to adapt the model to fit their situations—for example, by exploring the potential of solar power.

Tribal self-sufficiency means more than just creating some long-overdue economic justice; it promises environmental justice too. Harnessing the wind could mean that the old ways of compromising values for an infusion of capital are gone. No more allowing corporations or the government to use tribal lands for uranium or coal mining, or industrial hog farming. And it isn't just tribes that are looking at the model. Municipal utility districts around the country are looking at wind energy and learning from the Rosebud experience. More than just a catchy lyric, it appears that for Native Americans, and perhaps for everyone else, the answer really is blowing in the wind.

What You Can Do

Plug Into the Movement

Global climate change is a huge challenge. But there are many small things you can do that can make a big difference in reducing our carbon emissions. Here's a list to start with.

• *Change your transportation habits.* Our over-reliance on the automobile is the main reason the United States is the worst producer of greenhouse gases. By using mass transit instead of a car, you can make your single greatest contribution to reducing global climate chaos. Walking and using a bike are not only better for the environment, they are much safer for you than traveling by car. If you must drive a car, use one that gets good gas mileage. The average car emits as much carbon dioxide as the average house. To compare gas mileage of various cars, go to www.fueleconomy.gov.

• *Take Action on the Home Front.* Switch your light bulbs to compact fluorescents. Then change out your refrigerator and washer and dryer to more efficient models. More energy-efficient appliances will cut down on your utility bill, and will eventually pay for themselves; visit www.energystar.gov to learn about energy-conserving appliances. Also, unplug appliances when not in use; if just 100,000 Americans would plug in their DVD players only when watching a movie, it could prevent 5,000 tons of carbon dioxide from being emitted. For portable electronics, use rechargeable batteries. The average battery requires 50 times as much energy to manufacture as it will eventually deliver.

• *Check Out Energy Action* (www.energyaction.net), a coalition of several dozen organizations from across the United States and Canada, led by youth to strengthen the student and youth clean-energy movement in North America.

• *Get Involved in a Local Energy Group.* Relocalize.net can put you in touch with local groups across the country that are developing a broad range of tactics to deal with the coming post-carbon era. Another group with good energy resources is www.resource-solutions.org.

• *Learn More.* A good resource on energy issues is the Rocky Mountain Institute (www.rmi.org), which promotes "the efficient and restorative use of resources to make the world secure, just, prosperous, and life-sustaining."

Section Five

The Freedom of Everyone to Be Enterprising

A quiet massacre has been taking place in America. In recent decades, thousands of locally owned enterprises have been knocked out of business by big-box retailers such as Wal-Mart, Target, Price Club, and Home Depot. Because of their size, these large corporations are able to source their products cheaply—often in places like China, where workers' rights are limited and wages are low—and they can sell at prices that undercut the mom-and-pop sector. Across the country, the impact can be seen in the empty store-fronts along our Main Streets.

Academic studies have shown that areas with a higher percentage of big-box stores suffer from decreased economic prosperity and other social ills. For example, an October 2004 study of Chicago's north-side neighborhood of Andersonville found that locally owned businesses generated 70 percent more local economic benefit per square foot than chain stores.[1] A 2006 paper in the *American Journal of Agricultural Economics* revealed that counties with a Wal-Mart store, when compared to those without, showed decreases in "social capital": Voter turnout was lower, civic participation suffered, and there were fewer "social capital generating" organizations such as churches, nonprofit groups, business associations, and political organizations.[2] A study of Wal-Mart's expansion in Southern California found that Wal-Mart's lower wage scales would reduce the income of grocery workers by up to $1.4 billion per year.[3] What's good for one company's bottom line may be bad for society at large.

The business model of the big-box retailers is also environmentally harmful. The suburban sprawl of the giant stores turns green fields into parking lots and contributes to the overconsumption of resources, resulting in landfill problems. Stacy Mitchell, author of the authoritative *Big Box Swindle*, told us that the sprawl malls seduce people into bad environmental behavior. "Two big issues have to do with transportation: the shipping of the products and the consumers driving long distances due to the suburban location of the large stores with their huge parking lots. The very location of the stores out of town where people must drive to reach them creates a huge amount of pollution. In contrast, a local retailer is structurally more compatible with a lessened carbon footprint."

There is, however, another way of doing business. The big-box style of low prices at any environmental or social cost is starting to encounter competition from grassroots entrepreneurs, who are developing a more thoughtful way of managing the economy. Sometimes called the "triple bottom line," this more conscience-led capitalism seeks to synergize environmental restoration, social justice, and financial sustainability. Triple-bottom-line management recognizes that yes, businesses need to make a profit, but those profits should not come at the expense of people or the planet. Put another way, the triple-bottom-line model is all about balancing economy, equity, and ecology.

This more comprehensive measure of business success—injecting democracy into the marketplace—is spreading. Stacy Mitchell documents a movement that is growing rapidly. She told us, "Between when I started to work on this and now, the level of activity has exploded. I am finding it hard to keep track of all the activity going on around the country." Another indicator of success is the growth of the Co-Op America Business Network, which now includes more than 3,000 enterprises—including Burt's Bees, ClifBar, Patagonia, and Working Assets—committed to "using business as a tool for social change."

In this section, we tell the stories of such businesses. Fetzer Vineyards and Terra-Cycle are proving that you can make handsome profits by saving nature rather than destroying it. They are having no trouble attracting customers and investment capital to their earth-friendly products and practices. We also look at successful worker-owned cooperatives, whose enthusiastic employees are showing how weaving democratic principles into the workplace makes for a more productive business.

Countering the power of large corporations is not just happening one enterprise at a time. Independent merchants, recognizing strength in numbers, are coming together to encourage support for local stores. The Vest Pocket Business Coalition of Salt Lake City, whose story we share, is just one of the many local business alliances standing up to the large corporate retailers that have been grabbing market share. The Coalition was so successful in Salt Lake City that it expanded statewide, in a state not known for progressive politics.

We are at a tipping point. People are learning to synergize the green of money and the green of nature to strengthen both. As Tom Szaky, the CEO of Terra-cycle, told us: "I didn't start my company to save the environment. I started it to prove you could make money saving the environment."

Putting Mom and Pop First

Utah Promotes Local Business and Town Character

"It comes down to living in a place, everyone sharing the same things in common, the air, the water, the local culture. To have a real sense of community we must take care of each other on some level, and value what makes each place unique."

—Gavin Noyes, Director, Local First Utah

With the invasion of "big box" chain retailers, everywhere is looking a lot like everywhere else. As local businesses struggle to compete against deep-pocketed retail corporations and unfair government subsidies to major chain stores, local economies are being hollowed out, and Main Streets once filled with quirky independent merchants now look like Anytown, USA. Some say we're being "chained to death." Rather than launch yet another anti-chain campaign, local businesses in Utah decided to demonstrate the power of cooperation. Under the banner of "buy local first," a small group of economic leaders banded together to redefine how business is done across the state. In just over a year, Local First Utah grew to include more than 800 local retailers, each with its own success story. Together they are telling the tale of how powerful, rich and vibrant a locally based economy can be.

As the horrific events of September 11, 2001 unfolded, a long, cold shadow was cast across a nation bound in helpless disbelief. Stricken with grief and grappling for the comfort of family, neighbors, colleagues and friends, people of all walks of life instinctively sought the solace of their community—however defined—in an attempt to absorb, explain and comprehend the magnitude of a world forever changed. At the heart of it was a driving need to be in the presence of like-minded souls, perhaps for no other reason than to reaffirm our own common humanity.

Across the United States, regular television programming was suspended, school classes were cancelled, local and national sporting events were postponed, and countless numbers of restaurants, shops and businesses closed their doors for the day as people made their way to the places and faces that best connected them to this humanity.

Throughout that nightmarish day, a quaint and homey bookstore on a quiet residential corner in Salt Lake City drew a steady and spontaneous gathering of shell-shocked patrons, neighbors and friends from across the city, as if it were projecting a silent beacon of consolation. They arrived at The King's English bookstore knowing that inside they would find what they were looking for. Perhaps it seems an unlikely gathering spot, but those compelled to its doors found some kind of solace in the shop's cushy chairs, the "confessional bench," and the not-so-orderly stacks of books lining the steps, the counters and the floors. They took comfort in the coziness of the nooks and crannies that give the place character. They took comfort in the warm and friendly faces they knew from regular visits, through years of lively discussions and laughter. And they took comfort knowing that the store's owner, Betsy Burton and her shop partner Barbara Hoagland, would, of course, be serving up tea and sympathy.

"We opened the store and people just kept showing up," Burton remembers. "They needed to talk. It was one of the busiest days we ever had, as busy as Harry Potter day. Not so much for book sales, but there was this need for sharing with the community that brought folks in."

It's safe to assume that during the traumatic hours of September 11, the Salt Lake City Borders did not serve the same function. Because whereas Borders just sells books, The King's English—like millions of other locally owned bookstores, cafes, newsstands, delis, and barber shops—offers something else: kinship. When it comes to the invisible strands that knit a community together, local business ownership makes a difference. Unfortunately, recent decades have witnessed an assault on many local businesses as giant chains have steadily snatched away their customers. If you don't factor in tax breaks and other government incentives paid to national retailers, the chains appear to offer lower prices, but at a cost that's also measured out in community cohesiveness. A place like The King's English, after all, is more than a bookstore; it's also a neighborhood center.

But there is a backlash brewing to the chaining of America. In an effort to promote the importance of independent businesses for the health of local economy and the preservation of regional flavor, many cities and towns are encouraging their residents to shop at local stores. One such effort is occurring in Utah, where an extraordinarily successful organization, Local First Utah, has formed to make the connection between patronizing local businesses and fostering a vibrant economy. With its slogan, "Buy Close By—Preserve Community," the Utah network is showing how vital local businesses are to our quality of life. In the process, they are fostering a model of economic of development that is at once utterly traditional and, in the 21st century economy, strikingly unorthodox.

A Ghost Town in the Making

Growing up, Burton had wanted to be a writer, which was one of the reasons why she opened The King's English, in 1977. "I thought it would be fun to write in the back and come out when the bell tinkled," Burton fondly recalled. "But the book business is complicated, and took so much time. And I enjoyed it."

Burton grew up in Utah. As a young girl not of the Mormon faith, life in a state where the Church of Latter-Day Saints shapes culture seemed, well, dull. Despite the grandiose natural beauty of Utah—the northern salt flats and mountainous winter resorts of the west, Monument Valley and the red rock canyons of the southern and eastern region—the young Burton couldn't wait to leave in search of bright lights and excitement.

But the mountains drew her back, and she soon discovered that for her it would always be home. "I love this place, it's so beautiful for one thing, but it's so anchored in community, so grounded in this sense of place. I feel wonderfully evolved into a community geek. I mean, what kind of existence would it be without community?"

That philosophy guides the way Burton does business. "I learned quickly that it's the same with customers," Burton told us. "You can't be exclusive, thinking Mormons or non-Mormons, liberals or conservatives. It's all us—the community—that's how it is. Over time customers become dear friends, you look forward to seeing them and vice-versa. It's not about selling books, it's about matching books and people. You get to know what they read, and can recommend books they will like, not just the ones you like. It's a relationship, not a chain store."

And for years that was exactly how it was, for The King's English and for the thousands of other local businesses that served the state—served the community. By the mid-1990s, however, something had changed. Utah was suddenly met with a "big box" invasion of chain retailers that seemed to arrive in swarms.

"The idea of big was really catching the public's imagination at that time, and the government was underwriting it," Burton said. "It made it impossible to compete."

As a bookseller, the chain store competition for The King's English came down to two mega-retail corporations, Barnes & Noble and Borders. Together, these two booksellers account for approximately one-half of all books sold nationwide. Their predatory practices are common among chain retailers pushing their way into new neighborhoods with a mind to crush the local competition. As Burton said, "They come in and immediately discount their books. They are so large, they can afford to discount deeply for a while to lure customers away from independent local stores. By the time they stop discounting, the public has already bought in, and the small shops are gone."

But it wasn't just the advantage of size that had Burton and a handful of her fellow small business owners angry—it was that the government, using their taxes, was helping transnational corporations to put the smaller shops out of business. For example, local governments will often offer chain stores millions of dollars in property tax rebates. Another method by which local governments attract major retailers is by helping to secure federal loans to underwrite the building of a new mall for giant "anchor stores"—malls that take away foot traffic from the independent stores often located in older downtowns. Sometimes cities will pay for part of the infrastructure improvements—such as sewer line extensions or parking lot construction—necessary to support the warehouse retailers.

Regardless of the specific incentive, city and state governments have become accomplices in helping big box stores to swallow local businesses. With public dollars going to help out-of-state corporations rather than locally owned shops, small retailers often collapse under the pressure. To prove the point, over just a couple of years, the number of independent bookstores in Salt Lake City dropped from 11 to only two.

Fearful of going out of business, Betsy Burton and a few other small business owners decided to take action. They were faced with a choice. They could either succumb to the power of the big box onslaught, or do what no one expected: stop seeing each other as the competition, and begin working together, marketing together, and develop a new approach—together.

Minding Their Own Business

"I was mad," Burton said. "We all were mad, because the government was underwriting the incursion in the marketplace, and using our local tax dollars to do it." The "we" was a rag-tag team of seven up-in-arms neighborhood retailers that came together in January 1999 to preserve the uniqueness and vitality of community-oriented businesses. They called themselves the Vest Pocket Business Coalition, and established as their mission—not just battling chain retailers—but also generating awareness of the contributions neighborhood businesses provide the community.

The Vest Pocket members talked to other business owners, many of whom were surprised to learn of the government's role in handing over the hometown advantage to big business. They also met with the city's development planners. "We told them they needed to stop abusing small businesses in this way," Burton said. "They told us they'd think about it."

Wreckonomics: The Local Cost of Doing Big Business

Unlike chain retailers, where local money leaves the community so fast it's like it was being sucked up to the mother ship (which, in a way, it is), local merchants are directly tied to our well-being. They enrich local culture, make contributions to local charities, bank and shop locally, and reinvest money in the community. And yet, corporate hype and government investment in big business have distorted this reality.

Here are a few of the ways in which our tax dollars support big business in hometown USA.

- Nearly all U.S. business subsidies go to non-local companies: $50 billion each year at the state and local levels, and another $63 billion from the federal government.

- In one Iowa study, between 1983 and 1996, chain stores (including Wal-Mart) increased sales by 42 percent. During that same period, overall retail sales in Iowa plummeted in small towns: by 17 percent in towns with 2,500-5,000 residents, by 30 percent in towns with 1,000-2,000 residents, and by 40 percent in towns with fewer than 1,000 residents.

- The St. Petersburg Times has noted that in Florida annual incentives paid to big business "could pay for nearly 11,000 new teachers, pre-kindergarten classes for 150,000 4-year-olds, and all of next year's tuition increase for more than 250,000 university students."

- According to Good Jobs First, in the last decade, Wal-Mart, the richest retailer in the world, received more than $1 billion in state and local government support in 244 separate deals. Some communities paid as much as $19-46 million attempting to lure the company to set up a distribution center in their locale.

- Maintaining corporate factories is another big sink for tax dollars that works on the same notion that bigger business is better for local communities. When the Maytag factory in Galesburg, Illinois threatened to leave for Mexico, $8.6 million in local sales tax and state grants was used to retrofit the plant, in addition to other tax breaks given to Maytag. Not long after the money was gone, so too was Maytag.

Excerpted from Michael H. Shuman, The Small-Mart Revolution: How Local Businesses Are Beating the Global Competition (San Francisco: Berrett-Koehler Publishers, 2006) www.smallmart.org

When the newly formed Vest Pocket Business Coalition held a meeting, more than 60 businesses came. They prioritized their complaints. "That's all we had then, just complaints," remembers Burton. They broke into committees to address the group's collective priorities, and got to work.

As one of its first activities, the group hosted a publicly televised mayoral debate on the issue of independent business preservation and government incentives for out-of-state corporation. The debate illustrated the level of support all the candidates gave to the idea of fostering local enterprises. It was an idea that resonated with the area's Mormons, whose church was founded on principles of self-reliance, as well as with other Utahns, who are proud of their history as a pioneer state. Then-mayoral candidate Rocky Anderson came out as an especially strong supporter of local merchants. As Burton told us, "Rocky is community minded, and was responsive to our message."

Once elected, Mayor Anderson, or just Rocky, as he is affectionately called by many SLC residents, was more than just talk. He worked with the Vest Pocket entrepreneurs to develop the Business Advisory Committee, which provides feedback to the mayor and the Department of Economic and Community Development around issues concerning local businesses. Prior to that, it seemed only the transnational corporations had a say in how business development in Salt Lake City was planned. Now, longtime independent businesses also had a voice within city government.

Several Vest Pocket members were appointed to the committee, and among other things, their presence allowed the local business community to know about new chain store development in time to take action. "By the time there is a public hearing, it's already too late, it's already underway," Burton said. "As part of the committee, we were able to hear about development in time to have input."

Working closely with local officials, it was clear that the group could be more effective if it could make a compelling case for putting local business first. Some Vest Pocket members connected with a national non-profit organization, the Institute for Local Self Reliance (ILSR), a group that provides technical assistance and information on environmentally sound development strategies. Stacy Mitchell, author and senior researcher at the ILSR had just written a book, "The Big Box Swindle," which put the Salt Lake efforts into a broader context, and provided the hard facts to support the gut feelings the community had about the big business takeover. "That book became our bible," Burton said.

As Stacy Mitchell told us, "At the gut level, business owners understand the issues, but how do you sell it to officials? Making the case as an economic issue and using real data, facts and figures, that's where it makes sense to officials and to the public too. So we [at ILSR] have an online clearinghouse of studies for local groups to use."

As Burton said, "When we showed these [ILSR] reports to the city managers, they could see that what we were saying was true—chain stores are bleeding money from the city. We were on the right track already, the reports just gave us more leverage."

In 2000, the Vest Pocket coalition found its voice in city politics when it discovered other allies, including the Sierra Club's Utah chapter and the local Audubon chapter, who were keen to halt development of a super-mall proposed near the airport. The planned mall would not only harm local businesses, it was also bad for the open spaces and habitat near the airport. Together, the merchants and their environmentalist allies stopped the airport mall—one of two proposed malls that threatened to ruin the downtown retail business community by redirecting traffic away from the walkable local business center. The other mall is being built.

Mayor Anderson was supportive of the Vest Pocket agenda, and defended the decision to halt at least one of the malls as a matter of local pride, stating that Salt Lake "has a charm and unique identity worth protecting." That kind of appeal to special regional flavor was a key part of the Vest Pocket campaign to halt the malls. For the fact is that chain stores can never be the keepers of local character; their very nature is to serve the world in a one-size-fits-all monoculture kind of way. Local businesses provide the charm and help distinguish one city from another. Having made that argument convincingly in

The Results Are In
Spending Dollars Locally = More Local Dollars

Is it fair to hand out tax dollars to big businesses that will use them to put local merchants out of business? Does it even make sense? A number of studies prove that money spent at local merchants generate more than three times the return to the local economy as money spent at a national chain.

Why? Local business owners typically hire other local businesses for support services. Chain retailers usually contract with national firms for services such as banking, marketing, accounting, legal support, and design. Profits, too, are spent locally when the owners live in the same community in which they do business, and local merchants are far more likely to support local charities. Jobs are better locally too: local businesses are more likely to pay living wages and to offer benefits and flexible work arrangements. Local stores are more likely to provide good customer service, such as stocking specially requested items and providing tailored services. Local businesses also help provide a sense of community, and engage customers beyond asking, "paper or plastic?"

the state's biggest city—convincing enough to stop a giant development—the Vest Pocket merchants were prepared to take their campaign beyond Salt Lake City.

Local Goes Statewide

By 2002, Vest Pocket included more than 200 businesses. The group produced and distributed 50,000 colorful maps—underwritten by a local bank with a $10,000 grant—promoting local businesses in partnership with the Convention and Visitor's Bureau, just in time for the Winter Olympic games. Things were moving ahead. However, as a vehicle for change, Vest Pocket did have some limitations. In terms of advocacy and addressing unfair regulations, and being the cage-rattlers against chain stores, it was great. But there was more that some in the group wanted to do.

As Burton told us, "We felt that we needed to have a community outreach component with an educational approach, and to do some good things for the entire state, to help blighted business districts get on their feet. There were three of us that decided we wanted to start something new, that would work with Vest Pocket, but that had a different mission."

Betsy Burton, Kinde Nebeker and David Nimkin spent the next year figuring out the plan, and applying for non-profit status. They conferred with BALLE, the Business Alliance for Local Living Economies, a membership-based national network that supports local business and promotes the "triple bottom line"—a concept that says profit should not come at the expense of people or the planet. BALLE, a fast-growing network, hopes to build chapters in every city across the country, aspiring to replace Chambers of Commerce as the place where local businesses can have their voice heard above the din of chains, parent companies and other big business forces that dominate many Chambers these days.

BALLE, and other networks like the American Independent Booksellers Association (AMIBA), joined the Institute for Local Self Reliance in providing the Utah group with free resources and assistance. BALLE offered the opportunity to network with hundreds of locally minded business owners willing to share their ideas and successes, and an eager ear to hear what was happening in Utah. The energy was increasingly positive. The Vest Pocket merchants were evolving from a group focused on how to survive the chains, to an organization centered on how to thrive beyond the chains.

The independent booksellers' association had already pioneered the idea that in the face of competition from chain booksellers—with their huge advertising budgets, subsidies, and their ability to sometimes discount below cost—independent booksellers could work together. Rather than competing among each other, the independent booksellers could combine forces and compete together against the chains, as a kind of united front. In cities across the country, AMIBA chapters had been using a collective marketing campaign to promote the notion of buying books from local vendors. The collective marketing concept, once thought crazy by independent booksellers, has worked, and helped keep locals competitive.

In July 2005, Local First Utah was born. Burton told us, "We felt strongly that each locally owned Local First network should be grassroots, that they should have to be a part of their own community or it wouldn't feel local to people. That's important."

Taking the campaign statewide was a natural step. The Local First Utah organizers felt that the concept would resonate with the state's residents, and connect with their pride of place. Gavin Noyes, who became Local First Utah's director in 2006, put it this way: "We are lucky in a lot of ways because we are working on an issue that has appeal in the LDS [Latter-day Saints] faith, which was founded on self-reliance. A lot of church culture has a basis in trying to develop a local economy. Good evidence of this is the banning of cigarettes, coffee, etc., which was done in part to cut sales leakage to the state. In part it was an attempt to localize the economy. When the pioneers came out here, they were also building a localized economy. People have been forgetting that, but now they are coming back around. So we're lucky—the notion has broad appeal in all areas of the state. People see the value."

For Local First Utah, success would rely on having an outreach strategy that matched Utah's culture: conservative, business-minded and cautious. "This is a very unique community—a conservative community, so when we decided to be statewide, we had to adapt some things," Burton said. "As much as many of us are behind 'going green,' outside of Salt Lake City, 'environmentalism' is a bad word. We thought we'd be more effective centered on business. ... Instead of working with an ardent group of businesses the way most of these networks begin, we wanted to pull in others from other parts of state, and that just takes time."

But there was nothing slow or soft about the organization's kick-off. It was, well, a party. In November 2005 more than 300 businesses had already signed on to the campaign for the inaugural "Buy Local Week," which enjoyed huge media coverage and participation from the community, local officials and businesses across Utah.

A kick-off press conference was held at the local and organic Spotted Dog Creamery. Spotted Dog owner and chef, John Winders, recalled the launch event: "There was a ton of media coverage, the mayor came, a bunch of local farmers and local producers were here for it, local artists, authors. We were thrilled to be a part of it, and to serve up some tasty local ice cream."

Mayor Anderson proclaimed Buy Local Week an official city initiative, and pledged $20,000 in support of the first year's budget for the work. Speaking on behalf of the Governor's Office of Economic Development, Martin Frey said at the kick off event: "You don't find our culture in some of the national chains. When our local communities prosper, everyone in the state prospers." The local morning news show highlighted the week by featuring a different Local First business each day, and not just in Salt Lake City, but also in more-conservative Provo and other locales. For nine days, local businesses offered special discounts for people who said, "I buy local first." The campaign was an overwhelming a success.

International Jazz, Local Flavor

For its next venture, Local First Utah decided to make the link between promoting tourism and the uniqueness of independent businesses by hooking up with Salt Lake City's annual International Jazz Festival, which brings 50,000 visitors to town. Local First decided to kick off an annual "Independents Week" timed for the week before the festival, holding a farmers' market and promoting a week of community events. Local First business owners promoted the festival, hanging signs in their shops, playing jazz music and giving away tickets to the festival. The festival promoters loved it, and so did the local businesses, who got spots in the festival's promotional materials, radio ads and concert programs.

From a tourist perspective, enjoying local flavor and regional character enhances the travel experience in a way eating at KFC or shopping at Pottery Barn would not. Tourists want to buy local gifts as mementos and eat at local restaurants, meet the shop owners and remember the occasion as something special and different. At least, Festival revelers seemed to feel that way, as the revenues from local merchants during Jazz week proved. "It made running the campaign so much easier to tie in with an existing attraction, and it really hit home that this was all about being part of a community, " Burton said. The Jazz Festival experience marked Local First's second strong success.

The positive message of Local First Utah has been a key factor in the group's success. It's not anti-big business, it's not even strictly "buy local"—it's local first. "It's not just about the economy, how strong it is. It's about values, and it's about choice," Local First Director Noyes said. "We want folks to realize they have choices, and to understand what decisions they are making in the marketplace. No one is saying you shouldn't shop at Wal-Mart. We're just pointing out the value that comes from having choices and knowing what your choices really are."

That point has been especially important outside of Salt Lake City. Ranchers Jamie and Linda Gillmor are one example of how the local first message plays in the state's communities. The Gillmors own and operate Morgan Valley Lamb, a sort of nomadic operation, in which the sheep spend summers in the high mountains of Northern Utah, and then enjoy winter pasture in the west desert. The Gillmors give nothing but the best to these contented grazers, no hormones or antibiotics found on commercial feedlots.

Jamie Gillmor is a third generation sheep farmer in a state that produces some of the highest quality lamb in the world. As Gillmor told us, "We ran

Nothing is Tastier Than a Spotted Dog
(Creamery, That Is)

Perhaps it's the lack of vices such as alcohol, coffee, and cigarettes, but Utah is number one in the nation when it comes to having a sweet tooth. And Utahns do love their ice cream. Chef John Winders of the Spotted Dog Creamery and his real spotted dog, Hopper, are in business to bring Utahns the best ice cream by using the organic and farm-fresh local ingredients, and giving back to the community in a variety of ways. Says Chef Winders:

Local is about quality: "Ice cream is big business. I'm competing with Häagen Dazs and Ben & Jerry's, which is now owned by the Unilever Corporation. We can't exactly compete with them on price, but we can on taste. We wanted to use real stuff, real peaches from the farmers market, fresh local dairy. The local angle was important to us. There's a real message there. And you can taste it—the closer to the cow, the better the ice cream. When you ship all over the world, the fresh ingredients lose something. Producing ice cream in small batches makes a taste difference too. We're able to try some local flavors that might not fly elsewhere, like making goat's milk ice cream."

Local is about giving back: "The kids love Hopper, we do a lot of events for local charities, particularly around pet adoption. Hopper is a rescued dog. We do lots of donations for a variety of local charities. It costs money, but then again it doesn't—this is our community, I want to support it. We're not saving the world, but you gotta give something back."

Local is about community: "It makes sense to be green, to be conscious of other needs besides profit. Transporting ice cream across the country in refrigeration units doesn't make sense. Getting it locally makes it taste better, sure, but it also uses less energy, helps preserve open space, creates local jobs, local wealth. The community supports buy local. In fact, I'd be out of business without the buy local angle. Local writers, chefs, everyone is doing it together, supporting each other. Most of it is word of mouth. Buy local makes sense, and it's not just about making a profit, it's about everybody feeling good doing the right thing."

Visit the Spotted Dog: www.spotteddogcreamery.com

a traditional commercial sheep operation for years," selling live sheep on the commodities market, where prices are determined not on quality, but by a variety of market factors outside of a farmer's control. "We got tired of the highs and lows of the commodity market," Jamie said. Most of their sheep were sold to processing centers in places like California, which then resold the "value-added" lamb meat to East Coast markets, and even back to Utah; though as Jamie told us, "most of the lamb eaten in Utah comes from New Zealand and Australia." Part of the global free-trade system involves the puzzling phenomenon of trading like-products between countries, and the movement of goods back and forth across the country, in the name of "efficiency."

But Utahns appreciate quality, which is what Morgan Valley Lamb is all about. A few years ago the Gillmors decided to capitalize on that notion and gave up the commodities game for a local approach based on a handshake business approach. "We started marketing to high-end chefs who know their customers appreciate high-quality cuts and value local sourcing. We have some of the finest restaurants in the world right here in Utah, and they love dealing with us. We took samples to regional grocers, and just began knocking on doors." The Gillmors also started marketing directly to the public at farmers markets in Park City and Salt Lake City, partnering with butchers, grocers and other businesses. "We do cooperative marketing. Like at the markets, we set up next to the marinade guy. We trade recipes with other businesses, chefs and our customers. We work with the wool growers association. At the State Fair, we set up a booth with Peggy Whiting who has a killer teriyaki sauce, and sold teriyaki lamb sandwiches, and pulled lamb shoulder with sauce. Folks went crazy for it. And it was fun."

No longer interested in selling their product as a "primary good," the Gillmors are committed to seeing what can happen when products are processed and developed locally, rather using than the system of cross country transport, refrigeration, and emphasis on quantity over quality. "I'd like to see the value added here in the state, and locally, and being part of something like Local First Utah is an important part of it. We have such a high quality product—that gets lost in the international system."

Jamie and Linda Gillmor are committed to using Utah products in their business. They know that without the local angle, they'd be back to selling sheep on the turbulent commodities market, with no control over their future or fortunes. With a voice that is low and a bit gravely, Jamie Gillmor laughs: "If anyone told me a few years ago we'd be doing this, I'd never have believed it. Linda is on the board of Local First Utah now. We love it, love the contact with the customers, and if something is wrong, they know they can just call me directly. They are not dealing with some bureaucracy. The buck stops right here with Linda and me."

There are plenty of businesses statewide that agree with Linda and Jamie Gillmor. Membership in Local First Utah continues to grow, with over 800 businesses from across the state signing up during the group's first two years.

And you can't argue with results. Local First Utah analyzed the 2005 holiday shopping season among members, and pitted those results against the national sales figures. As Noyes reported, "The locals who really tied themselves into the branding of Local First had a phenomenal year. Lots of them had record sales. One shoe shop salesman who has been in business for 57 years had his top sales year of all time." Those that did the most outreach, the ones who talked about the buy local work to their customers and posted the Local First Utah branding materials in their shop windows and on their websites, reported the effort was well worth it.

Local First Utah plans to continue growing, but they want to do things differently than traditional business by building up businesses in low-income communities. Of several programs started around the state, one project underway in Salt Lake City is particularly ambitious for a state not known for its multiculturalism. Local First Utah is working with community leaders and entrepreneurs in West Salt Lake—a neighborhood that is 60 percent Hispanic, and home to many Polynesian-Americans, Asian-Americans and African-Americans—to help strengthen the area's business sector by exporting the community's flavor to the rest of the city and state.

"We need to treat each community differently to bring about the changes we think are possible," Noyes said. "We want opportunity developed from the inside, to connect the community better with the businesses and help the businesses serve the community better. We also want to help draw in new folks to this part of town, to let the rest of Utah experience the vitality and unique culture that is there. Currently no one knows how rich an experience it can be."

Local First Utah has seen the future, and it's all about encouraging community. "Even in an area as beautiful as Salt Lake, which is so amazingly beautiful, a lot of people can look around here and not see anything of value, not treat it with value," Noyes said. "Part of our job is to help people to take those values and help grow the things in their communities that they love: local restaurants, preserving natural spaces, whatever people's passions are in their own communities."

CONVERSATION

Rocky Anderson

Ross C. "Rocky" Anderson is the mayor of Salt Lake City (SLC). He received a B.S. degree from the University of Utah and obtained his law degree from George Washington University. For twenty-one years, he worked as an attorney specializing in civil litigation. He also worked as a community volunteer, serving on the boards of several community-based nonprofit organizations. Anderson took office as Salt Lake City's mayor on January 3, 2000. He has initiated many innovative green policies in his city, and has been a leader in getting other city governments to adopt sustainability policies. He has also been a prominent voice calling for the impeachment of President George W. Bush.

Q: Given that our book is titled Building the Green Economy, what are the green accomplishments in Salt Lake City you are most proud of?

RA: We focus on sustainability in everything we do. In our budgeting, in our day-to-day city operations, in planning for the future, in what we do with the local business community, in what we do with local residents, and even with our tourists. We started with our municipal operations. Just before the winter Olympic Games in 2002, I made a commitment that we would at least meet the Kyoto goals in our municipal operations. Kyoto uses 1990 as the base year for reductions in greenhouse gas emissions, with a target year of 2012. We didn't have adequate data for that, so instead of saying 7 percent reduction in greenhouse gas emissions from the 1990 level, we increased it to 21 percent from 2001. Nationwide, there was about a 13 or 14 percent increase in greenhouse gas emissions during that period. The pledge was a 21 percent reduction in greenhouse gas emissions by 2012. We reduced our emissions by 31 percent and we did it in just three years.

Q: How did you do that? Was it mainly city vehicles?

RA: It was across the board. It was changes in our fleet. I got rid of a number of SUVs; that made a huge difference. We downsized our fleet everywhere we could. We used to have sedans that did traffic enforcement. Now we have these little three-wheeled vehicles that use one-eighth as much gasoline. We even use electric chariots: little vehicles that run on electricity and take the place of an automobile. If we didn't need large four-wheel-drive vehicles, we got rid of them and put smaller vehicles in their place. At the same time, we are utilizing alternative fuels whenever we can. We have 89 compressed-natural-gas vehicles in our fleet right now. My personal car is a CNG Honda Civic. I think that's really important in this region. We have the second largest number of natural gas outlets in the country in Utah. So it's very convenient. It costs about one-third as much for natural gas as regular gasoline at the pumps. It's all domestically produced. When you run natural gas there are almost no criteria pollutants: the kinds of air pollutants that create the air quality problems that we have in this region. Although I don't think natural gas is the long-term solution, it's a very good interim solution. It's much better than running on regular gasoline.

We retrofitted the lighting in our city and county buildings. We got rid of the incandescent lights, and we have a lot of them because we've got these beautiful chandeliers throughout the building. We put in compact fluorescent bulbs. That means saving about $33,000 per year. Much less electricity has to come from dirty coal-burning power plants, which provide about 96 percent of the energy in this region. Then we used about $12,000 a year from that $33,000 savings to purchase wind power. We not only dramatically conserved the amount of electricity that we were using but then we also shifted over to clean renewable production of the energy we do use. Those two things alone—changing out the light bulbs and then utilizing some of the savings for the purchase of wind power—reduces global warming emissions by the equivalent of about 1,100 tons of carbon dioxide a year. Then we changed the bulbs in our traffic lights, and we now save about $50,000 a year because of the massive reductions in electricity. These are the sorts of things that make a big difference—lights all over town that are on 24 hours a day, 365 days a year, you are going to have some significant savings.

The largest savings in greenhouse gas emissions that we've seen has come from our methane recovery program. It's at our water treatment plant and our landfill. We used to flare off the methane. I think that's fairly common around the country. Now we capture the methane and we use it to fuel cogeneration plants that produce a lot of electricity that doesn't have to come from coal-burning power plants. At our wastewater treatment facility, it goes into a nearby municipal electric-utilities system. And at our wastewater treatment plant, it provides about half of the electrical needs for the entire wastewater plant.

These innovations were an outgrowth of a sustainability inventory we did throughout the city government in every department, assessing what we could do to make a difference in terms of local and environmental impacts and global warming. Then we took what we learned from that to the business community. We created what we call an E2 business program—E2 stands for "environmentally and economically sustainable". In that program we go to businesses and do the same thing we did in each of our municipal departments: we do an inventory of what the business is doing with lighting, with their waste disposal, with their transportation, recycling, water use, all of that. And then we make recommendations and show them what they can do to make a difference both environmentally and economically. We now have around forty-five E2 businesses. They are very enthusiastic, their employees love it, their customers love it, and we give them a lot of really good recognition for it. And most of them see fairly significant cost savings by incorporating these measures in their everyday business.

We took it all one step further to our E2 citizen program. It's a lot like our E2 business program, but we encourage citizens to register online on our website, SLCGreen.com. We give them a whole menu of choices: things that everybody can do to reduce their carbon footprint. We encourage them to calculate their own carbon footprint. We ask them to commit to at least five of these measures to reduce carbon emissions from what they do in their everyday lives. We have over 550 E2 citizens throughout the SLC community. So it's been a real consciousness-raising effort as well as effecting significant reductions in carbon dioxide emissions.

Also, we have massively stepped up recycling programs: in one year we increased the recycled materials in our recycling program by over 80 percent. That was done by replacing the smaller curbside containers, where people had to segregate recyclable materials, with one 90-gallon bin where you can put all recyclable materials except for glass, and then put it out with your garbage. A lot of people are like me, they are putting out a lot more in their recycling bin than they are in their regular refuse bin.

Q: Are you seeing these policies being copied in other cities? Is there a general trend going on?

RA: I think there is a real trend among cities, certainly in terms of the recognition of the problem of global warming and making an initial commitment. There are now over 400 mayors throughout the country that have sighed on to a climate protection agreement. The U.S. Conference of Mayors has a climate protection center. I must say that all the work that we have done has been done through ICLEI, the International Council of Local Environmental Initiatives [www.iclei.org]. They have provided us with the technical expertise to establish our baselines to measure our progress and they are also providing us with ideas about how we can accomplish reductions. They've created a really good network among the cities that are really serious about this work.

I think the one thing that has been largely missing in the discussion about global warming and climate change up until now has been the real hope we have, because solutions are available. There are ways to conserve within our reach right now that make a huge difference. Corporate communities are saying that. Other nations are saying it. And as more and more cities get on board they are also experiencing a lot of the same kinds of successes we are.

I called Robert Redford before I went to the Buenos Aires UN conference on climate change. I knew of his longtime concern about global warming—he'd been a real activist very early on. So I called him and said, "How about we team up with ICLEI and bring in mayors from around the U.S. with a very action-oriented agenda?" We brought in the very best climate scientists and communication experts, and showed mayors best practices so they could go back to their communities and incorporate these things. And it has been successful beyond our wildest imagination. We've done it twice now and we hope it will be an annual event. We brought in probably 70 mayors form throughout the U.S. And there have been some wonderful success stories with mayors who were either very skeptical about global warming and weren't doing anything or it just hadn't been on their radar before Sundance. They came to Sundance and now some of those mayors are doing some of the best work in the country.

A couple of examples: Mark Begich, the mayor of Anchorage, Alaska. He came to Sundance the first year we held it. He left very well informed, and was completely sold on the necessity for taking local action. They now have methane recovery at their landfills. They have building standards that they have incorporated. They have gone through all of their municipal properties and have incorporated all these great measures. He has become one of the really great enthusiastic leaders among cities in this country. A few months ago he brought 30 U.S. mayors to Anchorage where they could see first-hand the dramatic devastation in the Anchorage area resulting form climate change: the receding glaciers, the destruction of forests. It was an amazing event. When I see this happening in just one year it's very heartening. John Hickenlooper, in Denver, is another standout mayor. He came to Sundance and has been a real star, doing some really great work on sustainability.

Q: Can you talk about the support you gave to the first buy-local week and how the SLC Vest Pocket business coalition developed?

RA: There are so many reasons why we should support our local businesses. We are seeing such a massive shift with all the big-box stores and the category killers, the homogenization or our nation in so many ways, with all these look-alike suburbs and even some cities, where you can't really tell one from the other because they're just covered with Starbucks and Barnes & Noble and Wal-Mart. We are really losing a lot in terms of our local economy. We know that locally owned enterprises have a better impact. They use local lawyers, local accountants, local advertisers, local designers, and those dollars keep regenerating in our community. Plus, they are the ones who show up to volunteer and really become active in a civic fashion, in ways that you don't see from the large chain stores. Chain store profits end up getting sucked out of the community.

Every time you buy a book on Amazon.com you are taking dollars away form our local booksellers. And pretty soon we are not going to have any of those local booksellers, which are really drying up all over the country. And with that we lose so much of the sense of identity and community that these places provide.

I think it's a matter of personal ethics. We just need to keep reminding ourselves every time we go to a Wal-Mart rather than to a local store that the mom-and-pop sector is having a very difficult time competing. Even if it costs you a little more, it's an investment in what it really means to have a community.

We had the Vest Pocket business folks. I actually talked to them since their founding about getting a consumer movement going—not just having an association of the merchants, but reaching out more to consumers and getting them to commit to this personal consuming ethic. So we have the Local First campaign, emphasizing to people how important it is buy locally whenever possible. And another aspect of all this certainly has to do with supporting those who produce locally. Food is the perfect example: when you can buy food that is locally produced, you are saving enormous amounts of emissions from not needing to ship the food long distances from where it's produced. There are so many advantages both economically and environmentally from buying from those who produce locally, and then when you do buy those locally produced products, purchasing them through locally owned businesses whenever possible.

Q: You issued a strong statement calling for the impeachment of President Bush. What do you say to people who say mayors shouldn't get involved in foreign policy and national policy?

RA: I used to think impeachment was a fairly radical proposal. I am now convinced that—given the incredible abuses of power, breaches of trust, violations of law, treaties, our own constitution, and the heinous human rights violations under this administration—impeachment of the president and vice president is the only way to communicate to the rest of the world that this does not represent American values. It's a very important statement for the future of this country. I want our children in later generations to know that all of these horrendous things have occurred—including this completely illegal and tragic war of aggression in Iraq—and that the people of this country came together and said, "That's not who we are." We cannot allow the kidnapping and torture of human beings in our name. And when the leader of our government does these things in blatant violation of our constitution, we are going to hold him accountable and we are going to make sure that he doesn't hold this office anymore.

As for people who say mayors shouldn't speak out on these issues, I hear that all the time. They should be ashamed as human beings, and as supposed leaders in the community. Because that's what leaders do—when there are constitutional and moral crises like the one facing this country, every single person in any leadership position has an obligation to speak out, to say, "No, we are not going to put up with this anymore."

Local communities are hurting right now. It's in our local communities where we are bearing the debt and treating the young people coming back from Iraq who have suffered from losses of limbs and mental illnesses. This president has been spending so many billions of dollars—I think it has reached 500 billion dollars—on this war in Iraq. I think that the real total is going to be close to two trillion dollars. We have seen during the Bush administration a 16 percent cut in community development block grant funding. This is for the lower income areas of our cities, the organizations that provide services for the people most in need in our communities, and now for the coming year president Bush has proposed another 21 percent reduction in community development block grant funding. This includes cuts in police funding: before the Bush administration, Salt Lake City was getting $4.5 million a year to help with our police department, and now we are getting about $2 million—more than a 50 percent cut for policing in our communities. So I find it really hypocritical when he talks about homeland security. Because homeland security, first and foremost, is hometown security. To the Bush people it's only a slogan; to me, it's a reality. It reflects a complete mis-prioritization of where we are headed as a country.

Green Grapes

Fetzer Winery Cultivates a Triple Bottom Line

"It's not just looking at the money. It's how you treat the people and the earth. It's part of a whole philosophy."
—Nicole Birdsall, Wine maker, Fetzer Vineyards

When wine maker Paul Dolan set out to make Fetzer Vineyards a model of ecologically sustainable and socially responsible business management, he turned to the winery's employees to help transform the business. Field hands, cellar workers, truck drivers, and bottling plant employees came up with ideas to reduce waste, improve efficiency, and protect the environment. By encouraging employee empowerment and urging workers to develop and implement solutions, Fetzer is tapping into one of our most important renewable resources—human creativity.

Fetzer Vineyards of Hopland, California is well known as a reliable producer of fine wines, consistently winning awards for its line of Rieslings, Chardonnays, and Merlots. The winery has received accolades from judges at the California State Fair, the New World International Wine Competition, and the tough critics at the *San Francisco Chronicle*. Founded in 1958, Fetzer has won *Wine & Spirits* magazine's Winery of the Year Award nine times.

Well-balanced wines aren't the only thing that distinguishes Fetzer, the eighth-largest premium winery. Since 1992, Fetzer has been a pioneer in environmentally sustainable business practices. The company is one of the largest growers of organic grapes in the world; it gets all of its energy from green sources; and it runs its trucks on biodiesel. Recognized as a zero-waste company by the State of California, Fetzer uses state-of-the-art practices to recycle the glass, paper, and cardboard used in its operations. The company recently installed the largest solar energy collector of any winery in the country.

Fetzer's commitment to reducing its ecological footprint is driven by the philosophy of the triple bottom line—balancing the economic needs of the company, the environmental needs of the planet, and the equity needs of employees and neighbors. By practicing that philosophy, this $200 million company is showing other corporations how they can do well by doing good.

For entrepreneurs and other businesspeople who are eager to balance their company's profitability with responsible social and environmental practices, the obvious question is: How did it happen? How did this multi-million dollar company, which is itself a subsidiary of a much larger corporation, manage to earn solid profits and make sweeping investments in protecting and restoring the environment?

The short answer: By building a corporate culture that values employee empowerment and encourages workers to speak up, develop solutions, and build on their own ideas.

"Corporate culture." "Employee empowerment." Those phrases could easily sound like the hollow buzzwords of a public relations office. But after speaking with a range of past and current Fetzer employees and visiting the company's wine making and bottling headquarters, it's clear that Fetzer's story is real.

"As wine makers, they are always trying new ideas and pushing it further," said Bob Scowcroft, executive director of the Organic Farming Research Foundation, a sustainable agriculture think tank that has received donations from Fetzer. "Somebody like this is making it work within their scale, and it makes you think, 'Hey, other approaches are viable.' They are one of the few that effected change from within, on the higher rungs, and it's tangible."

Fetzer's ability to tap into the ingenuity of its employees stems from the same basic ideal that underlies the successful political struggles profiled in this book—empowerment works. Give people a sense of their own agency, encourage them to see how they themselves are powerful, and they will take on the world—or their city council member, or the most complex challenges in their workplace. Fetzer has succeeded economically and environmentally by mining that most valuable of human resources: creativity. The company encourages its employees to express themselves, and the payoff comes in dividends for both the company and the planet.

"The first line of opportunity was with those people who were closest to me," Paul Dolan, who ran the company for twelve years, told us. "I felt that if I could help them embrace the possibility of what this newly designed company was, then they would share it with their people. Then they would have these ongoing discussions and explorations with their teams. It would expand their vision."

"Hints of Cantaloupe" vs. "Bland and Insipid"

Dolan is widely credited as the creative fulcrum of the changes that have occurred at Fetzer. A third-generation wine maker, Dolan joined the company in the 1980s to oversee the production of its wines. In 1992 he became CEO when the Fetzer family sold the label to Brown-Forman, the company most famous for bottling Jack Daniels. Dolan's rise to CEO came as he was pondering alternative models for running a large business, and the promotion gave him the chance to put his beliefs into practice.

For Dolan, a wine maker at heart and a businessman in his head, the epiphany of triple-bottom-line management came through the taste of grapes. In the 1980s, Fetzer started an organic fruit and vegetable garden near its tasting room to supply the vineyard's café. The exceptionally fresh and tasty produce from the garden soon prompted the company to experiment with converting some of its grape acreage to organic methods. One day Dolan was walking the vineyards near the company's home ranch when he sampled a grape from a Sauvignon Blanc vine. It had the taste he expected: "hints of cantaloupe," as he put it. A few hundreds yards later, he tried another grape of the same strain, and was badly disappointed. Its taste, he recalls, was "bland and insipid." The ideal grape came from organic vines; the poor tasting one had been conventionally grown.

To Dolan's specially trained palate, the difference was stark. The organic grapes were more full-bodied, simply better. The reason, Dolan believed, was that the conventional vines had been propped up by pesticides and herbicides and artificially supported by chemical fertilizers; their natural taste had been leached away. The organic grapes, in contrast, expressed the full range of biological life in the soil, water and air; they were complex. At that moment, Dolan decided to convert all of the company's grapes to organic.

"The driver for us was organics," Dolan said. "It was the one area that was the most easily translatable. Since wine is essentially an agricultural product, it was easy."

Dolan's experience with organic grapes prompted a rethinking of the company's entire operations. The winemaker-turned-CEO plunged into research about corporate responsibility. He sought out other eco-minded executives to help him see how he could chart a course for change. Paul Hawken's book *The Ecology of Commerce*, which coined the "triple bottom line" phrase, influenced him deeply.

"Once people said, 'Oh, we aren't using chemicals in our fruit,' then everything else sort of fell in line," he said. "The 100 percent green power, and the 97 percent recycled materials. Those things all sort of enhanced the story, like jewelry around the wrist."

After first converting all of its own grapes to organic, Fetzer began encouraging its dozens of suppliers to do likewise, offering growers technical courses on ecological vineyard management. (Fetzer relies on other growers for about 80 percent of its grapes.) When the company designed a new corporate headquarters, Dolan and his staff made sure it was sustainable to the core: The walls were built of reinforced rammed earth (a kind of adobe), the interiors were made almost entirely of natural materials, and the roof was equipped with a massive solar array. The company looked closely at its waste stream, and realized that it could recycle much of the plastic and cardboard used in its packaging. All of the vineyard's tractors and trucks started to run on biodiesel.

These and other innovations reduced waste and saved energy. Equally important, over time they saved money.

"Yes, it costs more, but the payback is incredible," Ann Thrupp, Fetzer's current Manager of Organic Development, told us during a conversation in the company's airy and natural light-filled offices. "That's the thing people don't understand. They say, 'Oh my God, it's so expensive.' But then you eventually save so much money.... One of the initiatives was cost-cutting. We realized that we were taking all of this trash to the dump, and we thought, 'We could save money by recycling.' In a way, it's common sense."

Your Ideas Count

Rank-and-file employees were the key to the energy-, waste-, and money-saving modernizations. While Dolan and his management team supplied the vision of change, the innovation relied on the line employees who, since they knew their piece of the company best, were the best equipped to give suggestions. For example, workers in the bottling facility were responsible for figuring out how to recycle packaging materials. The company's backhoe operator helped design the composting system. A vineyard worker came up with the water conservation plan.

"We have an atmosphere where the solutions bubble up from the bottom," Suzanne Zechel, the vineyard's Facilities Manager, said. "We have a culture that allows people to say, 'Duh—let's do it this way.' ... It's very important to feel like your ideas count. It's satisfying."

The Fetzer employees encapsulate their commitment to sustainability with the term "E3." That stands for "economy" (making a profit), "equity" (ensuring that workers are treated fairly), and "environment" (protecting and restoring the natural systems on which the business depends). It's a catchphrase that, say Fetzer employees, constantly echoes around the company's offices, warehouses, and vineyards.

"People like it here—it's a culture that's quite unique," Thrupp said. "It's just the little things. If you throw something in the trash that could be recycled, or if you don't print double-sided, people will say, 'That's not very E3.'"

Nicole Birsdaall, one of the wine makers for Fetzer's Bonterra label, which used 100 percent organic grapes (other labels are a mix of organic and conventionally grown, due to a shortage of organic grapes), agreed that the E3 mentality pervades company relations.

"It's not just looking at the money," Birdsall told us. "It's how you treat the people and the earth. It's part of a whole philosophy ... I've worked at other wineries, and for me, I feel like I have a healthy lifestyle because I'm happy here. I'm challenged every day to come up with solutions."

The principle seems obvious enough: Give employees a sense of ownership over their work, and they will do that work in a fashion that mirrors their broader values. After all, everyone wants to feel proud of their job; people don't like to think that their energy is directed toward some harmful end.

"For me, when I think what is E3, it's safety, having a safe place to work," Lucas Boek, the assistant Cellar Manager, said. "We're exploring new technology that will make it safer for our guys, and also save energy."

A Family Committed to Responsible Business

It's important to note, however, that even though they may feel a sense of ownership, in actuality the employees don't own the company. The Brown family of Louisville, Kentucky, does. And that ownership marks one of the most extraordinary aspects of the Fetzer story—the fact that Dolan and his staff were able to make all of their changes even though they were part of a larger, $2 billion, publicly traded corporation.

Why? The fundamental reason is that even though they were making huge investments in the most environmentally sensitive practices, Fetzer was profitable. During the 1990s, the company was consistently posting gains of 15 percent a year. Brown-Forman had little reason to get in Dolan's way.

"I remember going to my first [Brown-Forman] board meeting," Dolan said. "I had put together this little slide show about what we were doing. Afterward, they actually stood up and clapped. So I thought, 'This is just what they do here.' And then when we walked out of the room my boss said, 'They have never done that before.' I was an oddity. We were an oddity, especially in their business. But they could embrace it. They thought, 'If this guy can run the company, he can do whatever he wants.'"

There is another explanation for why Dolan was allowed free rein. Brown-Forman, though publicly traded, is still family-run, with the Brown family controlling a majority of the voting stock. This means that real people—not Wall Street cost-cutters—are looking at the company as a living organism, part of a family tradition, and not exclusively as a machine for making money.

The family control over Brown-Forman brings to mind a similar situation in a completely different industry: Newspaper publishing. *The New York Times* and *The Washington Post* are among the most thorough newspapers in the U.S., and certainly this is due in no small measure to being located in the financial and political capitals of the country. But the papers' commitment to excellence is also due to the fact that both publications are controlled by families. While these families certainly have their elite biases, they continue to believe in the public mission of journalism. Unlike the profit-obsessed managers at chains such as the Tribune Company, who have ruthlessly cut newsroom positions, the Sulzbergers and the Grahams appear content with modest returns on investment as long as they provide a quality product.

In short, family control is meaningful. What the distilling and newspaper examples show is that family-controlled companies are more disposed to balance the imperative of money-making with the public service demands of protecting the environment or providing accurate information. Family pride balances out the cold calculations of the bottom line. Directed by a human unit—the family—these companies are kept at a human scale, where social values other than profit accumulation remain central to the company business.

"A good analogy is a family farm," Rob Frederick, vice president of corporate responsibility at Brown-Forman, told us. "You think about keeping a farm for future generations. You want to make sure the farm is still there. ... There is still pressure from Wall Street, but I think we have a lot more independence and a greater degree of patience because we are a family company. Here you can still ask family members what they think. They want to be contributing to the community. Environmental values are very strong."

The values exchange is two-way. While the Browns' family values have given the Fetzer managers more latitude in their operations, the more "deep green" values of the Hopland employees have percolated up to the corporate headquarters in Louisville. Managers within Fetzer and Brown-Forman agree that successful innovations at the winery have had a powerful influence on the thinking within the larger company. For example, in 2004 Fetzer endorsed a successful ballot initiative in its home county of Mendocino to ban the cultivation of genetically modified (GMO) crops within county lines. Shortly thereafter, Brown-Forman announced it would not use GMO corn in distilling Jack Daniels, Southern Comfort, or any of its other brands. In that case, at least, the larger parent corporation followed the smaller brand's lead.

Sustainability Is a Process, Not a Destination

Within the wine industry, Fetzer continues to lead. In 2006, the company installed the wine industry's largest solar array on its bottling facility; enough to generate 1.1 million kilowatt hours annually. The company offers free training to its vendors on how to be more ecologically sustainable. And the company is a founding member of the California Sustainable Winegrowing Alliance. The alliance—which encourages members to share their knowledge of best environmental practices—is a powerful example of how businesses can find ways to cooperate, instead of always being caught in competition.

"We have competitive edge with being greener. Why would Fetzer want to share all of this [knowledge]?" Thrupp said. "But that's not the point—we want to have a broader impact on society."

To be sure, there are still improvements to be made. While Fetzer has been heralded as a model of stewardship, the company has seemingly paid less attention to the "equity" component of E3. Employees are offered on-site ESL classes, and vineyard workers and their families enjoy subsidized housing. Low employee turnover attests to a happy work environment. But the company has not made an explicit commitment to paying its workers a living wage.

That, says Ann Thrupp, shows sustainability is a process, not a destination. The company's practices will continue to evolve as even better and smarter systems are developed. And as before, that evolution will depend foremost on the creativity and values of the company's workers.

"There's always room for constant improvement," Thrupp said. "There are still a lot of conversations we need to have. Again, it's about creating a culture that inspires people to build a safe and healthy workplace. I get very inspired by all this." She motioned to the rammed earth walls and recycled materials interior of her office. "Just being in this building. It's inspiring."

No Boss

Worker-Owned Co-ops Redefine Office Politics

"We won't have achieved true democracy until we have workplace democracy."

—Tim Huet, author and attorney

Imagine you had no boss, no one ordering you around or thinking that his opinions were better than yours. You'd probably be a much happier and productive worker. You might also be a more engaged citizen. At least, that's what those in the worker-owned co-operative movement believe. They say that by introducing democratic principles into the workplace, we can deepen respect for democratic ideals in the broader society. Instead of wallowing in complaints, the co-operative visionaries are building the world they want to see—one business at a time.

Work sucks. Surely you've heard that before. Chances are you've muttered it yourself, a grumbled complaint at the end of a long, frustrating day. Let's face it: The nine-to-five grind can be grueling. More often than not, the dissatisfaction stems not from the work tasks themselves—whether writing reports or painting walls—but from the very atmosphere of the workplace. For many employees, there exists a disconnect between effort and reward; too many hours result in too little pay. That frustration is compounded by the insult of capricious office rules and arbitrary management decisions. Most employees are given little say over how to do their jobs, and for many people—who instinctively feel a powerful sense of their own agency—the daily orders from the higher-ups can feel like never-ending abuse.

The problem may not be that your boss is a jerk, but that you have a boss in the first place. Unless, that is, you are among the select number of Americans who are members of worker-owned and worker-managed co-operatives. In the breakneck, competitive environment that is the hallmark of U.S.-style capitalism, worker-owned co-ops are rare breeds. While they have managed to carve niches for themselves in many European economies, in the United States worker-owned co-operatives are hard to find. According to the U.S. Federation of Worker Co-operatives, there are some 300 enterprises in the country that meet the definition of a "democratic workplace." Employing an estimated 3,500 people, these companies generate about $400 million in sales a year. Not bad—until you recall that the United States is a $12 trillion economy.

Those involved in worker-managed enterprises say that co-ops—due to their unique success—have the potential to exercise an outsized influence over the larger economy. By providing a working model for how business can be at once economically profitable and socially responsible, these enterprises prove that democratic decision-making can be preferable to the traditional model of top-down hierarchies. In business, just like in politics, democracy is often the key to success.

Proponents also say co-ops can help drive the transition to a local, green economy. For co-ops are by definition locally rooted: If the workers control and manage all the capital, there is no such thing as absentee ownership. They are also—by temperament, if not intent—green. Because co-ops have no incentive for constant growth, they more efficiently use resources. If a worker can't have more than one vote per share, there's little reason to spin off a new franchise, and the business stays within the sustainable limits of the local environment. The demands of democratic decision-making keep co-operatives at a human scale, one that doesn't heedlessly gobble up resources from around the world.

This living example of democratic and ecological business practices is an essential part of the road map to a more sustainable and just future, say co-op promoters.

"I think a lot of the progressive movement is about protesting and criticizing," said Tim Huet, a writer and attorney who has been involved with several successful co-ops, among them the Bay Area-based Arizmendi Bakery and Rainbow Grocery. "If that's what you're doing all the time, that's what you become good at. But that's not what we need to create a better society. It's about asking, 'How do we bake bread for our community and how do we build homes for our communities?' And doing it daily. ... If we can't offer anything that's better, then criticizing is not going to get us anywhere. We need to develop the habits of mind that are going to be part of that better society."

For Huet and other co-operative pioneers, there is no better way to encourage those progressive habits of mind than by guaranteeing democratic control over the workplace. One of the most common complaints from employees is that their job fails to give them respect. Co-operative members say that by offering every employee a say in how to run the company, individuals at co-ops are given not only responsibility, but the respect that comes with it. Instead of being told what to do, workers themselves decide how they will do it. An informed and self-directed worker is a happy worker; and a business full of happy workers is a successful one.

"The bad thing about employee mentality is that you have no power," Huet told us. "The good thing is that you have no responsibility. If you are a worker-owner, you can't just sit back and criticize. You have to come up with solutions. I think people learn a lot from that."

The idea behind co-operatives is elegantly simple: workers should own the means of production. That phrase, with its unmistakably Marxist tone, might suggest that co-operatives are grounded in some kind of anti-business ethic. Successful co-ops are anything but. Their very reason for being is to provide goods and services to their clients and communities. There are co-operative restaurants, design and printing companies, bike shops, farms, coffee importers, magazines and light manufacturing and high-tech enterprises. The basic purpose is to exchange products for money. Co-operatives put a twist on that traditional market ideal by asserting that worker satisfaction, rather than merely profits, should be the baseline of success.

Happy Workers Are Productive Workers

Isthmus Engineering of Madison, Wisconsin, is one co-op that reveals how such success works. Started in 1980 by four young engineers, Isthmus today is a $12 million company that specializes in custom-built manufacturing equipment for big corporations such as John Deere, Proctor & Gamble, and Duracell Batteries. Though the enterprise has grown, it remains committed to its founding principle of being employee-run. Of the 49 employees, 25 are worker-owners; most of the others are on their way to becoming owners, a process that takes several years. The day-to-day management of the company is purely non-hierarchical. There are no supervisors or bosses telling other people what to do. Rather, the company organizes itself into project-based teams. This fluid structure, say Isthmus employees, gives each person a feeling that their contribution is important and their opinions respected.

"People just like the fact that they have control over their workplace," John Kessler, one of the Isthmus co-owners, told us. "I think a lot of frustration and stress in normal jobs is because people are just told or given an assignment, and are not given the power to affect how they do that. When we have a situation when somebody comes up with an idea, we listen to those ideas, we jump right on them. ... People work harder because they aren't being told to work hard."

Probably the most well known example of a worker-owned enterprise is the neighborhood food co-op, where shoppers are part-owners and often part-time employees as well. But as the Isthmus experience shows, co-operatives come in all shapes and sizes. There is no template—and that is the point. At its essence, a co-op is a creative arrangement that gives individuals power over their own actions. In practice, this means that each co-operative has to figure out on its own what kind of ownership and decision-making arrangement works best for its members.

Chroma Technology is an example of the different forms co-ops can take. The company does not perfectly fit the non-hierarchical ideal. There is a measure of seniority. Veteran employees hold a greater number of shares in the company, and so get more voting rights; it's not a "one person-one share-one vote" system. But neither does Chroma fit the description of an ESOP—or Employee Stock Ownership Plan. ESOPs are the most common form of employee ownership, a system in which the workers use their pension funds to buy and then control all of the shares in the marketplace. United Airlines is one of the best-known examples of the more than 11,000 ESOPs in the United States. But while employees with stock ownership plans may boast a measure of ownership, they lack the degree of worker control characteristic of co-operatives; there remains a management class that oversees the work.

Not so at Chroma where, like at Isthmus, employees are in charge of day-to-day decisions. That worker direction probably explains why Chroma—a $17 million manufacturer of optical lenses for medical equipment—has been ranked one of the best companies to work for in the state of Vermont.

"Ownership is clearly not enough from my perspective," said Paul Millman, one of the Chroma founders. Seventy members of the firm's 82-person staff are employee-owners. "I can own shares in AT&T, but I don't participate in the decisions at AT&T. Ownership is a good thing at any level. Ownership is a good thing for employees. But it's only a small step in terms of the real ownership society. The real ownership society has people participating in the decisions that owners get to make.

"[At Chroma,] people basically make decisions regularly, every day, and so they are part of the decision-making process constantly. Our profitability is really dependent on our efficiency. And I think that worker-owned co-ops are more efficient."

Millman says that the co-operative culture relies on frequent meetings; nearly every decision requires a multi-stakeholder conversation. He says that while the discussions can be long, the company makes up for the time by having all employees buying into the final decision. Since everyone is present when the decision is made, there is no post-decision quibbling; people get right to work.

Isthmus engineer Kessler sees the same dynamic at his co-op. "It takes a long time to make decisions, longer than it would take in a hierarchical structure. But I think we end up with a much better result. ... We hire electricians, programmers, engineers, professional people who are all coming from conventional corporate business. It's a different atmosphere. But once people get used to it, they wonder why we are the only ones doing it."

The Obstacle of Ignorance

A good question. If co-operatives work so fabulously, then why aren't there more of them in the United States? After all, the co-operative model of worker ownership and management is much better established in Europe. There are an estimated 1,000 co-ops in the United Kingdom, and more than 1,500 in France. Italy has a well-developed co-op system, as does Spain, where the Mondragón Co-operative in the Basque region is actually a federation of 150 smaller enterprises making everything from rice cookers to refrigerators. The Mondragón Co-operative is the seventh largest corporation in Spain.

U.S. co-operative members offer a range of explanations for why the system hasn't developed more here. Both Millman and Kessler offer cultural reasons for the small number of co-ops. Simply put, we live in a more aggressively competitive culture, one that puts a premium on individual success. Few American entrepreneurs are willing to subsume their ego to the imperatives of collective decision-making. "A consciousness that focuses on the common good is not something that is encouraged in the U.S.," Millman said.

There are also technical and legal obstacles to forming co-operatives, according to Huet. For example, the laws around co-operative ownership are ill-defined, creating a barrier for startups. And because the laws are murky, banks often hesitate to make loans to co-ops, choking off capital.

All three co-op veterans agree that simple ignorance is perhaps the biggest obstacle. The concept is foreign to most people, and so, when starting a business, co-op arrangements are not something entrepreneurs consider.

"It is not the first thing that comes to mind," Millman said. "It's not even the second or the third thing that comes to mind when people set up companies."

That may be changing. Huet says that there has been a sharp increase in the number of co-operative startups in the last decade. He attributes that increase to greater public awareness. As more and more co-ops distinguish themselves as successful enterprises, the number of new businesses considering organizing as co-operatives increases.

"I think when people hear the idea, it very much appeals to them," Huet said. "We hire people all the time who have never heard of worker co-ops, and once they get in they say, 'This is great.' ... Our success rate, compared to capitalist enterprises, is pretty good. But we don't have that same exponential growth as capitalist industries."

Democracy Beyond the Workplace

Co-ops' day-to-day success occurs through the simple task of providing quality goods and services, and doing so in a way that creates especially happy employees. But co-ops' potential benefits stretch much further. They don't just contribute to the well being of their member-owners and customers, but also to society at large. Co-op proponents say that if their numbers were greater, the economy and the environment would be in a much healthier state.

Strengthening the country's manufacturing base would be one result of a growth in co-ops. If there were more co-ops, there would be less offshoring. As Millman points out, no co-op member is going to vote to send her job overseas. Also, more co-ops would mean higher wages, for the obvious reason that the workers themselves determine their salaries.

There are also environmental benefits to co-operative arrangements. While many co-ops may not have explicit ecological worldviews, they are by nature more sustainable, says Huet. Whereas capitalist enterprises keep growing for the sake of growth—the "ideology of the cancer cell"—co-ops have no incentive to grow beyond their immediate size. This means that co-ops are better equipped to help manage scarcity when twenty-first century society faces shortages of critical resources.

"Take a bakery," Huet said. "If there is one person owning the business, and they pay $11 an hour even though each worker brings in $33 an hour in value, they are taking $22 from each worker. There's a huge incentive to create another bakery. But if a co-op creates another bakery, then each worker does not earn more. ... Co-ops actually get to a certain homeostasis, and then they stop growing. Which is exactly what we need to have a sustainable economy."

Beyond these benefits to the economy and the environment lies a less tangible, but more profound good: A deepening of democratic principles throughout society. Co-op proponents say that democratizing the office and the shop floor can have a ripple effect, strengthening respect for the ideals of collective decision-making and consensus.

The workplace is famously undemocratic. There is the boss, and there are the bossed-around. But it does not have to be this way. If we truly believe in freedom of association, freedom of speech and the right to "petition for a redress of grievances" in the public square, then why should we abandon those fundamental democratic ideals at the workplace door?

What would happen if you translated democratic principles to the office? Huet, for one, believes the effect would be nothing short of revolutionary.

"I don't think there is much hope for achieving even limited political democracy … if you don't have the everyday democracy of workplace democracy," Huet has written. "For me, worker co-operatives are not simply businesses; they are democracy demonstration projects, schools for democracy, laboratories for democracy … If you want peace and democracy overseas, you should care fiercely about establishing economic as well as political democracy domestically."

Most of us spend about half our waking hours at work. By encouraging democratic habits of mind in the workplace, co-ops can help spread democratic practices to other parts of our lives. In doing so, they will help create the kinds of political, economic, and social structures needed to preserve the planet and reduce social inequities. As this and other stories in the book show, democracy is the best antidote to despair, injustice, and environmental destruction.

"It's like democracy, you know," Millman said, reflecting on Chroma's structure. "There are easier ways of doing things. But in the final analysis, it's the most rewarding."

CONVERSATION

Omar Freilla

Though only 33 years old, Omar Freilla has already distinguished himself as a leader in the movement to create a sustainable and just economy. As the founder of the Green Worker Co-op in the South Bronx district of New York City, Freilla has laid out an exciting vision of how to balance economic needs with ecological wisdom. That vision rests on the basic principles of environmental justice—ensuring that no one community has to bear a disproportionate burden for society's toxins and wastes. The way to do that, Freilla believes, is by creating worker-owned co-operatives that will have no incentives to pollute. He spoke to us from his office in the Hunts Point neighborhood in the Bronx.

Q: How did you get the idea for the Green Worker Co-op? Was there any "aha" moment that you remember?

OF: There have been a couple of "aha" moments. The most recent came when I worked for Sustainable South Bronx. I was involved in a collaborative effort to try to attract green businesses into New York, with the hope and the desire that they would be locating in low-income neighborhoods. Unfortunately, it didn't go anywhere at the time. I realized that I wasn't really comfortable with the approach that we were taking as a group, which was to try to attract businesses—traditional, corporate-structured businesses—into an area from outside. I felt that an approach that produces even more results and maximizes benefits to an even greater extent would actually be building up business from within the community. And creating it as a worker-owned business. So that way the profits would actually stay within the community, and decisions would be made by people from the area.

Q: A key part of the vision is recycling and reusing all the waste produced in New York. How do you plan to turn trash into opportunity?

OF: Well, that's part of the vision. Our vision is to incubate and let fly a number of worker-owned businesses that are able to improve environmental conditions generally. It's not specific to waste. We just happened to latch on to this idea of creating a co-op that could reduce waste. This particular co-op would be salvaging building materials that would otherwise get thrown out and get sent to a landfill, or even worse, to an incinerator. We have latched on to that and really promoted that as an idea. The next co-op or the third one or the fourth one could be anything. It could be energy efficiency, doing anything related to improving environmental conditions. For us, the big issues in the South Bronx are reducing air pollution, and reducing waste.

Q: Why is it important to you to have a worker-owned co-operative? How does that fit in with your broader philosophy?

OF: There are two reasons. One is economic. It's about being able to maximize the resources within the community. We have an incredible amount of money that just cycles out almost immediately, as soon as it's generated. People don't make a lot of money, and the money we do make winds up going into stores that aren't owned by people in the community. In many cases, especially if you are talking about big chains, the money immediately flows out to some corporate headquarters and distant stock owners in other parts of the country and other parts of the planet. There's really no financial benefit coming back to the person who actually shops there or who works there, other than maybe getting a particular product. We felt that the worker co-op model is a great way to go.

Q: What is the second reason?

OF: Democracy. We live in a country that is counted as a great democracy, but in day-to-day life few of us actually experience it. We go to school and we go to work under conditions where people don't have a say in their day-to-day life; they don't have a say in the things that happen around them. And then people are surprised that there is little participation at the voting booth, or that people don't really take seriously this idea of living in a democracy. So that is a really big part of it, creating an opportunity for people to have ownership of their lives.

Q: We have an industrial economy that's built on extraction. How do you envision a different kind of economy that's more sustainable?

OF: I think there are lots of different pieces that need to be there. One is requiring that everything is counted for, that you don't have natural resources that are being exploited without any kind of accountability. But there is an even larger question of accountability in general: Not being able to exploit anything without being accountable to other people that use it.

My point is that you have corporations that get away with really noxious, destructive practices because the people that are being impacted don't count.

They don't count in the political structure or the economic structure. They don't have much clout, and that's why we see environmental racism and classism in poor neighborhoods. Communities of color wind up bearing the greatest burden of all the environmental horrors that are out there, whether it's places like the South Bronx, with high asthma rates, or the Gulf Coast, known as Cancer Alley because of all the oil refineries. As long as those practices are allowed to happen, as long as those companies and governments feel that they have a dumping ground, then there is no incentive to do things better.

So I think, first, you really need to close that gap. And we can't have a green society or a green economy as long as you have social and economic injustices. Because that's always going to allow for someone to be exploited. We live in a capitalist society. We have businesses that are out to make a quick buck and they will do that, regardless of what the latest ideology is or however many groups are out there trying to promote green as a win-win strategy. There are plenty of people than can make an even quicker buck by exploiting and taking advantage of people's weaknesses. As long as you have that, then, I don't see it as possible to get to some pure sustainable economy. I think sustainability requires social justice.

Q: Van Jones of the Ella Baker Center in Oakland, California, warns that in rushing to a green economy, people of color are at risk of being left behind. How do you make sure that doesn't happen?

OF: I think we need to be in the driver's seat. We need to be the ones taking control of resources and shaping the kind of world that we want to live in. That is the nature of what our organization is about. Our approach is very different for lots of other groups that are out there. We really feel it's necessary to create the model ourselves. I don't have much faith in our governments—local, regional or federal—or the benevolence of outside corporations to implement the things that we want to see and the way that we want to see them.

Q: Is this about creating a new game, since the old game is not working?

OF: Yeah, that's essentially what it is. I draw a lot of inspiration from every effort that I have ever come across where people in their communities have decided that they were going to take on their own development and really create their own economic structures under their own circumstances—from the Mondragon Co-operatives in the Basque region of Spain, to workers that have just taken over their defunct factories in Argentina, to Native Americans in the U.S. that are building their own energy co-ops and are doing different things to sustain their own economies. There are different things that are happening all over the country where people are trying to do that.

Q: You have written that, "We don't have the luxury to wait for alternatives. That's why we are creating them." What drives that sense of urgency?

OF: Asthma, cancer, every health problem and threat that is associated with the environment; pollution in the environment. All of that. If you are living with power plants and oil refineries and sewage-processing plants, you are also living with the horrible health threats and problems that those things generate.

Q: Twenty-five years from now, what do you want to see your neighborhood looking like?

OF: Lush, green, clear skies, happy people smiling. I'd like in twenty-five years for "worker co-ops" to be a household phrase. For people to understand what co-operatives are, and to know at least somebody in their family who is working in a worker co-op in the South Bronx; for these businesses to be green, environmentally friendly; and for the South Bronx not to be known as a dumping ground anymore, but instead to be known as a place where visions become reality.

"Your Business Plan Is Complete Garbage"

The TerraCycle Story

If you were starting a new business and everyone told you your business plan was complete garbage, you would probably give up. But not Tom Szaky. He knows his business plan is complete garbage, and he's quite proud of it.

Szaky is the young CEO of TerraCycle (www.terracycle.net), a liquid, organic plant food that comes in a spray bottle and works wonders feeding your plants and making them grow (trust us, we've used it). What makes TerraCycle unique is that it is garbage wrapped in garbage. The packaging is recycled plastic soda bottles rescued from the waste stream, and the plant food is worm poop. The company seeks to extend this principle of re-use through all of its operations. The sprayer tops are seconds from other companies, and the boxes TerraCycle uses to ship products in are misprints rejected by other firms.

TerraCycle outperforms rival products that are laden with questionable chemicals. And that's why Szaky does not harp on the organic nature of his product: "We want to beat the competition on their own terms," he told us. "Does our product make your plants grow stronger and healthier? Sure it does. And it just happens to be helping the planet at the same time." In a CNN interview, the 25-year-old Szaky put it this way: "We're not doing this to help save the environment. We're doing this to show that you can make a lot of money while saving the environment."

TerraCycle's success can be measured in strictly capitalist terms. The worm poop plant food line is selling briskly at 11,000 stores nationwide, including Home Depot, Wal-Mart, Whole Foods and Target. Sales in 2006 topped $1.5 million, and the factory in Paterson, New Jersey—an economically depressed city—is employing 40 people. The company is expanding its product line to include specialty plant food that is best for tomatoes, orchids, cactus, lawns, African Violets, roses, herbs, tropical plants, and more.

It all started back in 2001, when two college students, Tom Szaky and his buddy Jon Beyer, were visiting some friends who were using compost to stimulate the growth of a crop that is not yet legal. The friends raved about how compost improved the health of the plants and how it was made from what was formerly thrown out as garbage: food waste, yard trimmings, and other organic matter. Szaky and Beyer had a light-bulb moment, and decided to write a business plan.

In 2003, Szaky and Beyer entered the Carrot Capital business plan contest, which involved dozens of America's top universities and offered $1 million in seed capital to the winning team. TerraCycle won! But in a move that could be seen as either very principled or very foolhardy, they turned down the prize, even though they only had a few hundred dollars in the bank. The business consultants had pressured the TerraCycle boys to drop the ecological ethic of their plan: At one point, just before starting a television interview, one of the corporate advisors leaned over to Szaky and advised him to "tone down the eco-crap."

As it turned out, the two ended up not needing the prize money. They were soon getting plenty of publicity, and with it, plenty of investment capital. "We figured we could get lots of free media attention if we developed a product that was garbage wrapped in garbage," says Szaky. And they were right. The TerraCycle story has been covered by CBS and major print publications. Szaky was featured in a cover story for *Inc.* magazine.

The huge amount of publicity fomented by the uniqueness of the product has meant that TerraCycle has not had to spend money on advertising. Szaky likes to call it "guerrilla marketing": using free media coverage, school outreach campaigns, and word-of-mouth promotion based on the effectiveness of the product.

TerraCycle has also innovated in the way they obtain their packaging. They encourage schools, community groups and yoga studios to collect used soda bottles for them. Hundreds of elementary schools run environmental fundraising events, collecting thousands of bottles that are then used by TerraCycle to package their worm poop. They also partner with recycling centers to ensure a steady supply of the plastic soda bottles.

The young company still faces many hurdles: what to do with the bottle caps made redundant by spray tops; how to hire and retain good workers in one of the most depressed and violent cities in America; how to avoid growing too fast and collapsing. But judging from the smarts and high-voltage energy of CEO Tom Szaky—not to mention the success of the product—TerraCycle is destined for bigger and better things in the future.

CONVERSATION

Michael Shuman

Michael Shuman is an economist, attorney, and Vice President for Enterprise Development for the Training & Development Corporation (TDC) of Bucksport, Maine. He has written, co-written, or edited six books, including The Small-Mart Revolution: How Local Businesses Are Beating the Global Competition *(Berrett Koehler, 2006), and* Going Local: Creating Self-Reliant Communities in a Global Age *(Free Press, 1998). He lectures widely across the United States and is one of the most important thinkers writing about the local green economy.*

Q: What motivated you to write your recent book, *The Small-Mart Revolution,* **and what are some of the main points of the book?**

MS: In 1998 I wrote a book called *Going Local: Creating Self-Reliant Communities in a Global Age.* It got a very positive and broad response and helped promote the emergence of two business networks—the Business Alliance for Local Living Economies (BALLE), and the American Independent Business Alliance (AMIBA). So what started as anti-globalization in the 1990s morphed into engagement by progressive-minded small-business people. So when I saw the innovations that these grassroots groups were coming up with, I wanted to expand on the theme and explore all the innovative organizing going on in the small-business sector.

The book has three big themes in it. The first is to lay out all the reasons why locally owned businesses are much more reliable actors in promoting economic development in an equitable way. The second point is that small businesses are a lot more competitive than most people think. In many places small businesses are competing successfully against bigger retailers or bigger manufacturers or bigger banks, and I document the strategies they're using. And the third theme describes a coherent agenda on what communities can be doing to advance this local business revolution even faster.

The book examines how we should think differently about economic development, how we can promote local entrepreneurship, how coalitions of local businesses can be more competitive acting together than they might be if they operate just as individual firms. Then I talk about new ways of promoting buy-local campaigns and local investing (this is where some ideas for local stock markets have come out). And then finally, in public policy, I try to show that right now the economic development system is rigged heavily against local businesses. We're trying to get rid of those biases so that small businesses have as much chance of succeeding as large businesses do.

Q: In your book, *The Small-Mart Revolution,* **you say "The small-mart revolution is not about ducking globalization, it's about redefining it." Can you elaborate?**

MS: Some people have said, "If you're telling communities to withdraw from the world and be internally focused and less interested in global affairs, then this will be a colossal failure. We're in an era of globalization and we can't isolate ourselves from that." So the last chapter of the book shows that there are many ways that we can support local economies on a worldwide basis without falling into the trap of just getting involved in more conventional trade. That's what I mean by redefining globalization: promoting the globalization of mass movements, globalization of the sharing of ideas of public policy, sharing of small business technology so that every community that's engaged in this small-mart activity thinks of itself as having a duty to help other communities around the world to achieve a similar level of self-reliance.

Q: You contrast two very different models: local ownership and import substitution (LOIS) and the status quo position, which says, "There is no alternative" (TINA). Can you elaborate on this distinction?

MS: One of the questions that has dominated public discourse in the last ten years is, what kind of capitalism should we embrace? For discussion purposes in the book, I simplify the debate with two types of capitalism that I gave the names TINA and LOIS. TINA embodies the most conventional ideas about economic development. People with this perspective are trying to attract as many global companies (whether it be manufacturers or big-box stores) to come into their backyards, and they are trying to export as much as possible to the global economy. They're trying to convince the small-business community that the first two activities are somehow in the best interest of the local community.

The alternative is LOIS (locally owned import substitution), which is really saying that the most dynamic development stories are coming from communities that are mostly made up of locally owned businesses. They are trying to diversify their economies through greater degrees of self-reliance. There's a confidence in those communities that if you have a strong homegrown economy, then you can selectively participate in the global economy from a position of strength ra ther than one of vulnerability and weakness.

Q: You say that small firms produce 60 to 80 percent of all new jobs in the United States and 13 to 14 times more patents than large firms. Can you contrast locally owned companies and big corporations in terms of their impact on jobs and tax revenues?

MS: Let's focus on the local ownership piece for a moment. There are probably three big differences between local and non-local businesses that help explain why local ownership is so important. Local businesses don't run away as easily; they spend more of their money locally and thereby generate higher economic multipliers; and they tend to be smaller in size and thereby have a kind of a character that's more consistent with locally controlled economic development. Let me elaborate. The impact of local businesses not moving is that the wealth that they produce stays in the community for many years, often for many generations. It also means that the kind of catastrophe that one sees around the country when the big TINA firm leaves town is much less likely to occur. That catastrophe—if you're dependent on one big plant—can be enormous.

My current affiliation with the Training and Development Corporation in Maine came about in late 2002 after a paper company decided they wanted to shut down this hundred-year-old plant and to set up a new plant in Canada. The unemployment rate over the next year in this part of Maine grew to 40 percent. It was the equivalent of a nuclear bomb going off in that section of the country. So having a strong local business sector for your economy is an insurance policy.

On the second issue of economic multipliers, there have been about a dozen studies comparing local vs. non-local businesses—one study is by Dan Houston of Civic Economics—these studies have all shown that in terms of the economic multiplier, which is the building block for community economic development, local businesses generate two to four times more benefits than non-local businesses. That is because the local businesses spend their money locally. One great study of this was done four years ago in Austin, Texas. It looked at a hundred dollars spent at a Borders bookstore, compared to a hundred dollars spent at a local bookstore. Of the hundred dollars spent at Borders, 13 dollars stayed in the local economy and of the hundred dollars spent at the local bookstore, 45 dollars remained in the local economy. So in multiplier terms, every expenditure that one made at the local business led to roughly three times the local income, three times the jobs, three times the tax benefits. So it's not an inconsequential distinction between the two.

The last issue is the size and character of the local businesses. Local businesses are small and they tend to have their own unique character. So if you want to create diverse communities where people live close to school, shopping and work, it really takes smaller businesses to create a walkable community. When it comes to tourism, what attracts tourists is the unique character-driven kinds of businesses—not big-box stores that can be found anywhere. Then there is the phenomenon explained by Richard Florida in his book *The Rise of the Creative Class*. He presents empirical evidence showing that the strongest communities are those that have a lot of diversity, tolerance, fun, and jobs that are creative: scientists, artists, entrepreneurs, and the like. Diverse small businesses controlled by local people give lots of different opportunities for people to enter into the economy and take full advantage of their skills—that's a creative economy. A local economy is the one that is going to be more creative and generate jobs that can attract and hold the best and the brightest.

Q: Would you say there is a movement happening? What is the evidence that leads you to believe that there is a movement?

MS: *Time* had a cover story in early 2007 that said "Forget Organic, Eat Local." It is the zeitgeist of the moment. It's just one of the many pieces of evidence that this movement is gathering steam. Everywhere you go in this country you see signs that say "we are a local bank" or "we serve local food" or "we manufacture local jewelry." It is so universal now, cutting across every single political divide. I think this is an important trend in American culture. It is equally significant that a lot of non-local companies are trying to pretend they are local to take advantage of this trend. McDonald's has put out some posters and newspaper ads that say "Locally Owned" to give you the feeling that maybe they are a local food outlet. Borders now has sections of its bookstore that say "Local Interest." The local economy networks have expanded from zero to fifty networks in six years. Formally, there are fifteen thousand businesses that are members of these networks. But if you counted all of the local businesses in these fifty areas, it's more like a couple hundred thousand. I just saw another list that had networks that are in various stages of formation in another hundred places around the U.S. where there is some form of activity.

We are almost to the point where a majority of the country is now being influenced by these business alliances. It's not quite there yet but given the growth rate of these movements, I think it's not that far off that we'll see that. In my adult lifetime, I have never seen a movement that has grown so fast and appealed to such a broad range of people in this country.

What You Can Do

Buy Close By

When you spend a buck, you're doing far more than simply taking a dollar out of your pocket and giving it to someone else. Your purchasing decisions—what you buy, where, and from whom—have a ripple effect that influences the health and welfare of your entire community.

If you shop at Wal-Mart, or favor Starbucks over the local coffee roaster, you are sending money away from your hometown. Each dollar you spend immediately drains out of your community and heads to the corporate headquarters located far away, in Bentonville, Arkansas, or Seattle, Washington. Corporate chains are based on a model of wealth extraction. After all, if Wal-Mart didn't expect to remove more money from your community than it puts in, it wouldn't locate there, for the simple reason that it wouldn't be profitable.

Buying locally helps keep your dollars in your community, where it can do the most good. How? The main way is through the "multiplier effect": Neighborhood businesses tend to support other local enterprises, creating a positive feedback loop that strengthens the regional economy. A study of mid-coast Maine by the Institute for Local Self-Reliance found that local merchants made more than 50 percent of their expenditures with other state businesses, whereas their big-box competitors spent less than 15 percent of their money within Maine. To put it in environmental terms, buying locally is a way of recycling your hard-earned cash.

In a society dominated by commercial transactions, you have power as a consumer, especially if you are teamed up with millions of other people thinking globally and spending locally. Every time you buy something, you are casting a vote for the kind of economy you want to see. But you play many other social roles beside being a consumer. You are also a citizen, family member, worker or entrepreneur, neighbor, or student. Within each of these roles there are ways that you can help strengthen the local, green economy.

As a citizen (your most important role), you can support public officials who promote policies that strengthen green and locally owned enterprises. Organize a delegation of citizens to meet with officials to suggest policies that can reduce subsidies to the chain corporations and direct more local government spending to local enterprises. You can get plenty of good policy ideas at www. newrules.org.

As a family member, you can educate your family about the importance of supporting the local, green economy. Go food shopping together and look for organic, locally produced and Fair Trade Certified food. Organize a family meeting to discuss how you can keep more of your spending localized and green.

As a worker, you can encourage your company to consider an ESOP (Employee Stock Ownership Plan) which can be a step toward cooperative ownership. Help your workplace develop policies for purchasing supplies from local and green companies. If your workplace does not recycle and compost, you can organize it. If you help the company adopt technology that saves energy and water, it will save money that could be put into other things—like a pay raise!

As a businessperson, you can join one of the local business networks focused on keeping more money in the local economy. Contact BALLE (www. localeconomies.org) or AMIBA (www.amiba.net) for help in starting a chapter if there isn't one near you already.

As a neighbor, you can promote the subversive act of getting to know the people living near you. The best way to move beyond the counterfeit community of watching the same TV shows and buying the same commodities is to get to know people on a personal basis. Throw a house party and discuss ways you can work together to green your neighborhood. Planting trees in the sidewalks, for example, raises the standard of living for everyone.

As a consumer, you can shop consciously instead of unconsciously. Look for the Fair Trade Certified label on coffee, tea and chocolate (www.TransFairUSA. org) and the Certified Organic label on the food you buy (www.organicconsumers.org). Ask your local food vendors to expand the fair trade and organic products they offer.

As a student, you can work within your school to ensure your tuition dollars are being spent on green technologies like renewable energy, fuel efficient vehicles, and recycled paper. Create a green career for yourself by helping your school develop a sustainability plan. The skills you develop in that process will be in great demand as more corporations and governments go green.

If you take these actions with a kind heart and a big smile, you will be amazed at how much healthier you feel. Science has now proved that when you do an act of kindness toward another person, their serotonin levels go up, your serotonin levels go up, and anyone who observes that act of kindness has their serotonin levels go up. Being generous of spirit is in your best interest and also in the best interest of the community.

CONCLUSION

Building the Movement

The dominant economic model—the one built on turning nature into money—is sinking fast. It's like the Titanic after hitting the iceberg. We passengers have three choices. We can run around the ship yelling, "I protest, this boat sucks." We can continue to merely rearrange the deck chairs on the sinking vessel, tinkering with an obvious failure. Or we can get busy building a green lifeboat—solar- and wind-powered, made from recycled materials, and serving an organic buffet as people dance to cool music. When we pull up alongside, the passengers on the Titanic will happily jump to our boat.

That's the challenge before us—to make the green revolution irresistible. To do so will require a collective effort that enlists the majority of the earth's people. As our stories show, none of us can successfully do this work alone. Citizen activism is not a spectator sport; it's a participatory team effort. It requires that each one of us become a recruiter, eager to bring new people—friends, roommates, family, neighbors, co-workers—into the movement for an ecological transition. If we can energize enough people to get engaged, we can change the course of history.

Altering the course of history will take a huge amount of work. But it shouldn't feel like drudgery. The beauty of mass movements is the spirit of adventure and celebration that invigorates people. The word "inspiration" (a key goal of movement recruiters) comes from the Latin word *inspirare*: to breath into. Through inspiration we energize and invigorate others and create an alluring movement.

Humans are hard-wired for empathy. We all have what is known as limbic resonance—looking into the eyes of other mammals and communicating with them in some way. The limbic system of the brain is intertwined with the brain's pleasure center that transmits sexual gratification and the "high" from drugs. This helps explain why people who participate in movements for change often report getting high from social solidarity.

To create and sustain that natural high, the local green economy movement must focus itself on establishing connections. Nurturing connectivity among different causes and disparate communities can be our biomimicry, our way of mirroring the natural networks that form the basis for all ecology.

Each of the stories we have told is impressive. Yet they remain scattered examples. Their greatest weakness is that they are disconnected from each other. It's fair to ask: Do these stories together represent a movement?

The stories sketch the outline of a "greenprint" for society, a vision for how to integrate real democracy, environmental restoration, social justice, and financial sustainability. But whether that greenprint will become the main organizing principle for our species depends on whether the isolated efforts can come together and synergize. How to unite the toxic avengers, the local food producers, the independent merchants, and the political activists? Whether those interest groups will form a whole that is greater than the sum of its parts rests on the strength of the relationships we build and the connections we are able to make.

Community As Connection

Each of the previous stories speaks to the uniqueness of a community: different circumstances, different places, different approaches, and different people. Each story has specific lessons that other communities can learn from as we move toward the citizen-defined, local green economy. Despite their differences, these stories hold general lessons that tell us something about our broader shared experience. There are several lessons we draw from these stories.

The most obvious lesson involves the failures of the corporation. The transnational corporation is the institutional form that dominates our society, and it has two key features: It is not locally rooted (it has no patriotism to any specific location), and it systematically destroys the environment because it only values nature as a means to profit (e.g., lumber is more valuable that a living tree).

Despite our political and cultural differences, all people share a common humanity; what we have termed life values. The desire to protect ourselves and our families from harm is part of that natural operating system, and that desire makes us all environmentalists to some degree—no one wants to live near a toxic refinery. So the opposite of the corporate-driven, nature-destroying model is the local green economy, where communities calculate the quality of life by deciding the value of the place we call home. Some of the stories we've told lean more toward the green end of the spectrum; others are more about local control. But they all share a common commitment to prioritizing basic human needs—clean air, safe water, healthy food, and basic liberties—above the imperatives of the marketplace.

Some of our stories revolve around a regulatory system or legislative mechanism, processes that broadly favor large corporations. The inherent imbalance of these decision-making methods has forced citizens of varying political sympathies to question the limits of our democracy and the relationship between our government and corporate elites. In some cases, this skepticism has led communities to bypass the regulatory "parts per million" framework all together, opting instead to push for radical reforms that get to the root of the big question: Who should decide—local communities or corporations? Citizen activists have found that they have a greater chance of success at the local level than at the state or federal levels, where wealthier forces often drown out their voices. We do have a few allies in the higher reaches of government, but access at those levels is usually dictated by the large amounts of money needed to finance election campaigns. A fundamental premise of all the struggles we document is that the people who have to live with the results of policy-making should be the ones to control the decision-making process. Just as the people making mass transit policy should be bus riders, so too should the people making air quality rules be those who have to live next to the refineries.

Many of the successes of the local green economy movement have bypassed government altogether. With little or no help from government, social entrepreneurs have created their own organizations to install windmills, build useful products, and grow food. The entrepreneurial spirit of the 21st-century grassroots activists represents a sharp break from 20th-century political organizing. Instead of trying to take over the government to reform the economy from the top down, today's progressives are trying to take over the economy from the bottom up—and then use that economic strength to reform the government from below.

True to their grassroots nature, the struggles we document were sparked by immediate injustices. In the course of addressing a local issue, our citizen activists came to rely on outside assistance for success. The local community may have lacked the knowledge to build a windmill, to test for air quality, or to pass a city resolution defending civil liberties. And so they reached out to larger, more established organizations for help. This reveals the crucial role that national organizations can—and must—play in creating a green economy. Technical assistance, however, must spring from a spirit of mutual respect; national groups must be careful not to eclipse local efforts. Balancing local passion with outside expertise is a delicate dance. For victory to occur, such connections between grassroots and national organizations are vital.

The key word there is "connections." Community is, at its essence, all about connections, the relationships you have with your grocer and your neighbor and the people at your favorite deli. Without such connections, the community at the heart of these victories would not have been possible. Our stories illustrate the power of community to build change, and how the very act of struggle creates—or recreates—communities that had been absent or fractured. As the protagonists in our stories told us repeatedly, the community discovered or developed in the pursuit of justice did not recede after the victory. In fact, it was part of the victory, the most highly valued outcome of the success—even among groups who had previously been adversarial, such as loggers and conservationists in our Oregon story.

Another obstacle overcome by the heroes and heroines of our tales is the commodified definition of success, daily pounded into our heads by ubiquitous advertising, that says the highest attainment of the individual is measured *quantitatively* by the number and prices of the things you own. The sub-text of our stories—people redefining the very meaning of life—is radical in the best sense of the word: getting to the root of what matters. By making new, personal connections, communities have redefined success to be a *qualitative* measure of our relationships with other people and Mother Nature.

Some would say that we have never had a true democracy in this country, but the people in our stories are proving the cynics wrong. They are setting the rules for themselves, and they are doing so all over the country. Folks that have never fought city hall before are taking a stand. They are making a mental connection between their quality of life and the political processes that determine how they live.

Despite the potential for movement-building inherent in our successes, many of these efforts remain a well-kept secret, uncovered mostly through word of mouth or Internet sleuthing. They are disconnected from each other. By connecting these struggles, we can unlock a powerful, kinetic energy. Forgive us for stretching our earlier Titanic metaphor, but these stories can be seen as more than isolated free floating ice sheets. Linked together, they reveal the tip of a huge iceberg: average citizens awakening to the power of participatory democracy.

It is here that national groups can provide more than random assistance to locals in distress. National groups can help link these groups, creating a network of mobilized communities. National groups can also provide vigilance at the state and national levels where locals can't detect threats to their hard-won victories. Rather than fighting local communities one by one, corporations find it more efficient to work quietly with lawmakers to strike down whole classes of laws designed to protect the environment, health, and safety. Corporate-influenced preemptive laws at the state and federal levels can, for example, prohibit municipal and county governments from passing laws that ban corporate hog farms, regulate water discharges, and prohibit GMOs. As communities take local action to protect their welfare, corporations are trying to cut off those efforts by leveraging influence in the state and federal political bodies where their power is stronger. National groups are best situated to be the watchdogs for these sly miscarriages of justice. They can sound the alarm, enabling citizen networks to apply pressure on lawmakers before a single sweep of a legislative pen wipes out the hard work of dozens or even hundreds of communities.

This is already happening. But there is much more that can be done if national groups see the self-interest in assisting local efforts. Residents fighting to redefine their communities are connecting the single-issue silos that fragment the progressive movement. As we have seen, residents fighting toxic sludge, farmers protecting the food chain from GMOs, and neighbors seeking access to healthy food all came to identify corporate agribusiness and the regulatory-legislative framework as the source of their problems. These diverse communities underwent similar political awakenings that shifted their worldview. Because of the new political space created by these campaigns, national groups can find new allies at the local level. Thus, a powerful political synergy is created when local networks, mobilizing at the grassroots, collaborate with national groups exposing the workings of elite policy making.

The Honeybee Economy

The key to creating a humane, sustainable future lies in redefining what we mean when we say "development" and "progress." One of the keys to redefining development is asking the question: How does capital get invested? Whether the issue is job creation, immigration, environmental destruction, or gender equity, it requires looking at the question of how capital gets invested. This leads to two subsidiary questions: First, who is at the table when the decisions get made? Is it just old, rich, white, male corporate executives? Or is it the bouquet of humanity, where all interests are represented democratically? Second, what are the core values driving the process? Is it to maximize corporate profits by turning nature and human creativity into money? Or is it to meet all social needs and save the environment? The answers will determine the fate of future generations.

The greening pioneers profiled in this book are developing a new model of capital accumulation. The investment model of the past has been based on exclusion. Banks and corporations control most of the money, and if you want some you have to pay them rent (interest). The ruling classes are able to exclude billions of people from the decision-making process because our current economic system tends to concentrate wealth into fewer and fewer hands.

Nature's model, on the other hand, is based on inclusion. It is a model of reciprocity and interdependence that rests on mutually beneficial relationships. Our biomimicry, then, should strive to create a kind of "honeybee economy." The honeybee does not hurt the flower when it makes honey; it helps the flower. The 21st-century version of that would tell the factory owner that it is okay to have a smokestack only if he or she is willing to live next door to the smokestack.

In the local green economy, we can replicate nature's model by returning profits to the community from which those profits were derived. Think of it as composting money. As Jim Hightower is fond of saying, capital is like cow manure. Concentrate it in a big pile and it stinks, but spread it out evenly and it makes things grow.

Agreeing to spread out the money requires a shift from the mentality of competition to the spirit of cooperation. It demands an optimistic view of human nature. We believe there is a sound basis for that optimism. We think that the green economy can anchor itself in a very basic ideal: "Do unto others as you would have them do unto you."

That could sound hokey until you realize that it is the closest thing we have to a universal human principle. Every spiritual tradition has some version of the Golden Rule. In Buddhism, it is: "Treat not others in ways that you yourself would find hurtful." In Islam, it is: "Not one of you truly believes until you wish for others what you wish for yourself." In Judaism, it is: "What is hateful to you, do not do to your neighbor." In Matthew 7:12, Jesus says, "So in everything, do to others what you would have them do to you; for this sums up the Law and the Prophets."

The trick is to expand the definition of "others" to include all life forms. We must realize that we can't exterminate, say, the red-legged frog any more than we would want the frog to exterminate us. We need to create a spirituality that has no "them." We need a worldview of just "us." And "just us" sounds a lot like "justice."

Growing a Green Movement

Because nature's core organizing principle is unity-of-diversity, we need to create institutions that can act as convergence platforms, bringing together the disparate parts of this movement to cross-fertilize and generate new synergies. In the spirit of launching a strategic dialogue, we propose the following institutions that could focus on networking the local green economy. These local networks could also be globally integrated to maximize the power of our self-evolving global brain. Each of the following institutions shares these characteristics: they are designed to synergize with each other; they achieve several social and environmental goals at once; they are designed to be adaptable to local conditions in most parts of the world; and they can be networked on a global scale.

The Green Guardians will organize school-age youth to green their school campuses and surrounding neighborhoods. In the process, the students, their teachers, and their parents will learn about: green building materials; heating and air-conditioning systems; water conservation and rain catchment; how to start and run a neighborhood recycling center; composting cafeteria waste (to go into the school garden that is growing food for the cafeteria); and how to develop materials for educating the general community.

The students can refine their community-organizing skills by going out to nearby merchants and residents to recruit them into community-betterment programs that clean up the neighborhood, plant trees, create pocket parks, introduce local restaurants to composting, teach local offices how to separate recycled paper (white paper can be sold), and how to create a sense of community—all with the clear moral authority of children leading the way.

Because the Green Guardians will be writing up their experiences and giving oral presentations on these vital subjects, they will develop one of life's most important skills, expressing yourself in words that can touch another person's heart. Students will be happier because this type of hands-on, relevant learning is way more interesting than sitting all day at desks in neat little rows. Teachers will be happier because if the children are actually excited about the learning process it will make the teachers' jobs much easier. Administrators will be happier because the children will come up with ways to make the school building run more efficiently, thus saving the taxpayers' money and making the administrators look good. And parents will be happier because their children will be learning their basic academic subjects while also developing practical skills that will be increasingly valuable as the environmental crisis deepens.

As the Green Guardians learn more advanced greening skills, they enter the first of a three-stage green workforce development program that also includes Green Careers courses in local community colleges, and apprenticeships and job placement in green social enterprises. Older Green Guardians get paid to receive professional training in green community service skills such as recycling, composting, tree planting, green building technology, computer skills, urban agriculture, conflict resolution and street safety, public education, and other important career skills.

By connecting talented youth with green organizations that can impart technical and social skills, and connecting them to green career courses at local community colleges, we can create a green workforce development program with potential ramifications for the country and the planet. After all, if there is to be a green economy, where is the green workforce going to come from? And by focusing initially on low-income youth, we ensure that the green train does not leave the station without the very people who have been left behind so many times in the past.

Green Careers Departments in community colleges will introduce students to the careers of the future. As the crisis of nature intensifies and the dollar impact is increasingly felt, work that saves resources and protects the ecosystem will go up in value. Community colleges are the most affordable form of higher education, and are therefore ethnically diverse and mainly working class. Many community colleges are already writing campus sustainability plans, and the students could be directly involved in this process: e.g., the water system portion would involve students and faculty researching and redesigning the water systems of their campuses; the energy portion would unite students, faculty and administrators in redesigning campus energy systems. This would ensure that the sustainability plan goes beyond being a mere document, to creating a core team of people with the skills and passion to put the plan into practice.

Green Careers Departments can introduce students to the wide range of career choices in the green economy: water purification and conservation technology, renewable energy, biofuels, mass transit technology, green building methods and materials, green sourcing of office materials, greening of events, urban planning issues such as how to make streets more bike- and pedestrian-friendly, and many more to be hatched by a Green Enterprise Institute.

Green Enterprise Institute: This is a collaborative platform for area colleges, green companies, nonprofits, and government agencies to incubate green community plans and green career skills, promote clean-tech research and green enterprise development, patent green technology, and green the campuses of schools, governments and corporations. The collaboration of these three primary sectors (government, enterprise, nonprofits) will result in benefits for all: new technology to reduce the effects of global warming, personnel with the necessary career skills, and financial models that reduce costs, increase revenues, and channel capital into the most productive areas for slowing humanity's negative impact on the environment.

Students and faculty can research the best aspects of existing campus sustainability plans and incorporate them into the work of the Green Enterprise Institute. The resulting strategic plan will be useful to hundreds of campuses and cities that have not yet embarked on this journey. If we develop a successful institutional model, we can help people in other cities replicate their own localized version of that model. An "open source" approach to institution building can spread the new system more rapidly than a hierarchical model.

What we are here calling a Green Enterprise Institute already exists in Canada. The Centre for Interactive Research on Sustainability (CIRS) in Vancouver (a collaboration between the University of British Columbia, the British Columbia Institute of Technology, Simon Fraser University, and the Emily Carr Institute) has created a living laboratory where entrepreneurs and academics come together to develop cutting edge technologies for saving people and the planet through eco-design. By using a consortium model, the CIRS spreads risk by sharing expenses, and synergizes human and material resources, benefiting all the participating institutions and the local economy of Vancouver.

Green Apprenticeships and Job Placement address the fact that it does no good to train people in green community development skills if they can't find a decent job after the training. Through organizations such as the Green Festivals, the Co-op America Business Network, BALLE, AMIBA, and many others, we can create a green jobs and apprenticeships network that will do the matchmaking between companies needing personnel with green skills and the job seekers wanting to fill those jobs. We list in the Resources section some of the best websites already doing this work.

Green Festivals (www.greenfestivals.org) are weekend events that expose tens of thousands of people to the fact that the green economy already exists and it is populated by fun-loving, openhearted people who care about future generations. Now operating in four cities (San Francisco, Washington, DC, Chicago, and Seattle), the Green Festivals can be replicated in other parts of the world in order to connect the general public to the burgeoning green economy. This weekend "party with a purpose" gives people a taste (literally) of the economy of the future. It combines commerce, education, and entertainment in a dynamic balance that fosters new values and ventures aimed at accelerating the shift to a green economy.

Global Citizen Centers (www.globalcitizencenter.org) will be brought to you by some of the same people who brought you the Green Festivals. The GCC is another institutional model designed to be a locally replicable platform where diverse sectors of the movement can unite and cross-fertilize to everyone's benefit. Here again, there is an existing model, Green Exchange (www.greenexchange.com) in Chicago. A planned San Francisco Green Exchange will feature offices of green enterprises and nonprofit social change organizations, an organic food court, a mind-body wellness center, a digital media center, an event space for educational and cultural events, and a green social enterprise incubator. This green showcase then becomes the base for developing Green Zones.

Green Zones are community-based networks bringing together diverse forces to raise the quality of life (socially and environmentally) in a whole neighborhood, with sustainability as a core guiding principle. There are several trends that can be bridged to make this exciting model of sustainability come to life.

The premier green building network in the country, the U.S. Green Building Council (www.usgbc.org), has produced a detailed set of design guidelines for greening entire neighborhoods (LEED-ND, which stands for Leadership in Energy and Environmental Design-Neighborhood Development). The Green Guardians youth group and their adult advisors can take that 100-page LEED-ND document, and involve the community in changing the technical language into a popular format, and distribute it throughout the neighborhood to be used as the People's Plan for Green Neighborhood Development.

There are a growing number of organizations, such as the Funders Network for Smart Growth and Livable Communities (www.fundersnetwork.org), committed to supporting sustainable neighborhood development. City governments of all political stripes look favorably on neighborhoods that can get their act together and raise the standard of living in their community.

This project can create a network of individuals and institutions with the requisite skills and resources to green a neighborhood such that people will come from other areas to see how you did it. Of course, you will gladly share the information in order to foster Green Zones around the world and link them in a global network of local best practices.

While we are talking about institution building, we would be remiss if we failed to acknowledge that the Green Party is the third largest political party in the United States, with hundreds of elected office holders. Although the Green Party has not yet lived up to its full potential, its policy proposals are miles ahead of the two main corporate parties. In some countries, such as England, the conservatives are trying to outflank their more liberal counterparts by taking stronger stands on the environment. Wouldn't it be sweet if the Democrats and Republicans tried to out-green the Green Party?

The Cathedral Builder's Mindset

Synergizing the diverse sectors of the local green economy will take time; movement-building doesn't happen overnight. While we must work urgently because the situation requires nothing less, we should recognize that some of us may not live to see the green vision reach maturity. Social activism requires perseverance and the understanding that we ourselves may not benefit from the sacrifices we make. "It is not always granted the sower to see the harvest," Albert Schweitzer once wrote. "All work that is worth anything is done in faith." For us to do the work that needs to be done without succumbing to discouragement or cynicism requires that we adopt the cathedral-builder's mentality.

When the masons laid the foundations of those large cathedrals in Europe that took centuries to build, they knew they would not see the final product of their work. The craftsmen understood that the endeavor was greater than any individual's lifetime. Yet those master builders took the utmost care in their labor, for they knew the entire construction would rest on their work.

That is the consciousness we need in laying the foundation of the locally owned, globally networked, green economy. We have to think beyond our own lifetimes in terms of the work we do. We must have the courage to be visionaries. As journalist I.F. Stone said: "If you expect an answer to your question during your lifetime, you are not asking a big enough question."

The cathedral builders, like Schweitzer's sower, worked on faith. Belief in ultimate success is what kept them going. If we believe, deep down in our hearts, that we can change the course of history, we *will* change the course of history.

Our challenge to you is: Do you believe? Do you have your mortar and your trowel in hand? Are you ready to get to work?

RESOURCES

We start with the groups directly related to sections of the book, followed by general groups that are working to democratize our economy and our politics. We apologize if we left out your favorite organization.

Section One
Toxic Avengers

Refinery Reform Campaign
www.refineryreform.org, (415) 643-1870
739 Cortland Ave., San Francisco, CA 94110

Communities for a Better Environment
www.cbecal.org, (510) 302-0430
1440 Broadway, Suite 701, Oakland, CA 94612

National Black Environmental Justice Network
www.nbejn.org, (202) 265-4919
P.O. Box 14944, Detroit, MI 48214

Community Environmental Legal Defense Fund (CELDF)
www.celdf.org, (717) 709-0457
675 Mower Road, Chambersburg, PA 17201

Section Two
Food & Water

Grupo de Agricultura Orgánica (GAO)
Tulipán 1011 e/Loma y 47, Apdo. Postal 6236C
Código Postal 10600, Nuevo Vedado
Ciudad de La Habana, CUBA
Phone: +53 7 845 387, Email: actaf@minag.gov.cu

Organoponico Vivero Alamar
Ave 160 y Parque Hanoi, Zona 6, Alamar
Ciudad de La Habana, CUBA
Tel: 53 7 930532
Email: ubpcalamar@agrinfor.cu and viveroalamar@sih.cu

Proyecto Comunitario Convservación de Alimentos
(Community Projection for Conserving Food)
Vilda Figueroa and José (Pepe) Lama)
Calle 96 No. 5501, E/ 55 y 57 Marianao
Apartado Postal 14039, Código Postal 11400
Ciudad de La Habana, CUBA
Tel: 53 7 260 4499
Email: conserva@ceniai.inf.cu

Applegate River Watershed Council
www.arwc.org, (541) 899-9982
6941 Upper Applegate Road, Jacksonville, OR 97530

LaDonna Redmond
Chicago State University, Department of Geography, Williams Science Bldg. 311
9500 South King Drive, Chicago, IL 60624

Organic Consumers Association
www.organicconsumers.org, (218) 226-4164
6771 South Silver Hill Drive, Finland MN 55603

Food Routes Network
www.foodroutes.org, (570) 638-3608
PO Box 55 - 35 Apple Lane, Arnot, PA 16911

LocalHarvest
www.localharvest.org, (831) 475-8150
220 21st Ave, Santa Cruz, CA 95062

Community Food Security Coalition
www.foodsecurity.org, (310) 822-5410
P.O. Box 209 , Venice, CA 90294

American Community Gardening Association
www.communitygarden.org, (877) 275-2242
c/o Franklin Park Conservatory
1777 East Broad Street, Columbus, OH 43203

Organic Farming Research Foundation
www.ofrf.org, (831) 426-6606
P.O. Box 440, Santa Cruz, CA 95061

Section Three

From Mean Streets to Green Streets

Participatory Budgeting Project
www.participatorybudgeting.org.uk, Tel: 0161 236 9321
c/o Church Action on Poverty, Central Buildings
Oldham Street, Manchester M1 1JT, UK

Ella Baker Center for Human Rights
www.ellabakercenter.org, (510) 428-3939
344 40th Street, Oakland, CA 94609

Program on Corporations, Law and Democracy
www.poclad.org, (508) 398-1145
P.O. Box 246, S. Yarmouth, MA 02664

Bill of Rights Defense Committee
www.bordc.org, (413) 582-0110
8 Bridge St., Suite A, Northampton, MA 01060 ·

Section Four

Power to the People

Sierra Club Cool Cities
www.coolcities.us

ICLEI - Local Governments for Sustainability, USA Inc.
www.iclei.org (510) 844-0699
436 14th Street, Suite 1520, Oakland, CA 94612

KyotoUSA
www.kyotousa.org, (510) 704-8628
800 Hearst Ave., Berkeley, CA 94710

Rosebud Sioux Tribe Utility Commission
www.rosebudsiouxtribe-nsn.gov/
877) 837-8729 or (605) 747-4097

Intertribal COUP (Council on Utility Policy)
www.intertribalcoup.org, (605) 945-1908
P.O. Box 25 Rosebud, SD 57570

NativeEnergy
www.nativeenergy.com, (800) 924.6826
823 Ferry Road, P.O. Box 539, Charlotte, VT 05445

Section Five
The Freedom of Everyone
To Be Enterprising

Local First Utah
www.localfirst.org, (801) 828-0676
P.O. Box 576, Salt Lake City, UT 84110-0576

Vest Pocket Business Coalition
www.vestpocket.org, (801) 596-8977
P. O. Box 521357, Salt Lake City, Utah 84152-1357

U.S. Federation of Worker Co-ops
www.usworker.coop, (415) 379-9201
P.O. Box 170701, San Francisco, CA 94117-0701

BALLE (Business Alliance for Local Living Economies)
www.livingeconomies.org, (415) 255-1108
165 11th Street, San Francisco, CA 94103

Fetzer Vineyards
www.fetzer.com, (707) 744-1250
13601 Eastside Road, Hopland, CA 95449

California Sustainable Winegrowing Alliance
www.sustainablewinegrowing.org, (415) 512-0151
425 Market Street, Suite 1000, San Francisco, CA 94105

Green Economy

CoopAmerica.org features many services covering green shopping, fair trade, conservation, socially responsible business, green energy and climate action.

GlobalExchange.org features fair trade shopping, Independence from Oil activism, green economy projects such as GlobalCitizenCenter.org, and Reality Tours to economic development projects in many countries.

GreenFestivals.org, a joint project of Co-op America and Global Exchange, organizes large weekend events uniting hundreds of green companies, 100 speakers, live music, organic food and drink, and much more.

The Green Guide (thegreenguide.com) offers a bi-monthly e-newsletter and comprehensive practical information on how to green your life.

U.S. Green Building Council (usgbc.org) is the premier organization for establishing green building standards in the United States.

The Organic Consumers Association (organicconsumers.org) can help you find local news, events and green businesses that promote all things organic.

Advancedbuildings.org presents products and practices that improve the energy and resource efficiency of commercial and multi-unit residential buildings

GreenBiz.com is a treasure trove of resources on aligning the two greens: environment and enterprise.

grist.org is one of the best websites for environmental news and opinion.

Congress for the New Urbanism (cnu.org) The New Urbanism movement is rapidly spreading the concept of walkable, human-scaled neighborhoods as the building blocks of sustainable communities.

Green Jobs and Careers

Sustainablebusiness.com has many useful features: a comprehensive green resources section, Green Dream Jobs, and a Progressive Investor newsletter.

Treehugger has a number of cool services, including green job listings at http://jobs.treehugger.com!

Marie Kerpan is the founder of Green Careers, which helps people find jobs that support ecological, social and economic sustainability. www.geocities.com/greencareers

Renewable Energy Access (renewableenergyaccess.com) Includes, among its many features, a jobs section for employers and job seekers.

Revoking Corporate Power

The New Rules Project (newrules.org) provides research and policy innovation that empowers citizens and cleans up the environment. Offers dozens of models for rules encouraging democratization and sustainability by reporting on best practices .

Citizen Works (citizenworks.org) Provides a "toolbox" of techniques and information for activists and community organizers.

The Community Environmental Legal Defense Fund (celdf.org) has outstanding resources, including model legislation and a citizen's guide to researching corporations.

Program on Corporations, Law and Democracy (poclad.org) is a long-time leader in rethinking the role of corporations and the meaning of democracy.

Women's International League for Peace and Freedom (wilpf.org) WILPF produces a superb study guide, "Challenging Corporate Power, Asserting the People's Rights," available free (pdf) online.

The Aurora Institute (aurora.ca) educates and organizes on corporate power issues in Canada, whose corporate legal history has closely matched that of the United States.

The Alliance for Democracy (alliancefordemocracy.org) has local groups around the country confronting corporate power. See if there's an active group near you.

Community Economics & Business

American Independent Business Alliance (AMIBA) amiba.net. They strengthen community-owned businesses through IBAs (Independent Business Alliances).

Rocky Mountain Institute's Economic Renewal Program (rmi.org) shows businesses, communities, and governments how to create more wealth and employment, while protecting natural and human capital.

Business Alliance for Local Living Economies (localeconomies.org) BALLE is an alliance of businesspeople across the United States and Canada, who join local BALLE networks dedicated to building local living economies. BALLE comprises 48 such local business networks with more than 15,000 member businesses.

Center for Community Change is a good resource for researching community development block grants. (communitychange.org)

wiserearth.org and **wiserbusiness.org** are two excellent websites connecting progressive forces worldwide.

Political Reform

National Voting Rights Initiative (nvri.org) defends the constitutional rights of all citizens, regardless of economic status, to participate in the electoral process on an equal and meaningful basis.

Center for Voting & Democracy (fairvote.org) offers a huge array of information on several electoral reform issues and is the definitive resource on Instant Runoff Voting.

Brennan Center for Justice (brennancenter.org) provides information on legal issues in campaign reform, civil rights and poverty issues within the legal system.

Ballot Access News (ballot-access.org) offers a wealth of resources on issues relating to opportunities for independent and third party candidates and for citizen initiatives. They track news from each state as well as nationally.

Common Cause (commoncause.org) offers information on the corruption of democracy by the power of money, and ideas for improving elections.

Center for Responsive Politics (opensecrets.org) is a great resource for information on money in politics and campaign finance law.

The Sentencing Project (sentencingproject.org) confronts harms of the criminal justice industry, racial injustice in the system, disenfranchisement and more.

Public Campaign (publicampaign.org) is devoted to implementing publicly financed elections around the United States.

Initiative and Referendum Institute (ballotwatch.org) the premier source of information on Initiative & Referendum topics.

National Initiative for Democracy (ni4d.org) promotes direct democracy via ballot initiatives. A similar effort, vote.org, is organizing for more direct democracy.

Education

GreenTeacher.com is the website of Green Teacher magazine, featuring practical resources for educating youth ages 6-18 about environmental issues.

Rethinking Schools (rethinkingschools.org) a journal committed to the vision that public education is central to democracy. Written for a broad audience, RS emphasizes problems facing urban schools, especially issues of race.

AlfieKohn.org offers important perspectives on the dangers of high stakes tests, commercialism and many crucial education issues. Kohn challenges much conventional wisdom in a provocative and engaging way.

Consumers' Union (consumersunion.org/other/captivekids/index.htm) gives an in-depth critique of corporate influence on our children.

Health, Food & Environment

The True Food Network (truefoodnow.org) is a consumer network campaigning to ban genetically engineered foods by providing educational and activist resources.

Rachel's Environment and Health Weekly (rachel.org) addresses the roots of environmental problems in corporate power and the decay of democracy. Their newsletter is essential reading and has the full archives in both English and Spanish.

Family Farmer (familyfarmer.org) is an advocacy organization promoting family ownership and environmentally sound agriculture.

Cancer Prevention Coalition (preventcancer.org) challenges the dominance of the "find a cure" perspective and encourages focusing energy on stopping production of carcinogens.

Native Forest Council (forestcouncil.org) recognizes revoking corporate power as essential to preserving our National Forests and other public lands.

Wild Wilderness (WildWilderness.org) works to keep public lands public and undeveloped, with a focus on stopping corporatization of those lands.

Civil Rights

The Center for Constitutional Rights (ccr-ny.org) vigorously defends the U.S. Constitution and international human rights accords.

Ella Baker Center for Human Rights (ellabakercenter.org) focuses on street violence and police brutality, and promotes alternatives to incarceration.

The Constitution Society (constitution.org) is a basic source on the U.S. Constitution, and has thousands of documents and books online.

National Lawyers Guild (nlg.org) is a progressive association of lawyers assisting legal efforts to challenge corporate power.

Bill of Rights Defense Committee (bordc.org) is a national network of people who are taking action to restore protections guaranteed under the Bill of Rights and the U.S. Constitution.

Center for National Security Studies (cnss.org) is a non-governmental research organization working to prevent FBI and CIA violations of civil liberties.

Organized Labor

AFL-CIO (aflcio.org) is a 10-million member trade union federation comprising 54 national and international unions.

Changetowin.org was founded in September 2005 by seven unions and six million workers devoted to building an activist movement of working people in the United States.

American Federation of State, County and Municipal Employees (afscme.org) has extensive information on privatization issues.

Center for Economic and Policy Research (cepr.net) features resources on domestic and international economic issues from a progressive standpoint.

Center for Labor & Community Research (clcr.org) addresses worker ownership and alternative models of economic development.

Labor Notes (LaborNet.org) is an online communication hub for a democratic, independent labor movement.

Global Trade & Treaties

Global Exchange (globalexchange.org) works for global economic justice, fair trade and accelerating the transition to the green economy.

Public Citizen's Global Trade Watch (tradewatch.org) is a great resource for staying abreast of U.S. legislation relating to corporate globalization.

Economic Policy Institute (epinet.org) their trade & globalization page has excellent background.

Council of Canadians (Canadians.org) tracks corporate globalization and many justice issues of interest to Canadians.

Oakland Institute (oaklandinstitute.org) works to increase public participation and promote fair debate on critical social, economic and environmental issues.

Resource Center of the Americas (americas.org) focuses on Central & South American issues.

Third World Network twnside.org.sg has one of the most extensive resource collections on corporate globalization, especially.

Researching Corporations

Public Information Network (endgame.org) is a clearinghouse of information for researching corporations.

Community Environmental Legal Defense Fund (celdf.org) provides affordable legal services to community-based groups and local governments working to protect the environment and build sustainable communities.

Corpwatch (corpwatch.org) exposes corporate malfeasance worldwide and supports corporate accountability campaigns.

Independent News on the Web

Common Dreams (commondreams.org) a daily online collection of opinion, news and leaks from a progressive perspective.

DemocracyNow.org is an increasingly popular TV, radio and web news source from a progressive perspective. Includes headlines in Spanish.

Alternet.org provides daily news and commentary from a critical perspective.

truthout.org provides a wide variety of news, commentary and video clips about current political issues.

indymedia.org is a unique network of news sites in over 30 countries and eighty cities where any individual can post news, opinion pieces, photos and more, a great source for coverage of mass protests and direct actions.

Media Reform Information Center (corporations.org/media) features useful information about media consolidation and democratic media movements.

Index

X
Xavier University 23, 25

Y
Yale University 186
Young, Connie 95

Z
Zambia 86
Zechiel, Suzanne 225
Zinn, Ryan 80

Acknowledgments

With special thanks to Nancy Schaub, without whom this book would not have been possible.

Our deepest gratitude to our research and interview interns who gave so generously of their time and skills: Robbert van Overdijk, Abby Reider, Tamara Wattnem, Kailin Clarke, Whitney Merchant, Jessie Appleman and Allison Mahoney. Big shout out to our design advisors Kernan Coleman at Ranch 7, and Kami Griffiths.

We are also grateful to Peter Richardson, Jonathan Harris, Scott Jordan, and the rest of the PoliPointPress team for their enthusiasm and support.

Notes

Sick and Tired of Living Next to (S)hell:
Residents Force an Oil Giant to Pay for Toxic Terror

1. John McQuaid, "Unwelcome neighbors: How the poor bear the burdens of America's pollution—Transforming the Land," *The Times-Picayune*, May 21, 2000.

2. www.refineryreform.org/downloads/LouisianaGreen58.pdf

3. Ibid.

Sludge Busters:
Porter, Pennsylvania Sets New Rules for Corporations

1. John Tuohy, "CDC sounds a warning on risk of sludge," *USA TODAY*, July 13, 2000.

Green Acres in the Windy City:
Urban Farming Grows Food Justice in Chicago

1. LaDonna Redmond, "Creating local food options in an urban setting," http://www.newfarm.org/features/1104/urban_farm/index_print.shtml.

2. Ibid.

3. Robert E. Pierre, "Chicago Neighbors Plot A Way to Healthier Food," *The Washington Post*, August 14, 2002.

Seeds of Change:
Dakota Farmers Give Monsanto the Boot

1. Larry Remele, Education & Interpretation Division, State Historical Society of North Dakota. This summary history of North Dakota appeared in the 1989 *North Dakota Blue Book*, a publication of the North Dakota Secretary of State. The history was originally written in 1988.

2. "Non partisan league ... U.S. History" Initiative & Referendum Institute at the University of Southern California http://www.iandrinstitute.org/North%20Dakota.htm

3. Charles M. Benbrook, "Genetically Engineered Crops and Pesticide Use in the United States: The First Nine Years," BioTech InfoNet Technical Paper n.7, October 25, 2004.

4. Ted Nace, "Breadbasket of Democracy." *Orion*, 2006. http://www.orionsociety.org/pages/om/06-3om/Nace.html

5. Ibid.

Loggers and Lizards Find Common Ground:
Saving an Oregon Watershed

1. Kathie Durbin, "The progress of freewheeling consensus jeopardized as feds pull back," *High Country News*, vol. 26, No. 19, October 17, 1994, http://www.hcn.org

Breaking the Chains:
Parents and Locals Transform a Juvenile Prison

1. "The Juvenile Justice Reform Act of 2003: A Summary," www.jjpl.org/PDF/Act_1225_summary.doc.

2. James Austin, et al., "Alternatives to the Secure Detention and Confinement of Juvenile Offenders," http://realcostofprisons.org/materials/Alternatives_to_Juv_Incarceration-10-05.pdf.

3. Jasmine Tyler, et al., "Cost Effective Corrections: The Fiscal Architecture of Rational Juvenile Justice Systems" (Washington DC: The Justice Policy Institute, 2006). http://www.justicepolicy.org/reports/CostEffectiveYouthCorrections306.pdf

4. "Building Blocks for Youth," http://www.buildingblocksforyouth.org/issues/

5. Bervera, Xochitl. "Families and Friends of Louisiana's Incarcerated Children." Applied Research Center, 2003. http://www.arc.org/pdf/281pdf.pdf.

Culture Shift in the Land of the Giants:
A California County Redefines Corporate Rights

1. http://www.duhc.org/Who_Rules.html

2. Porter, PA (story on page 35) was the first U.S. city to pass an anti-corporate personhood ordinance.

Harnessing the Saudia Arabia of Wind:
The Rosebud Sioux Bring Renewable Energy to the Dakotas

1. U.S. Department of Labor, Bureau of Labor Statistics, originally published March 3, 2004.

2. Energy Information Administration, "Energy Consumption and Renewable Energy Development Potential on Indian Lands," http://www.eia.doe.gov/cneaf/solar.renewables/ilands/ilands_sum.html, Table ES2: Indian Lands With Highest Potential for Central Station Development.

3. Carlye Adler, "Turning Point: A South Dakota tribe's utility rides the wind to a brighter and cleaner future," *Fortune Small Business*, February 1, 2005.

4. Lisa Chamley, "Turbines generating dreams for tribe," *Pierre Capital Journal*, September 15, 2005 at www.rapidcityjournal.com, and http://www.climateemergency.org/joomla/index.php?Itemid=163&id=208&option=com_content&task=view.

5. Winona LaDuke, "Tribal leadership for the next energy economy," *Indian Country Today*, March, 2005.

6. DOE Wind Power Pioneer Interview: Dale Osborn, DISGEN Corp., http://www.eere.energy.gov/windandhydro/windpoweringamerica/filter_detail.asp?itemid=681

7. Carlye Adler, op.cit.

8. Ibid.

Section 5 Introduction:

The Freedom of Everyone to Be Enterprising

1. http://www.civiceconomics.com/Andersonville/

2. Stephan J. Goetz and Anil Rupasingha, "Wal-Mart and Social Capital," *American Journal of Agricultural Economics*, December 2006.

3. Dr. Marlon Boarnet and Dr. Randall Crane, "The Impact of Big Box Grocers on Southern California: Jobs, Wages, and Municipal Finances," Prepared for the Orange County Business Council, 1999.

About the Authors

Described by *The New York Times* as the "Paul Revere of globalization's woes," Dr. **Kevin Danaher** is a cofounder of Global Exchange, Executive Director of the Global Citizen Center, and Executive Co-Producer of the Green Festivals in San Francisco, Washington, DC, Chicago and Seattle. He is the author or editor of eleven books, including *Ten Reasons to Abolish the IMF and World Bank* (Seven Stories Press), and (with Jason Mark) *Insurrection: Citizen Challenges to Corporate Power* (Routledge).

Shannon Biggs directs the Local Economy project at Global Exchange. As a former senior staffer at the International Forum on Globalization (IFG) she wrote for and edited IFG publications, and was a lecturer on International Relations at San Francisco State University. She holds a Masters degree from the London School of Economics in economics, empire and post-colonialism.

Dubbed a "rebel with a cause" by *TIME* magazine, **Jason Mark** is an author-activist who helped launch the national Freedom from Oil campaign. His writings have appeared in *Orion*, *The Nation*, *Grist*, *Alternet*, and *E*, among other publications. He lives in San Francisco, where he co-manages an urban organic farm (www.alemanyfarm.org) and edits the environmental quarterly *Earth Island Journal*.

About Global Exchange

Global Exchange is an international human rights organization promoting social, economic and environmental justice. For twenty years, our nonprofit enterprise model has created a diverse range of educational methods.

• Our *Reality Tours* take people to nations of the global south with a "reverse Club Med" approach: get out of the hotel and meet the development groups, farmers' organizations, womens' groups and others creating grassroots, democratic development.

• Our *Fair Trade stores* in San Francisco, Berkeley, Portland and on-line (http://store.gxonlinestore.org/) educate consumers by introducing them to fair trade crafts produced by development projects throughout the global south. By providing these grassroots groups with a market for their products, we give them a source of revenue independent from foundations and governments.

• Our Green Festivals (co-produced with Co-op America) are now in four cities: San Francisco, Washington, DC, Chicago and Seattle. These weekend events bring together hundreds of green enterprises, nonprofit environmental and social justice organizations, and tens of thousands of attendees who believe in accelerating the transition to the green economy (greenfestivals.org).

• Our Freedom from Oil campaign is pressuring the auto industry to adopt a zero-emissions plan. We are also mobilizing students on hundreds of campuses across the United States and Canada who are pressuring their administrators to green their practices and reduce their campus carbon footprints.

• Our peace work—in collaboration with Code Pink: Women for Peace—plays a leading role in the anti-war movement, pressuring the politicians to bring our troops home and shift resources from the military to meeting social and environmental needs (codepink4peace.org).

• Our Mexico program is building links of solidarity between progressive forces in the U.S. and Mexico, educating citizens and legislators to push for more just relations between our two countries.

• Our corporate accountability campaigns have forced sweatshop companies to raise their wages and improve their working conditions. Our extensive website has free tools for organizing against corporate domination.

**TO FIND OUT ABOUT THESE AND OTHER PROGRAMS,
PLEASE VISIT OUR WEBSITE: www.globalexchange.org**

Other Books from PoliPointPress

The Blue Pages: A Directory of Companies Rated by Their Politics and Practices. Helps consumers match their buying decisions with their political values by listing the political contributions and business practices of over 1,000 companies. $9.95, PAPERBACK

Cowboy Republic: Six Ways the Bush Gang Has Defied the Law, by Marjorie Cohn. Shows how the executive branch under President Bush has systematically defied the law instead of enforcing it. $14.95, PAPERBACK

Best Care Anywhere: Why VA Health Care Is Better Than Yours, by Phillip Longman. Shows how the turnaround at the long-maligned VA hospitals provides a blueprint for salvaging America's expensive but troubled health care system. $14.95, PAPERBACK

The Spirit of Disobedience: Resisting the Charms of Fake Politics, Mindless Consumption, and the Culture of Total Work, by Curtis White. Debunks the notion that liberalism has no need for spirituality and describes a "middle way" through our red state/blue state political impasse. Includes three powerful interviews with John DeGraaf, James Howard Kunstler, and Michael Ableman. $24.00, HARDCOVER

House of Ill Repute: Reflections on War, Lies, and America's Ravaged Reputation, by William Rivers Pitt. Skewers the Bush Administration for its reckless invasions, warrantless wiretaps, lethally incompetent response to Hurricane Katrina, and other scandals and blunders. $16.00, PAPERBACK

Cable News Confidential: My Misadventures in Corporate Media, by Jeff Cohen. Offers a fast-paced romp through the three major cable news channels—Fox CNN, and MSNBC—and delivers a serious message about their failure to cover the most urgent issues of the day. $14.95, PAPERBACK.

The Raw Deal: How the Bush Republicans Plan to Destroy Social Security and the Legacy of the New Deal, by Joe Conason. Reveals the well-financed and determined effort to undo the Social Security Act and other New Deal programs. $11.00, PAPERBACK

10 Steps to Repair American Democracy, by Steven Hill. Identifies the key problems with American democracy, especially election practices, and proposes ten specific reforms to reinvigorate it. $11.00, PAPERBACK

In Conflict: Iraq War Veterans Speak Out on Duty, Loss, and the Fight to Stay Alive, by Yvonne Latty. Features the unheard voices, extraordinary experiences, and personal photographs of a broad mix of Iraq War veterans, including Congressman Patrick Murphy, Tammy Duckworth, Kelly Daugherty, and Camilo Mejia. $24.00, HARDCOVER.

Jacked: How 'Conservatives" Are Picking Your Pocket –Whether You Voted For Them or Not, by Nomi Prins. Describes how the "conservative" agenda has affected your wallet, skewed national priorities, and diminished America—but not the American spirit. $12.00, PAPERBACK

The Great Divide: Retro vs. Metro America, by John Sperling et al. Explains how and why our nation is so bitterly divided into what the authors call Retro and Metro America. $19.95, PAPERBACK

For more information,
please visit www.p3books.com

About This Book

This book is printed on Cascade Enviro100 Print paper. It contains 100 percent post-consumer fiber and is certified EcoLogo, Processed Chlorine Free, and FSC Recycled. For each ton used instead of virgin paper, we:

- Save the equivalent of 17 trees
- Reduce air emissions by 2,098 pounds
- Reduce solid waste by 1,081 pounds
- Reduce the water used by 10,196 gallons
- Reduce suspended particles in the water by 6.9 pounds.

This paper is manufactured using biogas energy, reducing natural gas consumption by 2,748 cubic feet per ton of paper produced.

The book's printer, Malloy Incorporated, works with paper mills that are environmentally responsible, that do not source fiber from endangered forests, and that are third-party certified. Malloy prints with soy and vegetable based inks, and over 98 percent of the solid material they discard is recycled. Their water emissions are entirely safe for disposal into their municipal sanitary sewer system, and they work with the Michigan Department of Environmental Quality to ensure that their air emissions meet all environmental standards.

The Michigan Department of Environmental Quality has recognized Malloy as a Great Printer for their compliance with environmental regulations, written environmental policy, pollution prevention efforts, and pledge to share best practices with other printers. Their county Department of Planning and Environment has designated them a Waste Knot Partner for their waste prevention and recycling programs.